THE MYTH OF
MATRIARCHAL
PREHISTORY

The Myth of Matriarchal Prehistory

Why an Invented Past
Won't Give Women a Future

CYNTHIA ELLER

Beacon Press

BOSTON

Beacon Press
25 Beacon Street
Boston, Massachusetts 02108-2892
www.beacon.org

Beacon Press books
are published under the auspices of
the Unitarian Universalist Association of Congregations.

05 04 03 02 01   8 7 6 5 4 3 2 1

This book is printed on recycled acid-free paper that contains at least
20 percent postconsumer waste and meets the uncoated paper ANSI/NISO
specifications for permanence as revised in 1992.

Text design by Elizabeth Elsas
Composition by Wilsted & Taylor Publishing Services

Monica Sjöö, "Poem in Memory of and in Tribute to Marija
Gimbutas," *Goddessing Regenerated* 5 (Summer/Fall 1996): 30.
By permission of Monica Sjöö and *Goddessing Regenerated*.
June Rachuy Brindel, ritual poem in *Ariadne* (New York:
St. Martin's Press, 1980), 119. Courtesy of June Rachuy Brindel.

Library of Congress Cataloging-in-Publication Data
Eller, Cynthia.
        The myth of matriarchal prehistory : why an invented past
    won't give women a future / Cynthia Eller.
        p. cm.
    Includes bibliographical references and index.
    ISBN 0-8070-6792-X
    1. Women, Prehistoric.   2. Religion, Prehistoric.
3. Matriarchy.   4. Matrilineal kinship.   5. Patriarchy.
6. Feminist theory.   I. Title.
GN799.W66 E49 2000
306.83—dc21
                                                    99-057360

FOR JON AND SOPHIE

Over the last few months, this untaught history had become a lump in my throat, a forgotten piece of my female heart that had begun to beat again. Now here in the stone circle I felt it even more, like a sad, sad sweetness, like a sorrow and a hope melded into one.

—Sue Monk Kidd

The real political question . . . as old as political philosophy . . . [is] when we should endorse the ennobling lie. . . . We . . . need to show not that . . . [these lies] are falsehoods but [that] they are useless falsehoods at best or—at worst—dangerous ones.

—Kwame Anthony Appiah

CONTENTS

CHAPTER I

Meeting Matriarchy

Once while I was browsing through *On the Issues*, a feminist magazine, I happened upon an advertisement for a T-shirt: "I Survived Five-Thousand Years of Patriarchal Hierarchies," it proclaimed (see Fig. 1.1). This same birthday for patriarchy, five thousand years in the past, was mentioned several times in a lecture I attended in 1992 in New York City. I heard this number very frequently in the late 1980s and early 1990s; I was researching the feminist spirituality movement, and five thousand is the most common age spiritual feminists assign to "the patriarchy." Perhaps I shouldn't have been surprised to hear it yet again. But I was: the speaker was Gloria Steinem, and I hadn't figured her for a partisan of this theory.

As I later learned, Steinem had been speculating about the origins of the patriarchy as early as 1972, when she told the readers of *Wonder Woman* this story:

> Once upon a time, the many cultures of this world were all part of the gynocratic age. Paternity had not yet been discovered, and it was thought . . . that women bore fruit like trees—when they were ripe. Childbirth was mysterious. It was vital. And it was envied. Women were worshipped because of it, were considered superior because of it. . . . Men were on the periphery—an interchangeable body of workers for, and worshippers of, the female center, the principle of life.
>
> The discovery of paternity, of sexual cause and childbirth effect, was as cataclysmic for society as, say, the discovery of fire or the shattering of the atom. Gradually, the idea of male ownership of children took hold. . . .
>
> Gynocracy also suffered from the periodic invasions of nomadic

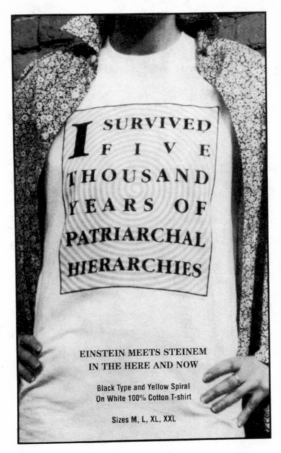

FIG. I.I
T-shirt dating the
advent of patriarchy to
3000 BCE.

tribes. . . . The conflict between the hunters and the growers was really
the conflict between male-dominated and female-dominated cultures.

. . . women gradually lost their freedom, mystery, and superior position. For five thousand years or more, the gynocratic age had flowered in
peace and productivity. Slowly, in varying stages and in different parts of
the world, the social order was painfully reversed. Women became the
underclass, marked by their visible differences.[1]

In 1972, Steinem was a voice in the wilderness with her talk of a past
gynocratic age; only a handful of feminists had even broached the
topic. The second wave of feminism was young then, but for most
feminists the patriarchy was old, unimaginably old.

Too old, some would say. The patriarchy is younger now, thanks
to growing feminist acceptance of the idea that human society

was matriarchal—or at least "woman-centered" and goddess-worshipping—from the Paleolithic era, 1.5 to 2 million years ago, until sometime around 3000 BCE. There are almost as many versions of this story as there are storytellers, but these are its basic contours:

- In a time before written records, society was centered around women. Women were revered for their mysterious life-giving powers, honored as incarnations and priestesses of the great goddess. They reared their children to carry on their line, created both art and technology, and made important decisions for their communities.
- Then a great transformation occurred—whether through a sudden cataclysm or a long, drawn-out sea change—and society was thereafter dominated by men. This is the culture and the mindset that we know as "patriarchy," and in which we live today.
- What the future holds is not determined, and indeed depends most heavily on the actions that we take now: particularly as we become aware of our true history. But the pervasive hope is that the future will bring a time of peace, ecological balance, and harmony between the sexes, with women either recovering their past ascendancy, or at last establishing a truly egalitarian society under the aegis of the goddess.

Not everyone who discusses this theory believes that the history of human social life on Earth happened this way. There is substantial dissension. But the story is circulating widely. It is a tale that is told in Sunday school classrooms, at academic conferences, at neopagan festivals, on network television, at feminist political action meetings, and in the pages of everything from populist feminist works to children's books to archaeological tomes. For those with ears to hear it, the noise the theory of matriarchal prehistory makes as we move into a new millennium is deafening.

My first encounter with the theory that prehistory was matriarchal came in 1979 in a class titled "Minoan and Mycenaean Greece." While on site at Knossos, our professor—an archaeologist with the American School of Classical Studies in Athens—noted that the artifactual evidence on the island of Crete pointed toward Minoan society being matriarchal. I don't recall much of what he said in defense of this assertion or what he meant by "matriarchal." All of this is overshadowed in my memory by the reaction of the other members of the class to the professor's statement: they laughed. Some of them nervously, some derisively. One or two expressed doubt. The general sentiment went something like this: "As if women would ever have run things, could ever have run things . . . and if they did, men surely had to put an end to it!" And, as my classmates gleefully noted, men did put an end to it, for it was a matter of historical record, they said, that the civilization of Minoan Crete was displaced by the apparently patriarchal Mycenaeans.

There were only a dozen or so of us there, ranging in age from teens to forties—Greeks, Turks, expatriate Americans—about evenly divided between women and men. The men's reactions held center stage (as men's reactions in college classes tended to do in 1979). I don't know what the other women in the class were thinking; they either laughed along with the men or said nothing. I felt the whole discussion amounted to cruel teasing of the playground variety, and I was annoyed with the professor for bringing it up and then letting it degenerate from archaeological observation to cheap joke. I left that interaction thinking, "Matriarchal? So what?" If a lot of snickering was all that prehistoric matriarchies could get me, who needed them?

Having thus washed my hands of the theory of prehistoric matriarchy, I didn't encounter it again until the early 1980s, when I was in graduate school doing research on feminist goddess-worship. I heard the theory constantly then, from everyone I interviewed, and in virtually every book I read that came out of the feminist spirituality movement. This matriarchy was no Cretan peculiarity, but a worldwide phenomenon that stretched back through prehistory to the very origins of the human race. These "matriarchies"—often called by other names—were not crude reversals of patriarchal power, but models of peace, plenty, harmony with nature, and, significantly, sex egalitarianism.

There was an answer here to my late adolescent question, "Matriarchal? So what?"—a thoroughly reasoned and passionately felt answer. Far from meaning nothing, the existence of prehistoric matriarchies meant everything to the women I met through my study of feminist spirituality. In both conversation and literature, I heard the evangelical tone of the converted: the theory of prehistoric matriarchy gave these individuals an understanding of how we came to this juncture in human history and what we could hope for in the future. It underwrote their politics, their ritual, their thealogy (or understanding of the goddess), and indeed, their entire worldview.

As a student of religion, I was fascinated with this theory, with its power to explain history, to set a feminist and ecological ethical agenda, and incredibly, to change lives. Of course I knew theoretically that this is precisely what myths do—and this narrative of matriarchal utopia and patriarchal takeover was surely a myth, at least in the scholarly sense: it was a tale told repeatedly and reverently, explaining things (namely, the origin of sexism) otherwise thought to be painfully inexplicable. But to see a myth developing and gaining ground before my own eyes—and more significantly, in my own peer group—was a revelation to me. Here was a myth that, however recently created, wielded tremendous psychological and spiritual power.

My phenomenological fascination with what I came to think of as "the myth of matriarchal prehistory" was sincere, and at times dominated my thinking. But it was accompanied by other, multiple fascinations. To begin with, once the memory of the derisive laughter at Knossos faded, I was intrigued with the idea of female rule or female "centeredness" in society. It was a reversal that had a sweet taste of power and revenge. More positively, it allowed me to imagine myself and other women as people whose biological sex did not immediately make the idea of their leadership, creativity, or autonomy either ridiculous or suspect. It provided a vocabulary for dreaming of utopia, and a license to claim that it was not mere fantasy, but a dream rooted in an ancient reality.

In other words, I had no trouble appreciating the myth's appeal. Except for one small problem—and one much larger problem—I might now be writing a book titled *Matriarchal Prehistory: Our Glorious Past and Our Hope for the Future*. But if I was intrigued with the newness and power of the myth, and with its bold gender reversals, I was at least as impressed by the fact that anyone took it seriously as history. Poking holes in the "evidence" for this myth was, to rely on cliché, like shooting fish in a barrel. After a long day of research in the library, I could go out with friends and entertain them with the latest argument I'd read for matriarchal prehistory, made up entirely—I pointed out—of a highly ideological reading of a couple of prehistoric artifacts accompanied by some dubious anthropology, perhaps a little astrology, and a fatuous premise . . . or two or three.

When I picked up my research on feminist spirituality again in the late 1980s and early 1990s,[2] I got to know many women involved in the movement, and I felt largely sympathetic toward their struggles to create a more female-friendly religion. But I continued to be appalled by the sheer credulousness they demonstrated toward their very dubious version of what happened in Western prehistory. The evidence available to us regarding gender relations in prehistory is sketchy and ambiguous, and always subject to the interpretation of biased individuals. But even with these limitations, what evidence we *do* have from prehistory cannot support the weight laid upon it by the matriarchal thesis. Theoretically, prehistory could have been matriarchal, but it probably wasn't, and nothing offered up in support of the matriarchal thesis is especially persuasive.

However, a myth does not need to be true—or even necessarily be *believed* to be true—to be powerful, to make a difference in how people think and live, and in what people value. Yet even as I tried to put aside the question of the myth's historicity, I remained uncomfortable with it. It exerted a magnetic appeal for me, but an even stronger magnetic repulsion. Eventually I had to admit that something was behind my constant bickering about the myth's historicity, something more than a lofty notion of intellectual honesty and the integrity of historical method. For certainly there are other myths that I have never felt driven to dispute: White lotus flowers blossomed in the footsteps of the newly born Shakyamuni? Moses came down from Mount Sinai with the Ten Commandments carved into two stone tablets? Personally, I doubt that either of these things happened, but I would never waste my breath arguing these points with the faithful. Truth claims seem beside the point to me: what matters is why the story is told, the uses to which it is put and by whom.

I have been a close observer of the myth of matriarchal prehistory for fifteen years now and have watched as it has moved from its somewhat parochial home in the feminist spirituality movement out into the feminist and cultural mainstream. But I haven't been able to cheer at the myth's increasing acceptance. My irritation with the historical claims made by the myth's partisans masks a deeper discontent with the myth's assumptions. There is a theory of sex and gender embedded in the myth of matriarchal prehistory, and it is neither original nor revolutionary. Women are defined quite narrowly as those who give birth and nurture, who identify themselves in terms of their relationships, and who are closely allied with the body, nature, and sex—

usually for unavoidable reasons of their biological makeup. This image of women is drastically revalued in feminist matriarchal myth, such that it is not a mark of shame or subordination, but of pride and power. But this image is nevertheless quite conventional and, at least up until now, it has done an excellent job of serving patriarchal interests.

Indeed, the myth of matriarchal prehistory is not a feminist creation, in spite of the aggressively feminist spin it has carried over the past twenty-five years. Since the myth was revived from classical Greek sources in 1861 by Johann Jakob Bachofen, it has had—at best—a very mixed record where feminism is concerned. The majority of men who championed the myth of matriarchal prehistory during its first century (and they have mostly been men) have regarded patriarchy as an evolutionary advance over prehistoric matriarchies, in spite of some lingering nostalgia for women's equality or beneficent rule.[3] Feminists of the latter half of the twentieth century are not the first to find in the myth of matriarchal prehistory a manifesto for feminist social change, but this has not been the dominant meaning attached to the myth of matriarchal prehistory, only the most recent.

Though there is nothing inherently feminist in matriarchal myth, this is no reason to disqualify it for feminist purposes. If the myth now functions in a feminist way, its antifeminist past can become merely a curious historical footnote. And it *does* function in a feminist way now, at least at a psychological level: there are ample testimonies to that. Many women—and some men too—have experienced the story of our matriarchal past as profoundly empowering, and as a firm foundation from which to call for, and believe in, a better future for us all.

Why then take the time and trouble to critique this myth, especially since it means running the risk of splitting feminist ranks, which are thin enough as it is? Simply put, it is my feminist movement too, and when I see it going down a road which, however inviting, looks like the wrong way to me, I feel an obligation to speak up. Whatever positive effects this myth has on individual women, they must be balanced against the historical and archaeological evidence the myth ignores or misinterprets and the sexist assumptions it leaves undisturbed. The myth of matriarchal prehistory postures as "documented fact," as "to date the most scientifically plausible account of the available information."[4] These claims can be—and will be here—shown to be false. Relying on matriarchal myth in the face of the evidence that challenges its veracity leaves feminists open to charges of vacuousness and irrelevance that we cannot afford to court. And the gendered stereotypes upon which matriarchal myth rests persistently work to flatten out differences among women; to exaggerate differences between women and men; and to hand women an identity that is symbolic, timeless, and archetypal, instead of giving them the freedom to craft identities that suit their individual temperaments, skills, preferences, and moral and political commitments.

In the course of my critique of feminist matriarchal myth, I do not intend to offer a substitute account of what happened between women and men in prehistoric times, or to determine whether patriarchy is a human universal or a recent historical phenomenon. These are questions that are hard to escape—feminist matriarchal myth was created largely in response to them—and intriguing to speculate upon. But the stories we spin out and the evidence we amass about the origins of sexism are fundamentally academic. They are not capable of telling us whether or how we might put an end to sexism. As I argue at the end of this book, these are moral and political questions; not scientific or historical ones.

The enemies of feminism have long posed issues of patriarchy and sexism in pseudoscientific and historical terms. It is not in feminist interests to join them at this game, especially when it is so (relatively) easy to undermine the ground rules. We know enough about biological sex differences to know that they are neither so striking nor so uniform that we either need to or ought to make our policy decisions in reference to them. And we know that cultures worldwide have demonstrated tremendous variability in constructing and regulating gender, indicating that we have significant freedom in making our own choices about what gender will mean for us. Certainly recent history, both technological and social, proves that innovation is possible: we are not forever condemned to find our future in our past. Discovering—or more to the point, inventing—prehistoric ages in which women and men lived in harmony and equality is a burden that feminists need not, and should not bear. Clinging to shopworn notions of gender and promoting a demonstrably fictional past can only hurt us over the long run as we work to create a future that helps all women, children, and men flourish.

In spite of overwhelming drawbacks, the myth of matriarchal prehistory continues to thrive. Any adequate critique of this myth must be based on a proper understanding of it: who promotes it and what they stand to gain by doing so; how it has evolved and where and how it is being disseminated; and exactly what this story claims for our past and our future. It is to this descriptive task that the next two chapters are devoted.

CHAPTER 2

Popularizing the Past

Many different types of women are attracted to the idea that prehistoric societies were goddess-worshipping and woman-honoring. Among the myth's adherents are academics and artists, career-minded women and stay-at-home moms, longtime feminists and young women just beginning to entertain the idea that they are living in a man's world. Generalizations one might want to make about feminist matriarchalists almost always fail: most are white, but not all; most are middle class, but some are working class or poor; many are well educated, but some are not; most were raised as Christians, but then most Americans are. They are married, single, lesbian, bisexual, and straight, with no one status dominating. The way in which the myth of matriarchal prehistory extols motherhood is clearly attractive to mothers of young children who feel they do not get the respect they deserve,[1] but then some of the myth's most vocal partisans are childless. Many feminist matriarchalists are religiously inclined, especially those who are affiliated with the feminist spirituality movement, where feminist matriarchal myth first came to be articulated in the early 1970s. But other feminist matriarchalists are quite secular: they see religion playing a key role in the past but they themselves remain religiously unaffiliated and spiritually inactive. Demographically, feminist matriarchalists run the gamut. Still, it is fair to say that the myth is most at home in white, middle-class, well-educated circles, and particularly among women who are interested in religion and spirituality.

Matriarchal myth is primarily a Western phenomenon, most popular in the United States, England, Germany, and, to a lesser extent,

Italy. The story itself is almost always centered on European prehistory, but there are exceptions: for example, Riane Eisler has recently inspired a search for matriarchal prehistory in China, which has resulted in the publication of a substantial anthology titled *The Chalice and the Blade in Chinese Culture.*[2]

This study is based almost entirely on texts produced by those who champion the myth of matriarchal prehistory. This is a rich and varied literature ranging from glossy art books to novels to poetry, and including paintings, conference talks, performance art, music, and even email. In general, I make no distinction between the tenured professor examining cuneiform tablets, the novelist spinning out imaginative fantasies of prehistoric Europe, and the New Age practitioner writing impassioned letters to spiritual feminist publications about her past lives as a priestess in Neolithic Europe. Once one is immersed in this literature, it becomes clear that the distinctions between these women are not so great as they at first seem. Underneath their variety lies a clear and consistent narrative that no amount of archaeological research, fictional imagination, or recovery of past lives changes very much. Indeed, what substantive differences there are between feminist matriarchalists rarely cause much internal dispute. Those who enunciate the most peculiar theories—that men evolved from extraterrestrials or that human females reproduced parthenogenetically for most of the history of the species—are more often the object of benign neglect than vitriolic attack. The only reason then that I give greater authority to one voice over another is because it best captures the most popular version of feminist matriarchal myth, not because the professional status of the author demands any special respect.

There are undoubted differences in the importance this story has for the various women who tell it. Because this book relies on those who invest significant time in telling the myth of matriarchal prehistory in prose, poetry, art, or song, it focuses mainly on the myth's enthusiasts: women whose experiences with matriarchal myth have been deep and profound, sometimes leading them to rethink their most basic life choices, if not to spend years studying archaeological artifacts and ancient Sumerian texts. Feminist matriarchal myth reaches well beyond the inner circle of its devotees, however. This more mainstream audience holds the myth a good deal more lightly, though at the same time giving it a cultural prominence it would not otherwise have.

None of the women who champion this version of Western history call themselves "feminist matriarchalists," and none refer to the story they tell as "the myth of matriarchal prehistory." The terms "feminist" and "prehistory" would probably not raise many eyebrows, but "matriarchy" and "myth" are much more controversial.

The term matriarchy has had a tortured history. As classicist Eva Cantarella points out, those using the term have meant everything from the political rule of women to matrilocal marriage to the worship of female divinities. And that is just those who have *used* the term. Those who have been *accused* of talking about "matriarchy" cut an even wider swath. Partisans of the myth usually resist the term because of its connotations of "rule by women"—a mirror image of patriarchy. As Mary Daly puts it succinctly, matriarchy "was not patriarchy spelled with an 'm.'" Most feminist matriarchalists are quick to explain that matriarchy should be understood instead as "the ascendancy of the Mother's way," or as "a realm where female things are valued and where power is exerted in non-possessive, noncontrolling, and organic ways that are harmonious with nature."[3]

Substitute terms are frequently offered ("gylany," "gynocracy," "matricentric," "gynocentric," "matristic," "gynolatric," "partnership," "gynosociety," and "matrifocal" have all been proposed), and they are intended to capture various shades of meaning: that prehistory was a time when mothers were the hub of society; or that women were powerful whether or not they had children; or that women and men shared power. But none of these substitute terms has attained common currency. The term prepatriarchal has been advanced recently,[4] but it is too vague to capture the specificity of the prehistoric societies feminist matriarchalists imagine. These societies are not just whatever happened to exist before patriarchy arrived on the scene. Even if sexually egalitarian, they are said to have been characterized by strongly differentiated sex roles. And however "female" and "male," "feminine" and "masculine" are defined for prehistoric societies, whatever is female or feminine has pride of place. A few partisans of matriarchal myth have complained about the imprecision and unfortunate connotations of the term "matriarchy" but have used it anyway, and I follow their lead here.[5] "Matriarchal" can be thought of then as a shorthand description for any society in which women's power is equal or superior to men's and in which the culture centers around values and life events described as "feminine."

The term myth is even more difficult to reinterpret to suit feminist matriarchalists' self-understandings. Probably the most commonly intended meaning of "myth," at least when it is used casually, is "not true." (For example, if a women's magazine promises on its cover to reveal "six myths about male sexuality," what you will learn when you look inside is that what you thought you knew about male sexuality is false.) But the theory that prehistory was matriarchal and goddess-worshipping is presented as fact, not fiction. It is only omitted from standard history texts, feminist matriarchalists say, because academics are trapped in a patriarchal worldview, suffering the consequences of a huge cover-up of matriarchy that started with the patriarchal revolution and has continued right up to the present.[6] Given these views, it would seem more accurate to call matriarchal prehistory a "hypothesis" or "theory." However, some feminist matriarchalists back away from the stronger truth claims suggested by these terms. As Anne Carson remarks, "Let it be myth then. . . . Whether the Golden Age of Matriarchy ever existed in history is not important: what is important is that the myth exists *now*, that there is a story being passed from woman to woman, from mother to daughter, of a time in which we were strong and free and could see ourselves in the Divine, when we lived in dignity and in peace."[7]

This suggests another layer to feminist matriarchal thought: that the story is sufficiently important to some feminists that they are unwilling to discard it simply because its status as historical truth is insecure. Mara Lynn Keller illustrates this by laying out the matriarchalist vision of prehistory and an "androcratic" one and asking, "which would be the more truthful, reliable, morally valuable and wise theory to choose?" "Truth" is thus only one consideration among others. Besides, "metaphoric truth," says Donna Wilshire, which "speaks to such a deep core of our common humanity and the meaning of life" is *"more real than factual reality* [her emphasis]."[8]

In other words, feminist matriarchalists know how badly they want their myth to be true—badly enough that they are willing to continue to believe it (or at least make use of it) even if the evidence does not really support it. But they also typically believe that it *is* true, and that they don't need to engage in any deceit to promote it as such.[9] This is a level of historical truth that is very characteristic of myth in the contemporary West. For us, myth seems to work best if we can at least provisionally believe it to be true. For example, the vast majority of practicing Christians believe that a man named Jesus lived, was crucified by the Roman authorities, and rose from the dead. Most Christians do not demand historical documentation of these events because it is the promises the Passion narrative makes about God's forgiving love that make the story valuable. But the story *could* be historically true, and those who find it useful generally believe it to be so, even if they must resort to faith rather than evidence. Similarly, the majority of practicing Jews, while not necessarily swearing by every boil and frog and locust in the Exodus story, nevertheless believe that the Jewish people were in captivity in Egypt and were led out by Moses into their own land. This story is generally told to illustrate the steadfastness of God's covenant with the Jewish people—not to establish the factual nature of this historic migration. But it *could* be true, and again, it is believed to be true by most of those who relate the story.

Going on these examples, contemporary myths need not have the sort of ontological certainty that we assign to things like gravity or mathematical formulae, but to carry the sort of psychic weight they are asked to bear in people's lives, they must be, at the least, plausible.

In theory, the golden era of prehistoric matriarchy may have happened just as feminist matriarchalists say. The scattered remains left to us from prehistoric times are open to a variety of interpretations, and there is simply no evidence that can *definitively* prove the matriarchal hypothesis wrong. But is the myth of matriarchal prehistory plausible to those not already ardently hoping that it is true? I will argue that it is not. It does not represent historical truth; it is not a story built or argued from solid evidence, and it presents a scenario for prehistory that, if not demonstrably false, is at least highly unlikely. But to stop at this is to miss a much deeper truth about the *kind* of story that feminist matriarchalists are constructing. Scholars of religion are more apt to think of myths as stories that impart profoundly value-laden messages in dense, image-rich language. And by this definition too, the myth of matriarchal prehistory is myth. It is a narrative designed to grasp hold of an audience's consciousness and thereby fulfill certain social and psychological functions: in this case, feminist functions.[10]

FEMINIST FUNCTIONS OF MATRIARCHAL MYTH

Women who respond enthusiastically to matriarchal myth do so at least in part because it offers them a new, vastly improved self-image. It teaches them about their "innate goodness," their "own natural majesty." It has, says Charlene Spretnak, "reframed our conceptualization of femaleness" and given us "the gift of ourselves."[11] This basic message of female self-respect is brought home again and again in feminist matriarchalist art and literature. Martha Ann and Dorothy Myers Imel set it out as the dedication to their massive reference work, *Goddesses in World Mythology*:

> *To all the women in the world who were unaware of their heritage.*
> *You are descended from a long line of sacred females*
> *who have been respected and honored for thousands of years.*
>
> *Remember and make it so.*[12]

In encountering the goddess of prehistoric times, women are said to be given "imagery and permission to see the divine within . . . as a woman."[13]

This has been a key function of feminist matriarchal myth from the outset: to redeem and revalue "the feminine," a task that seemed particularly timely since liberal feminism, associated with the early women's liberation movement of the 1960s, spared little attention for the special qualities of women. Liberal feminism focused on winning women the same rights that men were already believed to have: to pursue and succeed within a full range of careers, to combine work with childrearing, to have full legal rights; in short, to be recognized as citizens of the democratic state, heirs to the promise of equal opportunity for all. For many feminists, this agenda did not go nearly far enough. And so deeper analyses were ventured from at least two quarters: radical feminism and cultural feminism.[14]

Radical feminists, many of them fresh from the male-dominated New Left movements of the 1960s, were dismayed at the prospect of women attempting to assume roles equal to men's within late industrial capitalism. This, in their thinking, would merely lend more support to an economy and government that was poisoned at its roots, not only in terms of race and class—issues with which the New Left was already engaged—but in terms of sex. What emerged from radical feminist analyses was the assertion that hatred, exploitation, and brutalization of women were not mere epiphenomena in patriarchal capitalist society—easily cured by admitting women into the ranks of the powerful—but were the very foundations upon which the system was built. Radical feminists like Ti-Grace Atkinson, Shulamith Firestone, Kate Millett, Andrea Dworkin, and Mary Daly zeroed in on issues of misogyny and sexual violence as the bottom line of patriarchal society and counseled that a feminist revolution could never be won simply by putting women in factory lines and boardrooms alongside men.

In the course of making this analysis, radical feminists reflected at length on how women were placed in society vis-à-vis men, and how specifically female roles in sex and reproduction were implicated in and incorporated into structures of male dominance. But it was cultural feminists who turned most forcefully to the question of who women *are*. Like radical feminists, cultural feminists were appalled at the thought of women inadvertently buying into patriarchal culture by taking on men's traditional roles. But the key source of their distress was the fear that women would be distanced from their true, female selves. The consequences of this loss were not only personal, but deeply communal, and therefore political. Femininity, traditionally defined, was simply *better* than masculinity. It was the morally preferable alternative to be followed in creating a new social order. And women, as the carriers—whether by biology or history or both—of these "feminine" values, had a vital role to play in forging a more peaceful, harmonious, beneficent world.[15]

Feminist matriarchalists have their deepest kinship with cultural feminism (also called "difference feminism" owing to its analytical reliance on differences between women and men). In the tradition of first-wave feminists such as Elizabeth Cady Stanton, Matilda Joslyn Gage, and Charlotte Perkins Gilman (who all also referred to a past age of gynocentrism), feminist matriarchalists believe that the values and dispositions associated with women—if not women themselves—need to play a key role in reforming society.[16] Much of feminist matriarchal myth is given over to identifying and celebrating "the feminine" and searching for ways in which women can more fully be it and model it for society. Prominent among the arenas where "feminine" values are supposed to restore proper balance is environmental policy. Like other ecofeminists (some of whom, it must be noted, are hostile to matriarchal myth), feminist matriarchalists draw parallels between the treatment of women and the treatment of the environment, an analogy that is underlined by the contrast between prehistoric matriarchal societies, which lived in harmony with nature, and patriarchal societies, which exploit natural resources, in effect "raping the earth."[17]

But feminist matriarchalists have roots in radical feminism as well.[18] Interest in matriarchal prehistory was in part a direct outgrowth of radical feminism. And over the past three decades, feminist matriarchalists have retained a lively concern with issues at the heart of radical feminism—sexual harrassment and violence toward women (rape, child abuse, wife battering)—and have been comparatively less interested in issues of equal employment, government-subsidized day care, or legal nondiscrimination, matters more closely tied to liberal feminism.

Messages of female specialness, appealing in the early 1970s, are perhaps especially appealing now, in an era of feminist stocktaking. Many of the basic demands of liberal feminism have either been met or acknowledged as valid concerns. Women are employed outside the home in steadily increasing numbers; they have been admitted to previously all-male colleges and are making significant inroads into previously male professions such as medicine and law. "Sameness feminism," that which argues that the only thing women require is equal treatment with men, has achieved a knee-jerk acceptance in many quarters of the popular media: "Look," television commercials seem to proclaim, "girls can wear cleats, women can carry briefcases! It is a brave new world!" The other side of the coin remains pertinent though: the same popular media that champion women's athleticism and economic success continually run talk shows and made-for-television movies about female victims of incest, rape, and spousal abuse. And cleats and briefcases aside, women are still relentlessly judged—by themselves as much as or more than by anyone else—against ideals of femininity and motherhood. In such an environment, "equality with men" seems neither attainable nor especially desirable. Liberal feminism is then easily regarded by many feminists as a failure (though, in fairness, it has had little time in which to prove itself). Now, as we begin a new millennium, women are still women, and men are still men. Arguably then, feminists need a way to recognize inequities between women and men and recommend policies to rectify them within the highly gendered universe we continue to occupy.

This is just what feminist matriarchal myth does in assigning to male values a troubling interlude of violence and abuse of women, and to female values a long, prosperous era of peace and harmony with nature and a glorious coming era of the goddess's return. The myth provides an analysis of sexism, a social agenda, and a mechanism for social change that is not nearly so beset with failure and frustration as political activism. Feminist matriarchalists certainly engage in political activism, usually individually rather than as a group; the key exception being their use of what might be called "spiritual activism." This spiritual activism is enacted effortlessly every time the story of matriarchal prehistory is told, every time the name of the goddess is spoken. For the aspect of prehistoric matriarchies that feminist matriarchalists are most seeking to reinstate in the present is their value system, embodied in goddess religion, which honors women and nature as sacred. In contrast, patriarchal religions are held accountable, more than any other single factor, for instituting a social order oppressive to women and nature.

That religion should have had such an impact in making both matriarchies and patriarchies what they were (and are) is no accident. This is simply the nature of religion, feminist matriarchalists say, which is deeper and more basic than other social institutions.[19] Though on one level this is frightening (religion seals the triumph of the patriarchy), it is also encouraging. One could scarcely ask for a better ally in the feminist revolution: without guns or seats in Congress, feminist matriarchalists can hope to change the world; and not just superficially, but profoundly.

The note of hope sounded here points to what is probably the central function of the myth of matriarchal prehistory. It takes a situation that invites despair—patriarchy is here, it's always been here, it's inevitable—and transforms it into a surpassing optimism: patriarchy is recent and fallible, it was preceded by something much better, and it can be overthrown in the near future.

In this way, matriarchal myth provides a solution for a problem that radical feminism, to some extent, created. In radical feminist analyses, patriarchy was not simply the practice of sex discrimination or male dominance. Instead "patriarchy" became the one-word alias for an entire system of thinking, living, and being, of which the oppression of women was only the tip of the iceberg. Patriarchy, it turned out, was also about racism and heterosexism and capitalism; it was about technological excess, the irresponsible use of natural resources, and the exploitation of the Third World. This was on the macro level. On the micro level, patriarchy ran even deeper. It infected the way people thought and felt, discouraging intimacy and sensitivity in favor of logic and rationality.

This vision of "the patriarchy" is truly horrific. Patriarchy is monolithic, it is universal, it permeates everything. Clearly, one needs to juxtapose something equally large and solid against it if there is to be any hope of dislodging it.

For feminist matriarchalists, that something is matriarchal prehistory. The long era of matriarchal peace and plenty is the bulwark feminists can rest upon as they regard the patriarchal present and hope for a new age. It roots feminism "in the nature of being" and declares that "inevitable warfare and man's famous inhumanity to men, women, children, and everything else on this planet is not our only heritage." This connection between past precedent and future possibility is stated explicitly in narrations of the myth of matriarchal prehistory. If no precedent is available, feminist matriarchalists tend to conclude that the "feminist onslaught on the fortress of 'It has always been so' " is doomed to failure.[20]

As precedents go, the one offered by the myth of matriarchal prehistory is remarkable. It does not say that in the very distant past, there was a small group of people who were able for a short time to construct a society that gave women status and freedom and did not make war on other people or the natural world. Quite the contrary: according to feminist matriarchal myth, matriarchy was universal, it endured for all the millennia in which we were human, and was only supplanted very recently. It positively dwarfs the patriarchy, which is, in contrast, a "relatively short, albeit melodramatic, period."[21]

This is the preeminent way in which feminist matriarchalists combat the terrible strength of the patriarchy: they set it alongside the matriarchal era and comment on its diminutive size. Heide Göttner-Abendroth, author of a four-volume opus on matriarchal prehistory, imagines a timeline of human history two meters long, on which "man's rule" occupies only the last millimeter. As if the disproportion in matriarchy's favor weren't already commanding enough, feminist matriarchalists seem to experience an unstoppable desire to expand it even farther. In their voluminous work *The Great Cosmic Mother*, Monica Sjöö and Barbara Mor tell us on page 46 that "the mysteries of female biology dominated human religious and artistic thought, as well as social organization, for at least the first 200,000 years of human life on earth." By page 235, "the original Goddess religion" is said to have "dominated human thought and feeling for at least 300,000 years." On page 424, as they arrive at the end of their recounting of the myth of matriarchal prehistory, this number has increased to 500,000 years. Some feminist matriarchalists go even farther. Diane Stein says the matriarchal era began on the lost continent of Mu, when "people began incarnating on the earthplane ten and a half million years ago." Meanwhile, Matthew Fox contrasts the "original blessing" of the 18 billion years of the cosmos's existence as over against the appearance of sin "with the rise of the patriarchy some four thousand to six thousand years ago." [22] Patriarchy is thus reduced to a veritable blip on the radar screen, inspiring in feminists great hope for its future overthrow.

INTO THE CULTURAL MAINSTREAM

Feminist matriarchalists get this encouraging word out in a variety of ways, from ostensibly dispassionate popularizations of archaeologist Marija Gimbutas's findings to much more impressionistic means.

Art plays a special role in tellings of the myth of matriarchal prehistory. This is in part because the most compelling evidence of matriarchal prehistory for contemporary feminist observers is that of prehistoric female figurines. But art is attractive for reasons beyond its evidentiary power. It is an excellent medium for communicating mythic themes, and for reaching larger audiences. With this in mind, matriarchal myth has become the subject of museum exhibits, slide shows, glossy art books, and even "goddess cards" intended for divination or meditation. [23] Some of these media draw on feminist art of the past thirty years, in addition to the more typical fare of prehistoric "goddess" figures. This feminist art is itself a way in which matriarchal prehistory is communicated to a contemporary audience. For example, Monica Sjöö's painting *God Giving Birth*, first exhibited in London in 1968, consists of a large woman, face half-black and half-white, in the act of childbirth, her child's head emerging from between her legs. This painting initially touched off a storm of controversy, which only encouraged the production of art pieces expressing

FIG. 2.1   Hélène de Beauvoir's *Second Encounter with the Great Goddess*, 1982.

similar themes. Increasingly, this art has incorporated images from archaeological sites believed to date to matriarchal times. This trend
was already evident in 1982, when Hélène de Beauvoir painted her
Second Encounter with the Great Goddess, in which a naked woman
holding a snake in each hand is positioned alongside the prehistoric
Minoan "snake goddess" (see Fig. 2.1). More recently, Ursula Kava-
nagh, an Irish artist, has created a series titled *Matriarchal Listings* based
on her travels to "ancient Goddess sites" in Ireland, England, Italy,
Sardinia, Malta, and Sicily.[24]

The myth of matriarchal prehistory is also communicated in performance art. The most notable example of this is Mary Beth Edelson's *Your Five Thousand Years Are Up* (premiered in La Jolla, California, in 1977), in which eight shrouded female figures circled a ring of
fire, chanting about women's rebirth and the end of patriarchy. A
more recent example is Donna Wilshire's *Virgin Mother Crone*, still being performed and now published in book form. In this piece, Wilshire assumes three personas of the ancient goddess. Singing, dancing
with scarves, and playing drums and rattles, she invokes a prepatriarchal world into which she invites her audience.[25]

Though visual art predominates, there are other artistic render-
ings of matriarchal myth as well. Roberta Kosse's oratorio, "The Re-

turn of the Great Mother," composed for women's chorus and chamber orchestra (released on the Ars Pro Femina label in 1978), tells the story of matriarchal prehistory musically. Drummer Layne Redmond and her New York-based group the Mob of Angels find inspiration in ancient images of women playing drums, women they believe to have been priestesses of the goddess performing a vital function for cultures that respected women's power. Matriarchal myth has even entered the alternative rock world through two albums by the band Helium: *Pirate Prude* and *The Dirt of Luck*.[26]

More common than musical renditions of matriarchal myth are poetic ones, some of epic length, and fictional tellings such as Marion Zimmer Bradley's *The Mists of Avalon*, set in Arthurian Britain, and June Rachuy Brindel's *Ariadne*, set in Minoan Crete.[27] The most ambitious fictional telling of matriarchal myth is Mary Mackey's *Earthsong* trilogy, consisting of *The Year the Horses Came* (1993), *The Horses at the Gate* (1995), and *The Fires of Spring* (1998). In these novels, based on Marija Gimbutas's work, goddess civilizations carpet Neolithic Europe, living in peace and harmony with nature, only to collapse under the violent onslaughts of nomadic horse-riding invaders (the "beastmen") from the Russian steppes (the "Sea of Grass"). Like other fictional accounts, Mackey's trilogy focuses on the moment of culture contact, when the matriarchal civilizations find themselves under attack (not surprising when one considers that there is no plot to the myth of matriarchal prehistory until there is trouble in paradise). Marrah, a young girl descended from a matrilineage of priestesses, and newly initiated into womanhood, becomes attached to Stavan, son of a great chief from the Sea of Grass. She quickly converts Stavan to the ways of the goddess people (great sex proves an excellent teacher), and together they struggle to keep the patriarchal nomads from invading the goddess lands.[28]

Another potent vehicle for matriarchal mythology is the "goddess pilgrimage." Some feminist matriarchalists have crafted their own itineraries for these trips, no longer a heroic task with the publication of *Goddess Sites: Europe*, a travel guide offering "breathtaking descriptions of hundreds of sacred sites . . . complete with maps, photos, and detailed travel instructions." In addition, there is now a mini-industry of pre-packaged tours led by experts in matriarchal myth such as Donna Henes, Joan Marler, Vicki Noble, Willow LaMonte, and Carol Christ (see Fig. 2.2). The Spring 1997 issue of *Goddessing Re-*

TURKEY
Home of the Great Goddess

Sacred Sites in:
Istanbul
Cappadocia
Troy
Ephesus
Aphrodisias
Çatal Höyük
and more. . .

Encounter the Great Goddess in her
ancient homes.
Experience the riches of Anatolia.
Visit Konya's Sufi center.
Four Star Hotels.
August and December departures

Dr. Rashid Ergener, lecturer/guide

AnaTours-Mythic Travel
1580 Tucker Road
Scotts Valley, CA 95066
831-438-3031
Visit our website
www.anatours.com
email: info@anatours.com

FIG. 2.2
Sample advertisement for a
"goddess pilgrimage" from
AnaTours.

generated lists twenty-seven separate "goddess tours" for 1997 and 1998. Favorite sites are Malta, Crete, Turkey, England, and Ireland, though there are also tours to Hawaii and Latin America. Tours are mainly led by American women, though there is also at least one German-led tour to Crete and Malta.[29] Not all women who embark on these adventures are committed matriarchalists, but few return from their summer vacations as agnostic toward prehistoric matriarchies as they may have been when they left.

Those without the money or time to make such pilgrimages can go along in spirit by watching *Goddess Remembered*, a video recounting the myth of matriarchal prehistory through conversations with prominent feminist matriarchalists and footage of sites in Malta, England, and Crete. This video, sponsored by the National

Film Board of Canada, is one of its most popular ever and continues to be featured as a part of pledge campaigns. Study guides are also available to introduce newcomers to the myth of matriarchal prehistory. *Cakes for the Queen of Heaven*, a curriculum originally developed under the auspices of the Unitarian Universalist Association, has spread to many more mainstream churches. Like *The Partnership Way*, developed as a study guide for Riane Eisler's *The Chalice and the Blade*, *Cakes* familiarizes participants with matriarchal mythology through slides, art projects, meditations, rituals, and discussions.[30] Those who want to incorporate their newfound knowledge of goddesses and matriarchal myth into their daily lives can choose from a number of illustrated journals, appointment books, and calendars, or subscribe to periodicals such as *Metis*, *Goddessing Regenerated*, or *Matriarchy Research and Reclaim Network Newsletter*. Goddess reproductions are also quite popular and available from a number of sources (see Fig. 2.3). For some users, these no doubt carry a spiritual significance unrelated to matriarchal mythology, but for most they are tangible representations of a time when all women were held in high esteem.[31]

If most of these books, videos, pilgrimages, and so forth seem to cater to a group of insiders, it is important to note that they all include an element of outreach. And certainly there is evidence that these efforts have borne fruit in more mainstream social locations. For example, *Megatrends for Women*, published in 1992, proclaims "The Goddess Reawakening" to be one "megatrend" and recites the basics of matriarchal myth in the relevant chapter. The National Organization for Women (NOW) has gotten in on the act as well, producing a pamphlet titled "Goddess Cultural Beliefs," which includes assertions about prehistoric women's control of "religious, social, political and legal institutions," their work as priestesses, their sexual freedom, and their close connection "to nature, its cycles, power and beauty." As recently as March 1999, the Lexington, Massachusetts NOW chapter celebrated Women's History Month with a presentation titled "Unearthing Pandora's Treasure: Voices of Women Proclaiming Our Sacred Past," which aimed to show how "feminist scholars in archeology, history and theology [have] reviewed the ancient past to find evidence of a time when god was a woman."[32]

One of the most fascinating populist feminist works advancing the myth of matriarchal prehistory is Judy Mann's *The Difference:*

LILITH

Goddess of the Underworld

This fearless and winged Goddess is approximately 4,000 years old. As the "Nigh Owl" she represents chthonic wisdom and death as a natural cycle of life. Exquisitely carved and detailed.

Hand Colored, Tan. 8" x 10" x ½". Ready to Hang. Gypsum.

Original: (Terra Cotta. Found in Sumer. Private Collection.)

$42.00

NILE RIVER GODDESS

Goddess of Renewal

This Egyptian Bird or Serpent Headed River Goddess is approximately 5,000 years old. She is associated with life-giving, renewing waters.

Tan in Color. 7" in Height. Gypsum.

Original: (Predynastic, Egypt. Brooklyn Museum.)

$25.00

Finely handcrafted walnut and brass stand available for Nile River Goddess. Add $12.00

ENTHRONED GODDESS

Earth Mother

This seated Goddess embodies the fecundity of the earth. Her incised throne-like body powerfully represents the pregnant Goddess. She is approximately 4,500 years old.

Light Brown Earth Tones. 7½" in Height. Gypsum.

Original: (Clay. Found in Thrace [Bulgaria]. Neolithic. Sofia Museum.)

$39.00

DREAMING GODDESS

Goddess of Inspiration

This Deaming Goddess is approximately 6,000 years old. She was found in the Hypogeum Temple on the Island of Malta in the Mediterranean. She portrays a monumental presence.

Terra Cotta in Color. 7½" x 4" x 4". Gypsum.

Original: (Clay. Neolithic. Valletta Museum, Malta.)

$35.00

"Your Goddesses are gorgeous! The Dreaming Goddess from Malta is one I've never seen before — especially evocative."

creativity

FIG. 2.3   A page from the Star River Productions catalogue showing a range of goddess reproductions.

Growing Up Female in America. Mann, a columnist for the *Washington Post*, undertook the task of investigating girlhood in America when she became concerned about the effect adolescence might have on her daughter (the much-discussed "Ophelia" syndrome, in which previously confident and brave little girls become timid and insecure teenagers).[33] Mann tells the story of her investigation as a series of encounters with theories and experts, focusing mainly on how girls are treated in educational settings. But Mann is restless to get to the root of the problem, and this drives her straight to prehistory. As she explains:

> It took a year of research before I learned this: If I really wanted to know why girls come out feeling second best, if I really wanted to know what makes it possible for rock musicians to make fortunes writing songs about dismembering women, for girls to be ignored in classrooms, in churches, in medical schools, in governments, I had to go backward in time to the dim memories that lurk on the borders of human beginnings. As I kept going further back into history, into antiquity, and finally into prehistory, I began to find out how things once were between men and women, and where and how men rose to dominance over women.[34]

The urge to return to roots is what drives many feminist commentators into the arms of matriarchal myth, almost in spite of themselves. If an author wants to give a sweeping chronological account of her topic, the first chapter is logically about prehistory: and the reigning feminist story these days is that prehistoric societies were goddess-worshipping and matriarchal. Thus Rosalind Miles's *Women's History of the World* tracks feminist political gains in terms of suffrage, divorce laws, and so forth, but begins "In the Beginning," with chapters on "The First Women," "The Great Goddess," and "The Rise of the Phallus." Nickie Roberts's *Whores in History* documents the history of prostitution in the West but starts with "sacred prostitution" in goddess-worshipping cultures. Shari Thurer's *The Myths of Motherhood* seeks to decenter current views of motherhood by showing how mothers have been regarded at other times in Western history, but she too begins with "the beginning of time," when "woman was an awesome being" who "seemed to swell and spew forth a child by her own law."[35]

Matriarchal myth is even making its way into school curricula. While it is true that one can go through twelve years of primary and secondary education, or even a college or graduate school career without being taught that prehistory was matriarchal (particularly if one majors in, say, engineering), the academic world is far from immune to the enticements of matriarchal mythology. Young women have told me that the myth of matriarchal prehistory has been presented to them as historic truth in high school classes in world history, religion, and women's studies. *Women's Roots*, by June Stephenson, now in its fourth edition, is a rendition of matriarchal prehistory designed to be read by high school students. At the college level, courses are offered about or with the premise of matriarchal prehistory, with titles like "Reclaiming the Goddess," "Herstory of the Goddess," and "The Goddess and the Matriarchy Controversy."[36] A 1995 text, *Women and Religion* by Marianne Ferguson, purporting to cover the broad terrain of interactions between women and religion, is actually a straightforward telling of the myth of matriarchal prehistory, from the mother goddesses of prehistory to the father gods of patriarchy.

Increasingly, matriarchal myth is being given some credence in college texts. For example, Rita Gross critiques the myth of matriarchal prehistory in her religion textbook, *Feminism and Religion*, viewing it as "extreme" and not well grounded in archaeological evidence. Yet she comes quite a distance to meet its partisans, arguing that it is reasonable "to conclude both that women were less dominated than in later societies and that female sacredness was more commonly venerated" in prehistoric times.[37] Gerda Lerner's *The Creation of Patriarchy*, though not strictly a textbook, is widely read in college courses. Lerner spends very little time discussing the nature of prehistoric societies, and she cannot, in fairness, be counted as a champion of matriarchal myth, since she explicitly disclaims a former stage of matriarchy. And yet it is impressive how even this careful and scholarly study ends up endorsing most of the major points of feminist matriarchal myth:

- patriarchy didn't always exist;
- unless we are aware of this fact, we cannot effectively combat it;
- patriarchy is now ending as a result of the planetary crisis to which it has brought us;
- the future is not determined, and could bring either improvement or disaster;
- women's involvement is crucial to lead the future in a more positive direction.[38]

The myth of matriarchal prehistory has not been adopted as the one true account of human history, taught to first graders and graduate students alike. But it is nevertheless making itself felt, and, especially in feminist circles, it is hard to avoid. It earns new converts every day, especially among a younger generation of girls and women not formerly exposed to it. There are even dedicated resources available to teach the myth of matriarchal prehistory to younger girls. For example, Jyotsna Sreenivasan's *The Moon Over Crete* is a novel for young readers that relates the story of eleven-year-old Lily and her flute teacher, Mrs. Zinn, who takes Lily 3,500 years back in time to ancient Crete where "Lily finds out what it's like for girls to be *important*." In *Why It's Great to Be a Girl*, Jacqueline Shannon offers fifty points of comparison between women and men in which women emerge superior: Point number 8 is that "anthropologists and archeologists credit females with the 'civilization' of humankind"; point number 50 is that "only females can give birth." Though Shannon does not explicitly invoke matriarchal myth, she asserts two of its familiar themes—women's invention of civilization and the female monopoly on childbirth—and quotes one of its earliest feminist proponents (Elizabeth Gould Davis) to support the first of these points.[39]

The myth of matriarchal prehistory is not without its critics. Some populist feminists have included critiques of matriarchal myth in recent books, and a number of more academic critiques have been included in books, articles, or reviews. Archaeologists and students of ancient history, long silent on this topic, have recently spoken out more frequently about matriarchal myth, almost always negatively. Matriarchal myth is also refuted on the Internet, in broadsides delivered mainly by a pair of self-appointed defenders of the universal patriarchy thesis: Steven Goldberg, author of *The Inevitability of Patriarchy*, and Robert Sheaffer. Goldberg systematically addresses any and all purported exceptions to patriarchal social relations as they surface; Sheaffer, in his turn, suggests that "the Goddess promoters" are "suffering from a case of False Memory Syndrome."[40]

But criticism of matriarchal myth has, for the most part, been restrained. It has not felt this way to the myth's proponents, of course; in 1991, Vicki Noble lamented the fact that though feminists have been uncovering "the ancient matriarchal past" for twenty years, "even fairly recently the *New York Times* was still able to find a female professor of history who would ridicule rather than review Riane Eisler's *The Chalice and the Blade*, making her position sound like a fantasy rather than documented fact." A recent festschrift for Marija Gimbutas is full of defensive reactions to criticisms of the myth of matriarchal prehistory, both perceived and real. Feminist matriarchalists worry that there is "a not-so-subtle backlash" against the work of Gimbutas, and that in due time "her name will be deliberately 'disappeared' in the quagmire of academic 'scholarly' discussion."[41]

Matriarchal myth is a source of some controversy then, but it is also a cultural resource that is tapped into by many who are not feminists, or not primarily feminists. This use of matriarchal myth is especially prominent among environmentalists. It can be found in books like Thomas Berry's *The Dream of the Earth*, Jim Mason's *An Unnatural Order*, and even in Vice President Al Gore's book, *Earth in the Balance: Healing the Global Environment*.[42] Some Afrocentrists claim that Africa was not only the source of ancient Mediterranean culture, but also of the matriarchal social order that was eventually obliterated by patriarchal Europeans.[43] The most recent appropriation of feminist matriarchal myth is Leonard Shlain's *The Alphabet Versus the Goddess*, which argues that it is was literacy—the development of written language—that led to matriarchy's demise. By requiring greater effort from the left brain, which Shlain terms "masculine," language undercut the work of the image-oriented, "feminine" right brain, which had produced matriarchal, goddess-worshipping civilizations.

The myth of matriarchal prehistory is proudly proclaimed by some feminists, tacitly acknowledged by others, and studiously ignored by probably the majority, who may not find it plausible or appealing but don't wish to break feminist ranks. Given that this story has become (if mainly by default) *the* feminist account of prehistory, and given too its increasing currency among environmentalists, Afrocentrists, and even cultural theorists like Shlain, it is imperative that we take the time to see how this story developed and found its way into feminist circles, and to examine the picture feminist matriarchalists paint of prehistory, the explanations they offer for its demise, and the hopes they hold out for the future.

CHAPTER 3

The Story They Tell

The myth of matriarchal prehistory speaks to what seems to be an extremely common human need to trace the origin of important, and sometimes controversial, social institutions.[1] Feminist matriarchalists are not the first to seek an origin story to account for the principal institutions of male dominance—government, religion, marriage. They were anticipated in this by at least five generations of matriarchalists before them. The story of women's glorious past, it turns out, has a past of its own, a rich, ambiguous, multilayered past that in its broadest contours dates back to classical Greece, and in its more recent genealogy reaches back through a 140-year-old conversation about the respective roles of women and men in prehistoric times.

When I began my research, I was under the impression that while there had been a few nineteenth-century scholars who broached the subject of matriarchy, the myth was really a late-twentieth-century feminist invention, heavily indebted to archaeological finds that nineteenth-century scholars knew nothing about. What I found was that the story preceded the archaeology—and the feminism—to a surprising extent. Furthermore, an enormous array of individuals turned out to have spent some time—or a lot of time—with matriarchal myth. There were names I knew: J.J. Bachofen, Friedrich Engels, E. B. Tylor, Elizabeth Cady Stanton, Matilda Joslyn Gage, Erich Fromm, Wilhelm Reich, Robert Graves. And there were names I had to learn: Julius Lippert, Lothar Dargun, August Bebel, Alfred Bäumler, Uberto Pestalozza, Iu. I. Semenov. From the shadowy background of matriarchal myth in medieval cartographers' efforts to sketch presumed matriarchal lands onto their maps, through to late-twentieth-century feminist workshops on the sacred symbols of prehistoric goddess religions, stretches a vast territory of conservatism and radicalism, archaeology and poetry, economic determinism and mystical goddess worship, all embodied in a recognizably single myth. The myth of matriarchal prehistory has found adherents among socialists, anthropologists, communists, fascists, psychoanalysts, sexologists, folklorists, religionists, and a whole host of other notable characters. It has been used to justify patriarchy and to overthrow it, to hustle women back to hearth and home and to place them at the helm of the ship carrying us into the future.

THE EMERGENCE OF FEMINIST MATRIARCHAL MYTH

Until the late nineteenth century in Western Europe, matriarchy served more as an occasional literary trope than a purported history. All this changed in 1861 with the publication of Johann Jakob Bachofen's *Das Mutterrecht* (*Motherright*). Drawing on classical Greek sources (which, as we will later see, were full of references to women's rule), Bachofen postulated an era of matriarchy ending in classical times with the rise of men and the "male principle." He was quickly joined by a whole group of scholars pioneering the new discipline of anthropology along evolutionary lines (including John Ferguson McLennan, William Robertson Smith, Sir John Lubbock, Herbert Spencer, Lewis Henry Morgan, and E. B. Tylor, among others). Here matriarchal myth attained a status of cultural dogma for thirty years or so in the late nineteenth century, a status that it did not again approximate until its adoption by feminists one hundred years later. With little need to protect themselves from outside criticism, evolutionary anthropologists were free to concentrate on such burning questions as whether fraternal polyandry preceded patriarchy and whether the Omaha-Crow system of kinship terminology indicated group marriage. So firmly did the myth of matriarchal prehistory grip late nineteenth-century European and American intellectual life that even someone like Sigmund Freud—whose origin myths are primarily a fantasy of fathers, sons, and brothers murdering, cannibalizing, and repressing knowledge about one another—felt compelled to find a place for matriarchy, sandwiching it somewhere in between the "brother horde" and the patriarchy.[2]

In the late nineteenth century, the myth attracted not only anthropologists, but also others with less mainstream political agendas: specifically, socialists and feminists. Karl Marx had become interested in anthropology in the last few years of his life and was apparently, at the time of his death, working his way toward his own view of prehistory. His fragmentary notes were taken up by Friedrich Engels, and between these notes and a wholesale adoption of Morgan's earlier *Ancient Society*, Engels produced *The Origin of the Family, Private Property, and the State*.[3] This, along with a handful of other works, served to institutionalize the myth of matriarchal prehistory as a socialist origin story. Soon after, first-wave feminists began to see the myth's potential to dislodge the idea that patriarchy was universal and inevitable, and several European and American women—most influentially, Matilda Joslyn Gage, and later, Charlotte Perkins Gilman—wrote their own accounts of matriarchal myth, based on the anthropological treatises of the time.[4]

Anthropologists dropped the idea of matriarchy rather abruptly around the turn of the century (with the important exception of Soviet anthropologists, who stuck close to matriarchal myth—in the tradition established by Engels—until at least the 1950s[5]). The matriarchal thesis was discredited not through attacks on the evidence underlying it (though there were some), but through challenges to its assumptions. The universalizing premises of evolutionary anthropology came under fire, and the armchair anthropology upon which the matriarchal thesis relied was rejected in favor of a new emphasis on fieldwork. But when anthropologists dropped matriarchal myth, there were others waiting to pick it up. Between 1900 and 1970, the myth found some interesting champions. Within the academy, classicists such as Jane Ellen Harrison and George Thomson found echoes of a prior matriarchal time in Greek myth and ritual; archaeologists and art historians (including some very prominent ones like O. G. S. Crawford) discovered the footprints of matriarchy and goddess worship in the artifacts they studied; and a few maverick anthropologists, particularly E. S. Hartland and Robert Briffault, refused to let go of matriarchal theories, in spite of the jeers of most of their colleagues. Sir James George Frazer's wildly popular study of comparative mythology, *The Golden Bough*, included in its later editions much speculation on prehistoric goddess worship. Meanwhile, psychoanalysts studiously wove matriarchal threads into their emerging theories.

Erich Fromm used matriarchal myth to argue against the inevitability of violence, aggression, and war; Wilhelm Reich used it to buttress his claim that sexual freedom, even promiscuity, would result in more peaceful and harmonious, less repressed and patriarchal societies; and in the Jungian wing of psychology, Erich Neumann (*The Great Mother*) and others added even more layers of archetypal symbology (beyond those already provided by Bachofen) to the supposed prehistoric transfer of power from goddesses to gods. Well-known poet Robert Graves sang the praises of the "White Goddess" and foresaw an apocalypse in which patriarchal repression and rampant industrialization would give way to a return of the prehistoric goddess.[6] Most of this use of matriarchal myth came from the political left or center, but those on the extreme right invoked it also. Neo-romantic philosophers and protofascists in Germany, working from 1900 to 1930 (and even through the years of the Third Reich), spoke of the matriarch and the goddess, steeped in blood and soil, and yearned for their return.[7]

This was a relatively quieter time for matriarchal myth than what preceded and followed it. There were many pockets of interest in matriarchal myth, but no entire disciplines given over to its seductive power. And yet it is impressive to note the tenacity with which matriarchal myth clung to thinking about human prehistory during these years. Will Durant's *The Story of Civilization*, a standard reference work in print for more than two decades (from the 1930s to the 1950s) restated themes that most anthropologists had dispensed with by 1905: "Since it was the mother who fulfilled most of the functions," Durant argued, "the family was at first (so far as we can pierce the mists of history) organized on the assumption that the position of the man in the family was superficial and incidental, while that of the woman was fundamental and supreme." Like matriarchalists before and since, Durant gave women credit for inventing agriculture, weaving, basketry, pottery, woodworking, building, and trade, and claimed that "it was she who developed the home, slowly adding man to the list of her domesticated animals, and training him in those social dispositions and amenities which are the psychological basis and cement of civilization."[8]

In 1963, a multivolume *History of Mankind* was even more outspoken about the possibility of prehistoric matriarchy. In her chapter on

Paleolithic and Mesolithic society, Jacquetta Hawkes admitted that "today it is unfashionable to talk about former more matriarchal orders of society," but in her chapter on the Neolithic, Hawkes claimed that "there is every reason to suppose that under the conditions of the primary Neolithic way of life mother-right and the clan system were still dominant. . . . Indeed, it is tempting to be convinced that the earliest Neolithic societies throughout their range in time and space gave woman the highest status she has ever known. The way of life and its values, the skills demanded, were ideally suited to her." [9]

Matriarchal myth emerged with new vigor in the early 1970s, as second-wave feminists began to take it over in earnest, engineering a decisive shift in its meaning in the process. Prior to this, most matriarchalists regarded the patriarchal revolution as either a signal improvement over matriarchy, or at least a necessary, if regrettable, step toward the progressive civilization of humankind. But by the mid 1980s, the myth of matriarchy had definitively become a myth of regress, of paradise lost. These days it is virtually impossible to speak of ancient matriarchies and their overthrow by invading patriarchs without drawing feminist, or at least quasi-feminist lessons from the story. [10]

The contemporary feminist version of matriarchal myth was not adopted wholesale from earlier sources. As matriarchal myth was disseminated within and outside the feminist community in the 1970s and early 1980s, it was tweaked and prodded, growing through trial and error, assertion and retraction. Some of the earlier feminist matriarchal narratives appear, from the vantage point of the late 1990s, distinctly quirky. For example, Elizabeth Fisher, writing in 1979, used the early Neolithic site of Çatalhöyük to illustrate patriarchy's gradual encroachment into human society. Today every matriarchalist "knows" that Çatalhöyük is one of the very best exemplars of prehistoric matriarchal society. Likewise, Elizabeth Gould Davis's *The First Sex*, published in 1971, named Mycenaean Greece as matriarchal, a claim that no one has made in the past twenty years. [11] The rough consensus that now reigns—the consensus that, for example, names Çatalhöyük matriarchal and Mycenaean Greece patriarchal—took on its characteristic form under the pressure of three key developments: (1) the steadfast rejection of matriarchal myth by most feminist anthropologists; (2) a burgeoning feminist spirituality movement intent on placing goddess worship in prehistory; and (3) the pioneering archaeological work of Marija Gimbutas.

The first of these developments prevented anthropological versions of matriarchal myth from gaining anything more than a toehold in academia, and indeed had a chilling effect on matriarchal myth in the mainstream women's movement as well. As early feminists looked hopefully to other, "primitive" cultures for signs of matriarchy, they asked for corroboration from their anthropologist sisters. In the main, they didn't get it. Around the same time that Elizabeth Gould Davis was enticing readers with her descriptions of the great women-ruled empires of prehistory, Sherry Ortner, in her highly influential article "Is Female to Male as Nature Is to Culture?" was calling women's secondary status "one of the true universals, a pan-cultural fact," and asserting that "the search for a genuinely egalitarian, let alone matriarchal, culture, has proven fruitless." Anthropological denials of matriarchy extended as well to prehistory. "Males are dominant among primates," a group of feminist anthropologists noted in 1971, "and at the 'lowest' level of human social evolution now extant, males are still dominant. There is no reason to assume that in the intervening stages of human evolution the same situation did not prevail." [12]

If this was anthropological dogma, it was not anthropological consensus. A small group of socialist feminist anthropologists were diligently at work throughout the 1970s and 1980s developing a matriarchal myth of their own by updating the work of Friedrich Engels in *The Origin of the Family, Private Property, and the State*.[13] But this version of matriarchal myth was, in the final analysis, far too tepid to feed appetites whetted by the early women's movement. The best these anthropologists could serve up was the notion that human beings in small-scale "band" societies treated women and men equally, until property ownership, an incipient state, agricultural technologies, or even intergroup trade came into existence. Such a matriarchy was thin to begin with and easily gave way before the smallest signs of what we have come to think of as social progress.

The feminist spirituality movement offered something far more attractive. The position spiritual feminists envisioned for women in prehistory was not the "relative equality" stipulated by socialist feminist anthropologists. On the contrary, prehistoric woman was said to have been respected for her special feminine contributions to the human economy, if not positively revered as an embodiment of the great goddess.

The beginnings of the feminist spirituality movement roughly coincided with the second wave of feminism in the late 1960s and early 1970s. Feminist spirituality's organizational flexibility and its hostility toward any and all religious dogma defy attempts to define the movement or count its membership.[14] There are no "average" spiritual feminists, but when they gather together, it is most often to celebrate solstices and equinoxes; to perform rituals centering on self-empowerment, nature, and the worship (or embodiment of) goddesses from cultures around the world; to assist one another in divination, healing, magic, and guided meditations; and to teach one another the movement's "sacred history": the myth of matriarchal prehistory.

The centrality of this last activity should not be underestimated. In much the way the Exodus and Passion narratives serve as synecdoches of Judaism and Christianity, matriarchal myth holds together the otherwise extremely diverse feminist spirituality movement. Not every spiritual feminist believes that matriarchal societies once existed, but then there are Christians—some of them influential theologians—who regard the historicity of Jesus's life, crucifixion, and resurrection as immaterial to the true meaning of Christianity. Exceptions notwithstanding, the myth of matriarchal prehistory is foundational for feminist spirituality. Goddess worship itself is sometimes taken as a shorthand for matriarchal myth: goddesses are proof of matriarchy, reminders of it, and calls to recreate it.[15]

Introducing religion into the matriarchal equation, as spiritual feminists did, freed up an enormous amount of imaginative energy for feminist matriarchal myth. The idea that a great mother goddess was our ancestors' first object of veneration had been proposed by archaeologists and historians of religion long before spiritual feminists began to speak of her.[16] Neopagans already believed themselves to be reviving this religion. But spiritual feminists drew new conclusions from ancient goddess worship: first, they argued that it was enormously beneficial to women, who were her priestesses; second, they insisted that the goddess had been worshipped to the near exclusion of gods (on which point they departed from other neopagans); and third, they claimed that the clearest sign of patriarchy's triumph was the end of this exclusive goddess worship.

Merlin Stone was the first to assemble these pieces of the prehistoric puzzle in a convincing fashion. In her 1976 book, *The Paradise*

Papers (later retitled *When God Was a Woman*), Stone explained that the many names given to goddesses in ancient myths should not obscure the point that "the female deity in the Near and Middle East was revered as Goddess—much as people today think of God." She reasoned that "a religion in which the deity was female, and revered as wise, valiant, powerful and just" would provide "very different images of womanhood" from those of patriarchy; and she pondered at the close of her book "to what degree the suppression of women's rites has actually been the suppression of women's rights." [17]

Now this was a matriarchal myth worthy of feminist attention. But one link was missing: credibility. Stone aimed to provide this; she did extensive research, but since she did so as an art historian, some doubted the veracity of her conclusions. Real archaeological confirmation, enough to satisfy feminists eager to apply the stamp of authenticity to matriarchal myth, remained a scarce commodity until spiritual feminists discovered and adopted the work of Marija Gimbutas—who in turn adopted them.

Born in Lithuania, Marija Gimbutas did her graduate work in folkore and archaeology in Lithuania and Germany in the 1940s, and in 1949 immigrated to the United States. Unemployed for a time, she eventually found work translating Eastern European archaeological publications for Harvard University's Peabody Museum. By dint of hard work, tenacity, and undeniable talent, Gimbutas finally began to be recognized as an archaeologist in her own right. She received numerous grants, published lengthy works on Central and Eastern European archaeology, and directed her own excavations there. In 1963, she accepted a professorship at the University of California at Los Angeles which she kept until her retirement in 1989. [18]

Relatively late in her career, Gimbutas began to talk about the goddess, and to describe her reign as an unusually peaceful and harmonious time in which women enjoyed prominence and power. Gimbutas made her way toward these conclusions through her long-standing interest in Indo-European origins, a topic that was very much in vogue in Europe when her intellectual interests were first forming. While working in the United States, Gimbutas began again to ponder the location of the Indo-European "homeland"—the presumptive place from which speakers of Indo-European languages spread out to conquer many lands (linguistically, if not militarily).

She almost couldn't help tackling these issues: she had tremendous linguistic expertise—she read twenty different languages—and the sort of encyclopedic knowledge of Central and Eastern European archaeological sites that permitted her to speculate effectively on "big picture" questions.[19]

Working on Indo-European origins led Gimbutas to wonder what Europe was like before the process of "Indo-Europeanization," and excavations she directed in southeastern Europe began to provide clues. Among the artifacts that these and other excavations uncovered were a wealth of female figurines which Gimbutas identified as goddesses. Her first book-length attempt to interpret these artifacts was published in 1974 under the title *The Gods and Goddesses of Old Europe*. Although this work predated Merlin Stone's, it went virtually unnoticed by spiritual feminists, probably because Gimbutas did not write about prehistoric goddesses from a feminist point of view. "I was not a feminist," Gimbutas said of herself, "and I had never any thought I would be helping feminists."[20]

However, it would be disingenuous to suggest that once feminists *did* begin to support Gimbutas (as they did with the republication of *The Gods and Goddesses of Old Europe* in 1982, under the reversed title *The Goddesses and Gods of Old Europe*), it did not affect the course of her work. Her later books, *The Language of the Goddess* and *The Civilization of the Goddess*, went further and further to meet the ambitions of spiritual feminists in search of a prehistoric golden age for women.[21] Gimbutas is now routinely hailed by feminist matriarchalists as the brilliant polymath who has scientifically proven the claim that prehistoric societies were woman-centered and goddess-worshipping, and destroyed only recently. She is, Vicki Noble says, the "archeological Grandmother of feminist scholarship." Feminist matriarchalists cite Gimbutas, thank Gimbutas, and intimate that they would be nowhere without her work. Judy Grahn, a feminist poet, reports that she sometimes places one of Gimbutas's books on her home altar and whispers, "Marija, may we understand where you were going as quickly as possible."[22]

It is hard to overestimate the significance of Gimbutas and her work to the contemporary feminist myth of matriarchal prehistory. Gimbutas loaned her impressive archaeological credentials to the myth at a time when other academic archaeologists were steadfastly unwilling to do so. Though there are many intelligent and well-read partisans of the myth, Gimbutas is the only one who is an archaeologist. Her very existence—to say nothing of her work—has done much to enhance the credibility of feminist matriarchal myth in the eyes of the more mainstream audiences that feminist matriarchalists have been diligently endeavoring to win. As some have put it, in parody of a Christian bumpersticker, "Marija said it, I believe it, that settles it."[23]

THE MATRIARCHY

Just when and where do feminist matriarchalists believe that matristic societies flourished? The standard answers to these questions are "since the beginning of time" and "everywhere." Some feminist matriarchalists assert that society itself—the grouping together of human beings on an ongoing basis—was a female invention, built up around women and their children, with men playing little or no role.[24]

Claims to universality aside, however, the story feminist matriarchalists tell of prehistoric matriarchy is much narrower in scope. Some feminist matriarchalists find hopeful glimpses of protomatriarchy among nonhuman primates, and from there make the claim that all species situated evolutionarily between our primate ancestors and modern human beings (australopithecenes, *Homo habilis*, *Homo erectus*, and so on) had a gynocentric social orientation.[25] Others suggest that the so-called Acheulean hand axes (teardrops of quartz or flint) produced in great numbers by *Homo erectus* from roughly 1.5 million years ago to 200,000 BCE were actually goddess images rather than the stone tools archaeologists typically take them to be. One Acheulean artifact has generated special interest: found in the Golan Heights region of contemporary Israel, it dates somewhere between 800,000 and 200,000 BCE, was probably made by an archaic *Homo sapiens*, and is said by feminist matriarchalists to be an image of "the divine feminine, the Blessed Mother."[26]

In general though, feminist matriarchalists find little in this long era of human beginnings to interest them. They are not envisioning bands of near-chimps when they imagine matriarchal prehistory, but rather people like us, creating stable and prosperous societies with women at their center. As a result, feminist matriarchalists typically claim human origins as matricentric, but then fast-forward to the European Upper Paleolithic (beginning around 40,000 BCE), when quite suddenly far more extensive archaeological remains appear, including carved and painted images of women. It is in the Neolithic era, however—after the development of farming, but before the development of advanced metallurgy, between roughly 8000 and 3000 BCE—that matriarchalists most often locate the height of matriarchal culture.

Geographically, in its actual tellings, the myth of matriarchal prehistory almost always confines itself to Old (southeastern) Europe, the Near East, and the Mediterranean.[27] Old Europe, though painstakingly treated site by site in Marija Gimbutas's work, generally becomes an amorphous mass in the work of other feminist matriarchalists. In the Near East, several sites are mentioned, but there is only one of any consequence, and that is Çatalhöyük, dating to roughly 6500 BCE and located in Anatolia (present-day Turkey). Finally, the Mediterranean yields up the jewel of matriarchal culture, Minoan Crete, and also Malta, which is increasingly being adopted as another matriarchal homeland. On the infrequent occasions when the myth of matriarchal prehistory moves off this familiar turf, it is most often to Western Europe, especially England and Ireland. The only other place that is mentioned consistently is India, which is said to have been invaded by the same patriarchal tribes that destroyed the goddess-worshipping matriarchies of Old Europe.

It is easy to see the ethnocentrism in these choices: most of the narrators of the myth of matriarchal prehistory are Europeans or Americans of European extraction, and these are the lands they came from or that they regard as their proper cultural origin. Feminist matriarchalists have been self-conscious about their ethnocentrism, but they have rarely endeavored to broaden their scope beyond the lands that most white people think of as their cultural and ancestral home.[28] Most efforts in this direction have been undertaken by those with non-European cultural roots: Latinas and Native Americans have searched the literature on preconquest America for evidence of matriarchy; African Americans have looked to Africa; Asian Americans have explored Asian prehistory; Indians have investigated their own archaeological sites and religious customs for remnants of matriarchal culture.[29] The most significant attempt to expand the myth of matriarchal prehistory beyond its home in the so-called cradle of Western civilization has been undertaken by a mélange of matriarchalists all devoted to including Africa within the scope of matriarchal prehistory—or, more often, to making Africa matriarchy's original home.[30]

Though narrowed somewhat in practice by the chronological and geographical choices that feminist matriarchalists have made, prehistory is still a huge, and, as I will later argue, largely blank canvas. Thus incredibly diverse scenarios can be painted upon it, depending on the predilections of individual thinkers. Amid this diversity, however, a number of themes appear repeatedly in feminist descriptions of prehistoric matriarchal societies: peace, prosperity, harmony with nature, appropriate use of technology, sexual freedom (including reproductive freedom), and just and equitable roles for women and men. These are all thought to be the products of values engendered by the religion of the goddess. Some matriarchalists refer unapologetically to this era as a "utopia" or the "golden age."[31] However, feminist matriarchalists are intent on bringing prehistoric peoples closer to themselves in imagination, so our ancestors are said to have had problems—there were "temper tantrums and . . . tribal scores had to be settled"[32]—but they did not have *our* problems, which are overwhelming. In a poem titled "Tea with Marija," Starr Goode recounts an afternoon spent in conversation with Gimbutas at her home in Topanga Canyon, and closes with the lines:

> I ask—what were they, our ancestors?
> Marija says—they were like us, only
> happy.[33]

The one feature of matriarchal society that is noted more often than anything apart from goddess worship is the harmony that existed between people and nature. Matriarchal peoples were "attuned to the seasons and to the earth"; they were able to "live together harmoniously, in meaningful and exciting intercommunication with all the creatures of earth, earth herself, and the energy-beings of moon, sun, planets, and the stars."[34] This is sometimes conceptualized as a sort of psychic unity, but usually it is described more prosaically as a responsible relationship between people and the natural resources upon which they depended, expressed in the use of sustainable technologies.

It is crucial to feminist matriarchal myth that these technologies (weaving, architecture, mathematics, and so on) arose in societies that did not discriminate against women. As Vicki Noble explains, "without class stratification, centralized government, taxation, technology, warfare, or slavery, these early Goddess-loving people were able to invent everything we consider relevant today (except plastic and toxic chemicals)." Frequently, the invention of these technologies (including that of written language) is credited specifically to women.[35]

The most important thing women are said to have invented during matriarchal times is agriculture. The standard lore is that women were gatherers (as opposed to hunters) in preagricultural societies, and that through their familiarity with plant life, they "conceived the idea of sowing and harvesting seeds and figured out how to do it successfully where they wanted to." In 1978, Merlin Stone advocated that feminists adopt a new dating system, according to which 1978 was actually 9978 ADA—After the Development of Agriculture—emphasizing the fact that, as Charlene Spretnak puts it, "it was women who developed agriculture . . . leading all of humankind . . . into the Neolithic Era of stable agricultural settlements."[36]

One thing we usually associate with advanced technologies is said to have been lacking in matriarchal societies: private property. Feminist matriarchalists are not unanimous on this point,[37] but the picture they paint of prehistory is one of groups of people pooling most of their resources together. Perhaps more important to feminist matriarchalists is the belief that people pooled their children together. As June Stephenson asserts, "All children were protected and nourished by all women, and all women were therefore mothers to all children." There was "no sharp division . . . between home life and societal life," says Jane Alpert.[38] In other words, the distinction between public and private, which many late-twentieth-century feminists have considered a central characteristic of (if not a precondition for) the oppression of women, was utterly lacking in prehistory.

Having friends to help share the burden of work and child care is certainly an appealing vision for many feminist matriarchalists. What is probably more universally appealing is how people had sex in prehistory: which is to say, a lot, with whomever they wanted, and with no harm to their reputation. Sex in the matriarchies was for young and old women alike, and sexuality and motherhood were not regarded as antithetical to one another. If marriage existed, it did not require sexual fidelity to a single partner. Orgasms—for women, at least—were multiple and intense, and attained, at times, religious heights.[39] Lesbianism was as easily accepted as heterosexuality, sometimes more so.[40] Certainly rape and sexual abuse were unknown.

Like matriarchal women, the goddess herself was worshipped as a sexual being. Sex is sometimes imagined as having been akin to a positive religious duty in matriarchal societies, institutionalized in the form of "sacred prostitution." As Merlin Stone enthuses, "among these people the act of sex was considered to be so sacred, so holy and precious that it was enacted within the house of the Creatress of heaven, earth and all life."[41] All this sex—much of it heterosexual—was remarkably free of the usual consequence. Women bore children, but not constantly or unwillingly.

Just as sex was sacred, so were all other aspects of daily life in matriarchal societies. "Secular and sacred life in those days were one and indivisible," according to Gimbutas. People walked about "filled with awe by the mystery of nature," and "every aspect of the daily domestic routine was considered holy and imbued with ritual intent." This sense of sacrality was concentrated in the figure of the goddess. The goddess had many roles, but she is identified most often as mother. She is the divine creatrix, she who gives birth to the universe and everything in it. Interestingly, she is also linked strongly to death: she is "the wielder of the destructive powers of nature."[42] When Ariadne embodies the goddess during a spring ritual in June Rachuy Brindel's novel, she recites this poem, which sums up the picture of the goddess held by most feminist matriarchalists:

> I am She that is Mother of all things
> The waters and the earth, the sky and the wind,
> The power of life and the power of death;
> The fires of heaven and earth, the sun, the moon
> And all the stars are My progeny,
> Women and men, cattle, eagles, serpents,
> Wrathful lion and gentle dove. At My will
> All things grow and fill the universe,
> die and are renewed. Within my bounds
> All beings arise and die, are good and evil,
> Merciful and wrathful. All are within my womb.[43]

Since the goddess and human women shared the capacity to give birth, it was only natural that women would hold roles as religious functionaries in prehistoric matriarchies. Feminist matriarchalists imagine women serving as "priestesses, healers, and wisewomen," as "female elders," as "diviners, midwives, poets . . . and singers of songs of power": they were "custodians of the spiritual life" of their cultures.[44] Whether or not these exclusively female religious roles were complemented by exclusively female political roles is a matter of some debate among feminist matriarchalists. Most downplay the issue of political leadership altogether, seeming to suggest that these cultures functioned so smoothly that they did not require specially appointed leaders. However, if prehistoric societies were not truly "matriarchal"—ruled by women—then what was women's status, and how did it differ from men's?

The standard answer to this question goes back again to the issue of motherhood. Matriarchal societies are typically portrayed as being centered around mothers, with households consisting first of a mother and her children, and then possibly extending to include her brothers or her husband. Children took their mother's name and kinship status (matriliny); husbands went to live with their wives or mothers-in-law (matrilocality); women owned or controlled their family's property, insofar as it existed. This is not simply a description of prehistoric social arrangements: it is a statement about what matriarchal societies valued. Matriarchal power is different from patriarchal power, feminist matriarchalists say, because it is based on a natural (as opposed to an arbitrary) kind of power, that of motherhood. "The mother cares for the baby until it is able to move about easily by itself, find food, and protect itself without her," Marilyn French explains. "The mother 'rules' by greater experience, knowledge, and ability, but the intention of her 'rule' is to free the child, to make it independent."[45] This is finally the answer to who had social power in prehistoric matriarchies: mothers did; and because they were *mothers*, it was power handled ably, delicately, and benevolently.

Where did this leave men in matriarchal societies? As Phyllis Chesler puts it, "There are two kinds of people: mothers and their children." Men could never become mothers in matriarchal society (or anywhere else, for that matter), so they would then seem to be forever the second kind of person: children. But since, as we have already seen, the women of prehistoric matriarchies were well disposed toward their children, these societies are said to have been good places for men. As Heide Göttner-Abendroth explains, "In the matriarchal world the man is at once son, husband, and hero and completely embedded in the universe of women, who lovingly direct everything." [46]

Men were not necessarily infantilized in matriarchal societies. Different versions of the myth of matriarchal prehistory give men greater or lesser roles to play as adults. Men are thought to have had important male-specific roles in matriarchal societies: usually hunting, trade, and herding. Some matriarchalists suggest that women's and men's worlds were largely separate. They had separate duties, separate social networks, separate religious activities, and sometimes even separate living quarters. [47] But other matriarchalists fantasize a culture in which women and men interacted constantly and harmoniously. Mary Mackey's characters in *The Year the Horses Came* rarely perform sex-segregated tasks; even trade and hunting are conducted in mixed-sex groups. Crucially, however, men in prehistoric matriarchies are rarely imagined as having any substantive structural power within the family; certainly nothing that could rival the authority of women as mothers.

One of the most common (and longest-lived) explanations for *why* prehistory was matriarchal is the notion that prehistoric people—or at least prehistoric men—were not aware of a male role in reproduction. With no connection drawn between sexual intercourse and conception, matriarchalists argue, children would have appeared to be the miraculous product of women alone. [48] This central attention to the fact of childbirth is the hallmark of virtually all feminist reconstructions of matriarchal society. "Woman, as her name implies," writes Janet Balaskas, "is the human with a womb." When feminist matriarchalists describe women's ability to bear children, they speak of "mystery," "miracle," "magic," and the "awe" and "reverence" that this inspired in prehistoric peoples. Feminist matriarchalists expand this to a more generalized reverence for all the sex-specific functions of the female body, including menstruation, lactation, and female sexual response. Menstruation is "bleeding without injury"; it is "primeval dragontime blood," a "shamanic death and rebirth every month" which indicates women's "intimate relationship with the mysteries of the universe," especially "the swelling and ebbing of the moon." [49] This rhapsody to the female body offered by Riane Eisler is fairly typical:

> Our Paleolithic and early Neolithic ancestors imaged woman's body as a
> magical vessel. They must have observed how it bleeds in rhythm with
> the moon and how it miraculously produces people. They must also have
> marveled that it provides sustenance by making milk for the young. Add
> to this woman's seemingly magical power to cause man's sexual organ to
> rise and the extraordinary capacity of woman's body for sexual plea-
> sure—both to experience it and to give it—and it is not surprising that
> our ancestors should have been awed by woman's sexual power.[50]

Together, women and the goddess, each the reflection of the
other, are thought to have formed a "mysterious female universe"
that reached out to encompass nature—which, feminist matriarchalists note, also brings forth life. Out of this synergy, say feminist
matriarchalists, a culture and a religion were born, the finest the
world has ever seen.

THE PATRIARCHAL REVOLUTION

The narrative of matriarchal myth wheels around abruptly to unmiti-
gated disaster with the rise of the patriarchy, as catastrophic an event
as one could imagine. Obviously, the difficult question is the simplest
one: Why? Why did this golden age fall, only to see the world
plunged into barbarism and misery? Feminist matriarchalists offer
two basic types of explanations for what caused the patriarchal revolution: internal and external. In the first model, critical things—
economy, the family—changed within matriarchal cultures, giving
rise to male dominance. In the second model, matriarchal cultures
were attacked and eventually defeated by patriarchal invaders, who
then substituted their own social institutions for those of the cultures
they conquered. These models are often mixed—certain factors predisposed matriarchal peoples toward patriarchy, but armed attack by
patriarchal invaders tipped the balance. In either case, the patriarchal
revolution is dated to roughly the same time: 3000 BCE.[51]

Among internal explanations for the patriarchal revolution, one
reigns supreme: the idea that men discovered, fairly late in the game,
that they played a role in human reproduction. Knowledge came,
some say, when humans began to domesticate animals and observed
a cause-and-effect relationship between sexual intercourse and conception.[52] Men, who had long envied the "body mysteries" of
women, took this opportunity to seize control of those aspects of re-

production which they could control—namely, the paternity of individual children—and debase those aspects they could not control (such as menstruation).

Male discontent—in this particular explanation for the patriarchal revolution—turns out to be a bit of a worm in the apple, since men were supposed to be content with their lot in matriarchal societies. Men *were* happy in matriarchal societies, feminist matriarchalists say, but they were also beseiged with a nagging sense of their own dispensability. They felt "marginal" or "empty," like outsiders; they lacked "the rich sense of herself that women had in those early times, because she was the childbearer"; they suffered a "primal jealousy" of "a woman's total commitment to her infant"; they "felt themselves to be essentially different" from women, not quite "flesh of the mothers' flesh, after all"; and they envied women's ability to menstruate, since it was associated with heightened "psychic awareness and inner vision." Under matriarchal conditions, feminist matriarchalists say, men's sense of inadequacy was carefully contained. As an old woman explains to Ariadne in June Brindel's novel of Minoan Crete, "in the old time, they were in awe and could be gentled." But now, she says, "they are all killers." In the most dangerous mimicry of menstruation, men develop warfare as a "parody of women's monthly bloodshed."[53]

The other leading internal explanation for the patriarchal revolution attributes it to the changeover from small-scale farming techniques (horticulture or "hoe agriculture") to large-scale agriculture ("plow agriculture") and herding. Plow agriculture generally required the use of irrigation systems and domesticated animals to pull plows, and, so the story goes, the superior upper-body strength of men. With the means of production thus effectively placed in men's hands, and farming raised to a level where surpluses could be produced and traded, all the conditions for patriarchal revolution were in place.[54] Then all that was required was for men to acquire the will to amass property and social power, use both to their advantage, and pass them to their own progeny. In this department, men were not lacking, though again it is not clear what prompted their avarice.

Animal husbandry has a particularly insidious role to play in this version of the patriarchal revolution. Not only is it sometimes credited with revealing the truth about paternity (especially to men, who are usually—though not always—said to have developed animal husbandry), but it is also thought to have advanced patriarchy by allowing men to practice techniques of oppression on animals that they would later perfect on women. Things previously unthinkable—forced labor, forced reproduction, confinement—became not only thinkable but doable once they had been done to animals. Further, by observing animals men saw that it was possible for one male to dominate an entire herd, an observation that they then transferred to human society.

All internal explanations for the patriarchal revolution tend to find fault with men. Of course, the myth of matriarchal prehistory is a highly gendered story, and the transition from "good" prehistory to "bad" history is, in its most unadorned formulations, a change from the peaceful, harmonious world of women to the awful, wicked world of men. And yet narrators of the myth are generally reluctant to blame men—at least not all men, or men as a class—for the patriarchal revolution, if only to leave room for a future which will include men without allowing them to dominate. Ironically, when faced with this dilemma, feminist matriarchalists most often turn to external explanations for the patriarchal revolution, particularly invasion theories, in which villains abound.

When it comes to patriarchal invaders, none can rival the popularity of the Kurgans from the Russian steppes (the term Kurgan was coined by Marija Gimbutas to name the invading patriarchs, and is drawn from a form of burial which Gimbutas takes to be the archaeological signature of the group[55]). This was the group situated to wipe out the matriarchal societies most favored in matriarchal myth: those in Old Europe, the Near East, and the Mediterranean. Two key characteristics of the Kurgans (apart from the obvious, that they were male-dominated) are usually mentioned: they were pastoralists, and they were nomads. The tension between the sedentary agricultural economy of the south (the matriarchies) and the nomadic pastoral economy of the north (the patriarchy) is constantly reinforced in tellings of the myth. So are other oppositions, including that the Kurgans were large, blue-eyed, and blond-haired, while the people of the matriarchies were smaller and darker.[56] Another, somewhat curious opposition is that between matriarchal women and Kurgan men. Though there were clearly men in the matriarchal societies, it was women who were central, whereas in Kurgan society, at least as it is narrated by feminist matriarchalists, women rarely surface at all.[57] Once these contrasting cultures come into contact, the result is predictable: the patriarchs "sweep down" on matriarchal cultures in "huge hordes" and "overrun" them, riding in on horses, animals which matriarchal peoples had never seen before.

This story, in its bare outlines, raises several obvious questions, ones which feminist matriarchalists strive—with varying degrees of success—to answer: Where did the Kurgans come from? How did they come to be patriarchal? What inspired them to invade the matriarchal cultures? How did they carry out their nefarious mission? How were they able to overwhelm the matriarchal peoples not just for a generation or two, but for all time up to the present day?

The question of where the Kurgans came from has a rote answer: the Russian steppes. Gimbutas has brought great precision to questions of the Kurgan homeland. She centers it in southwestern Russia where the Don and Volga rivers approach one another most closely, extending downward from there toward the northern shores of the Black Sea and eastward toward Kazakhstan and the northern shores of the Caspian Sea.[58] Rhetorically speaking—apart from any archaeological data confirming or disconfirming this theory—this is a terrific place to locate the patriarchal homeland. What is required is a territory big enough to be home to a largish population of marauding warriors; a place from which one can, without crossing enormous geographical barriers (such as oceans) reach Europe and the Near East; a region whose prehistory is neither noble nor well documented; and, finally, since no one wants to come from the place where patriarchy began, a land that is sparsely populated today. On all counts, the Russian steppes—"no man's land"—fit the profile.[59] Indeed, there is little evidence that most narrators of the myth of matriarchal prehistory know where the Russian steppes are. Maps are rare in feminist matriarchalist literature, and identifying geographical features are typically vague when given at all.[60] This is a notable omission in works whose entire premise hinges on the existence and spread of a group of conquering warriors hailing from a specific location. Furthermore, peaceful prehistoric matriarchies seem to have been everywhere, including Russia, and even, according to some matriarchalists, "on the vast steppes of Russia." Perhaps truer to the spirit of the myth of matriarchal prehistory is Riane Eisler's frequent insistence that the patriarchal invaders came from "the barren fringes of the globe,"[61] a place securely off the map of anywhere we might want to call home.

One cannot point to a map or invoke a stock phrase to explain how the Kurgans came to be patriarchal. This more complex question is given a variety of answers, including that herding animals or living in a harsh climate brought out the worst in men. But most frequently, there is no answer at all (which is not to say that feminist matriarchalists do not regard it as a valid question; on the contrary, they consistently state that *something* must have caused the Kurgans to become patriarchal, since all human societies were originally matriarchal[62]). As Merlin Stone notes, why the Kurgans became patriarchal is "a moot question," since they only come "to our attention" after they arrive "in the Goddess-worshiping communities of the Near and Middle East." Similarly, Gimbutas does not believe it correct to speak of "Kurgan people" until "they conquered the steppe region north of the Black Sea around 4500 B.C."—in other words, only after they were already launched on the path of patriarchal conquest.[63]

The Kurgans are the star players in invasion theories, but they did not have to patriarchalize the world all by themselves. They had help, occasionally from nameless nomads in other parts of the world, but most often from the Semites; specifically, the Hebrews. As Elizabeth Gould Davis explains, "it was these people, cultureless and semicivilized, who first upset civilization in the ancient East by overthrowing the city states and later by dethroning the ancient goddess and enthroning male strife in the form of Yahweh." Feminist matriarchalists speculate that the Hebrews, like the Kurgans, suffered the ill effects of nomadic pastoralism and a harsh climate. But they also accuse the Hebrews of having taken especially cruel steps to destroy goddess religion. The anti-Semitism implicit in this thesis—"blaming the Jews for the death of the Goddess"—has been much commented upon, but the belief that Semitic invaders helped to crush matriarchal cultures is still very much a part of the myth of matriarchal prehistory.[64]

There are a few remaining explanations feminist matriarchalists give for the patriarchal revolution. Matriarchal culture is sometimes said to have fallen apart owing to "famine, disease, [and] natural cataclysm," when "a series of violent volcanic eruptions, earthquakes, and tidal waves rocked the Mediterranean world." Men, with their superior physical strength, took on a new importance as economic scarcity produced intertribal warfare. A few feminist matriarchalists offer astrological explanations: patriarchy arises in the martial age of Aries and flourishes in the Piscean Age (which is "concerned with duality"), or else patriarchy is nothing more than the "dark moon phase of the Goddess," who in the immediate past five-thousand-year "lunation cycle" withdrew herself and all "feminine energies" from humanity. Another theory, offered rarely, and more in desperation than in earnestness, is that extraterrestrials landed on Earth in 3000 BCE. They either taught us all how to behave badly, or else joined us, becoming the males of the human species. More common, though still unusual, is the theory that men—or at least men as they are presently constituted—are the result of an unfortunate genetic mutation. This theory generally has little explanatory power for the patriarchal revolution because the mutations which created men are thought to have occurred well before 3000 BCE. However, Kristie Neslen, author of *The Origin*, offers an alternative mutation theory linked directly to the patriarchal revolution: Kurgan men, she suggests, mutated toward "a higher level of androgen and androgen sensitivity" and became more violent and aggressive than the men in the matriarchal cultures to the south, whom they were thus able to defeat with ease.[65]

Part of the problem is that behind the "historical" question of when and why patriarchy arose lies another, more fundamental and disturbing question: How could something as horrible as patriarchy come to exist in the first place and then continue to thrive? This question stems from a deep (and very common) need to explain evil in such a way that it does not swallow up all the good in the world. Feminist matriarchalists face this challenge in a variety of ways. Some claim that the patriarchal revolution was, quite simply, an accident: a very big, very bad accident. The foremost proponent of this viewpoint is Riane Eisler, who consistently refers to the patriarchy as "a bloody five-thousand-year dominator detour" from "the original partnership direction of Western culture." Since then, patriarchy has persisted largely through tradition. People are socialized to accept it as normal, and so they do. The solution is simple: in Eisler's words, we "allow our cultural evolution to resume its interrupted course."[66]

That humanity could descend to such depths of depravity and stay there for five thousand years by accident alone, however, is an inadequate answer for most. So feminist matriarchalists often struggle to find some way of comprehending the patriarchy that makes it, while terrible, nevertheless necessary or useful. One such way is to imagine the switch from matriarchy to patriarchy as a cycle which, over the long span of human history, is relatively benign. Another response is to argue that patriarchy had some redeeming features. Generally, these redeeming features are not specified; rather, there is simply the reassurance that patriarchal institutions "served their purposes, or they wouldn't have lasted as long as they did." More often, the whole question of how—and why—the patriarchy came to be is put off as mysterious or irrelevant. Indeed, some claim that dwelling on this question is a diversion, one that serves patriarchal interests. Feminist matriarchalists encourage their readers to stick to the point. As Kristie Neslen says, "Alas, each possible explanation for how patriarchy arose only seems to bring up more questions. Ultimately the 'why' does not matter as much as the 'how.' " [67]

The "how" of the patriarchal revolution is very similar across different versions of the myth of matriarchal prehistory. Once the patriarchal revolution was under way, it proceeded by means of warfare, slavery (including sexual slavery), and religion, through which the patriarchy consolidated its power and staked a claim in Western consciousness that is still deeply ingrained five thousand years later.

What guaranteed short-term victory for the Kurgans was the monopoly of force they commanded. According to feminist matriarchal myth, matriarchal peoples did not manufacture weapons of war; their villages and towns were undefended; and, perhaps most critical, they did not have the moral will to wage war: it went against everything in their value system. When (and if) they learned to fight back and defend themselves, say feminist matriarchalists, they were starting from too far back in the game. Some add that once the matriarchal peoples learned the arts of war, they were no longer what they had been: the virus of violence and male domination had entered them, and it was only a question of time before they became indistinguishable from their patriarchal enemies.[68]

With warfare comes slavery, and with slavery, a more perfect means of oppression. According to Gerda Lerner, when large-scale warfare first began, men who were caught in war were killed, while women, who were easier to control and who could be used to breed children, were enslaved.[69] Gradually, this basic form of relationship—that of master and slave—came to infect all relationships between men and women. As men discovered their role in conception, they wished to ensure that their property would go to their biological offspring. But in order to determine paternity with certainty, men had to restrict women's sexual behavior. Once a woman's sexuality "belonged" to one man (or in the case of prostitutes, to whichever man purchased it for the moment), she became, in a real if limited sense, his property.

The final mechanism for perpetrating a patriarchal revolution was religion. Patriarchal religion developed in two directions: the construction of a male-dominated pantheon and worship of a single male god. Feminist matriarchalists sometimes see this as an evolutionary development—first the patriarchs sapped female deities of their power, then later eradicated them—but these two types of patriarchal religion are related rather transparently to the two purported sources of patriarchal invasions: the Kurgans and the Hebrews. The Kurgans insinuated their propaganda into the psyches of matriarchal peoples by splitting the matriarchal great goddess into dozens of goddesses, each with her own "department." These goddesses were then married to Kurgan sky gods (or raped by them) to form a dual-gendered, male-dominated pantheon. The Semitic solution (documented, say feminist matriarchalists, in the Bible) was to erect a single male god called "Father" in the place of the great goddess of matriarchal times. Ultimately, this god takes more heat from feminist matriarchalists than do the Kurgan sky gods. It was not until "we began to worship one male god," some feminist matriarchalists say, that we truly "became patriarchal."[70]

PATRIARCHY AND BEYOND

How do women and men fare in patriarchy? In a word, poorly. Women's victimization is systemic. But men are banished from the garden as well, according to feminist matriarchal myth. No longer the cherished sons of the goddess, men are subject to cruel hierarchies of status among themselves, alienation from women and nature, and a painfully limited range of role choices.[71]

Feminist matriarchal myth does not imagine much change over time and place in the structure of patriarchy. Women's status has fluctuated over the past five thousand years but has never changed substantially from that established by the patriarchal revolution. However, under this smooth patriarchal exterior lies a subterranean river of goddess religion which emerges in folklore and nonelite religious practices, and even surfaces—albeit in disguise—in the patriarchal religions of the West (particularly in the person of the Virgin Mary). Matriarchal myth is replete with accounts of churches built on top of old goddess shrines, Catholic saints who are goddesses in disguise, and Christian holidays that are mere adaptations of pagan festivals.[72]

Most feminist matriarchalists regard the return of goddess-worshipping matriarchal cultures (in one form or another) to be a possibility, and some—though not many—regard it as a foregone conclusion. There is a very strong apocalyptic strain in feminist matriarchal myth that shows itself in dire comments about the possible death of the planet. But there is also some confidence that "patriarchal structures are cracking at the seams," that we are reaching "an evolutionary dead end." As Hallie Iglehart Austen tells us, "The world is more ready for her [the Goddess] than it has been for millennia and more in need of her than it has been for all of human existence."[73] It is an exciting and awful time to be alive.

It is often thought that women will play a special role in bringing about this enormous social revolution. They will balance out men's tendencies to be "aggressive, competitive, and possessive," and allow a new, more cooperative social order to emerge.[74] Others, however, suggest that the solution to the present predicament lies equally with men: either with their ability to recognize the damage they have done and to step aside and let women repair it, or, more positively, to follow in women's footsteps by adopting "feminine" ways of being, working in concert with women for social regeneration. The "rediscovery" of matriarchal prehistory is itself sometimes seen as a sign that the patriarchy will soon collapse and make way for something new.[75]

There is no single vision of what the future will be, but interestingly, there is near unanimity that it will not be a simple recreation of our prehistoric matriarchal past. If nothing else, our "much larger population" and "greater technological complexity" make it impossible, say feminist matriarchalists, to reproduce prehistoric matriarchies in the twenty-first century.[76] Pragmatic considerations are not the only ones operative here; some feminist matriarchalists do not wish to return to prehistoric matriarchies because they regard them as being "out of balance" in a feminine direction, just as patriarchy is imbalanced in a masculine direction. Matriarchy and patriarchy are thought to represent extremes, while the future has the potential of bringing a new, superior synthesis.

Most feminist matriarchalists, however, are unwilling to count the matriarchies as flawed. Certainly they are not as flawed as the patriarchy that followed. The future feminist matriarchalists seek is most commonly a recreation of prehistoric matriarchy on a "higher," more technologically advanced level: completing a circle back to matriarchy, as Barbara Mor and Monica Sjöö describe it, but at the same time, as on a spiral, revolving to "a larger circle." Just where women will stand in these future societies ranges from equality with men to special respect for women to being "dominant and listened to" under a form of government described as "a socialist matriarchy."[77] Some feminist matriarchalists indulge in involved fantasies of what a future matriarchal utopia would include; others never look too far beyond "the matriarchal counterrevolution that is the only hope for the survival of the human race."[78]

This, then, is the story that has given many feminists today an enhanced sense of self-confidence and pride in their femaleness, and a deep hope for the future of us all. With benefits like these, it is no surprise that the myth of matriarchal prehistory has attracted a substantial and enthusiastic following. But before we risk advancing it as either a desirable account of human history or a true one, it is important to explore the myth's gendered assumptions.

CHAPTER 4

The Eternal Feminine

The myth of matriarchal prehistory is a univeralizing story: once things were good, everywhere; now they are bad. And since the operative terms in matriarchal myth are gendered ones, what emerges by way of explanation is a robust, universal theory of sex difference. Matriarchalist assumptions about how sex determines personality, preferences, and values are sometimes only implicit, but they are always present. Though some interpreters earnestly attempt to avoid these implications of matriarchal myth, the myth continues to feed off of a very reductive notion of who women—and by extension, men—are.

SEX DIFFERENCES IN MATRIARCHAL MYTH

Feminist matriarchalist assessments of femininity and masculinity are rooted most strongly in a particular vision of female embodiedness. Feminist matriarchalists frequently refer to their bodies as a source of insight, knowledge, and power, a source more reliable than "what a woman might know with her mind." This embodiedness does not stop with the individual; women's bodies are said to be the "only true microcosm" of the universe. Female bodies are thus the vehicle through which we are supposed to recognize the value of the earth and of nature.[1] With near unanimity, feminist matriarchalists assert that these connections between women, bodies, and nature are not simply poetic metaphors or politically savvy conceptualizations, but a fact of life, based primarily on women's ability to reproduce.[2]

Reproduction, as we have seen, is perceived as miraculous by feminist matriarchalists. It is also thought to teach women an important spiritual lesson that is less available to men. When pregnant, women have "an Other inside." As the boundary between "me" and "not-me" becomes blurred, women come to appreciate that "everything is intimately connected, everything is oneness."[3] Beyond pregnancy, discussion of the skills and traits that mothers must develop to deal effectively with infants and children sometimes makes its way into matriarchalist discourse. Jane Alpert, for example, draws attention to qualities she sees issuing from the practice of motherhood, including "empathy, intuitiveness, adaptability, awareness of growth as a process rather than as goal-ended; inventiveness, protective feelings toward others, and a capacity to respond emotionally as well as rationally." More commonly, however, the emphasis is on childbirth itself. For example, when Marrah gives birth to twins in Mary Mackey's novel *The Horses at the Gate*, the first three years of the children's lives pass in less than twenty pages. Most of these pages concern the plottings of Marrah's enemies. All we learn of Marrah's first three years as a mother is that "the twins grew fat on Marrah's milk" and that she and her lover Stavan were occupied with training horses.[4] Clearly the actual work of motherhood takes a distant backseat to the miracle of reproduction.

This focus on childbirth has been troublesome to many feminists, even to those who are strongly attached to the myth of matriarchal prehistory. At one level it seems to suggest that unless and until women give birth, they are excluded from this most essential of female "mysteries." This has the potential to become quite a problem, since many feminist matriarchalists—probably more than the national average—are childless.[5] As a consequence, much effort is devoted to assuring women that the actual bearing of children is not necessary in order to express feminine creativity, fertility, and closeness to nature. As Meinrad Craighead explains, "whether or not a woman does conceive, she carries the germinative ocean within her, and the essential eggs." Whatever women create, be it "tissue in the womb or pictures in the imagination," it is created "out of our bodies."[6]

Since a female identity centered on childbearing is problematic, feminist matriarchalists have at times attempted to center it elsewhere, typically on menstruation. As Anne Carson explains, menstruation is "one feature of our bodies that all women can share and celebrate, whether we are heterosexual or lesbian, mothers or childless."[7] But the focus does come back unerringly to childbirth, probably because producing menstrual blood is simply not as impressive as producing a human being. Furthermore, childbirth is one of the few remaining fortresses of femaleness in a time when most of the accoutrements of female sex can be purchased for the price of hormones and a surgical operation. The ability to bear children is the only thing of great value that women have that "men could never take from them"[8]—or at least that they haven't taken yet.

Built on this foundation of childbirth is a larger structure of femaleness which concentrates on such traditional "feminine" virtues as nurturance and compassion. Women "tend to cluster," says Maureen Murdock. They "like being related, helpful, connected." In essence—and I choose that word with care—feminist matriarchalists portray women as naturally good, kind, loving human beings. Women "do not use their power to dominate or to subordinate," but rather "to increase the well-being of their environment." They "are naturally inclined to assume responsibility for the welfare of others," and they prefer "a more securely ordered, fruitful, lawful, ethical, and spiritual way of life."[9]

If this is what women are like, what should we expect from men? Mostly, it turns out, the opposite. Charlene Spretnak (drawing on the work of "neuropsychologists") says that men "excel at many visual-spatial tasks, daylight vision, and gross motor movements," but that "when it comes to grasping oneness and at-large bonding (i.e., active empathy with people beyond one's circle), most men are simply not playing with a full deck." Elizabeth Gould Davis puts it more bluntly: "Man is the enemy of nature: to kill, to root up, to level off, to pollute, to destroy are his instinctive reactions to the unmanufactured phenomena of nature, which he basically fears and distrusts." Aggressiveness, possessiveness, and competitiveness are all said to be male traits. Men are as capable of thought as women are, but what distinguishes them from women is that their rationality is the "cold, divisive, or killing calculation of logic."[10]

One matriarchalist vision of men puts them in the role of wild little boys who, under matriarchal control, would become harmless and amusing. Merlin Stone suggests that through goddess spirituality, women are saying to men, "Stop this pretense of glory and importance, and look at the mess you've made!" Barbara Walker imagines that without the monotheistic male God standing behind men, women would "simply laugh at male posturings of self-validation and assertiveness" and would respond to them "with nothing more than her ancient, casual 'Yes, dear, that's nice, run along now.'" Another matriarchalist vision casts men in a considerably more sinister role. In this view, men have no "energy" of their own and so must pirate it from women. They "literally and figuratively plug into" women, casting women in the role of "batteries" or "the Vampire's energy source."[11]

One wonders how women and men ever could have lived happily together, especially when what is wrong with men often seems to be quite permanent. Some feminist matriarchalists have described men as mutants whose "small and twisted Y chromosome" is "a genetic error" resulting from, perhaps, "disease or a radiation bombardment from the sun."[12] Other feminist matriarchalists find men's eternal secondariness illustrated in the development of human embryos. Claiming that all human embryos "are anatomically female during the early stages of fetal life," they conclude, with Rosalind Miles, that women are "the original, the first sex, the biological norm from which males are only a deviation." No wonder a T-shirt proclaims "T.G.I.F. (Thank Goddess I'm Female)," for who would voluntarily choose to be male?[13]

Feminist matriarchalist thought is not always characterized by these excesses of misandry. There are other, more prominent strains in matriarchal myth that take a far more accommodating attitude toward men (though not ultimately ones that put men on an equal footing with women). Many feminist matriarchalists emphasize the point that women—and also the goddess—give birth to males as well as females. When pregnant with boys, women contain maleness within themselves, and this is taken as a metaphor for the ultimate inclusion of men within a female universe. Men are embedded within nature, just as women are, though owing to the natural limitations of their bodies—their lack of firsthand experience of menstruation or childbirth—it is more difficult for them to achieve this insight.[14]

Some feminist matriarchalists try to provide—or at least allow for the existence of—positive male role models, the sort of men who might have lived and flourished in prehistoric times. The Motherpeace tarot deck, created by Vicki Noble and Karen Vogel, includes

"Sons" in each of the four suits who "represent positive male energy" and who can "help a person imagine positive ways of being male in a culture where 'male supremacy' has all but destroyed manhood." Just what these "positive ways of being male" are Noble does not say, though she remarks that it is "ugly and gross to equate masculinity with murder and rape, pillage, greed, and a mindless ransacking of the planet," and she articulates the hope that "some other manifestation of the Masculine" is "waiting to be revealed to us." As Monica Sjöö remarks, "boy children are not born patriarchs, nor is it through a natural process that men become such." [15] In other words, according to most feminist matriarchalists, men are not beyond hope.

In fact, many feminist matriarchalists do not regard maleness as a problem at all. In its place, "masculinity" is as important and valuable as "femininity"; the key is that the two must be in balance, not only in society as a whole, but in individual human beings as well, some say. All "creative and inspirational thinking, all nurturing, mothering and gestating, all passion, desire and sexuality, all urges towards connectedness, social cohesion, union and communion, all merging and fusion as well as impulses to absorb, to destroy, to reproduce, and to replicate" are included in the "universal archetype of the feminine," say Jennifer and Roger Woolger, but this does not mean that these qualities are closed off to men. Feminist matriarchalists sometimes invite men to encounter their "feminine side" or the "feminine within." Likewise they suggest that women have a "masculine side" with which they are more or less closely in touch. [16] "Masculine" and "feminine" thus become congeries of characteristics which, while arranged under gendered labels, have nothing to do with the potentialities of either gender or with physical sex.

Or so the theory goes. But it is very difficult to disconnect terms like masculine and feminine from male and female persons. When feminists were fighting the battle against the use of generic male terms, they pointed out, quite rightly, that so long as the same term was used to mean both male-specific and person-general, people would continue to "see" the normative person as male and woman as "other." Surely the same is true of the adjectives "feminine" and "masculine": apologetics aside, hearers will always call up mental pictures of the requisite sex when these words are in use. If feminist matriarchalists were truly eager to make the point that the characteristics we have labeled "feminine" and "masculine" were erroneously attached to sexed persons when they are actually the property of all regardless of sex, then one would think that they would simply dispense with the terms. The reason they do not is because they are *not* eager to lose the gendered connotations of the terms (in spite of occasional protestations to the contrary), and it is worth asking why.

In fairness, some feminist matriarchalists have made earnest attempts to discard the terminology of "the feminine." Starhawk, for example, has increasingly resisted the use of such terms, telling Mary Beth Edelson in 1989 that "'feminine principle' doesn't mean much—it's one of the many terms that makes us *think* we know what we're talking about when we don't. I think we should declare a moratorium on its use." [17] But most feminist matriarchalists do not want to sacrifice their special access to "the feminine" on the altar of gender neutrality; at least not yet. So they grope around for alternative terms (never very successfully), hedge themselves about with disclaimers, and then wade right back into the morass of gender stereotypes they profess some interest in escaping.

There can be no better exemplar of this phenomenon than Riane Eisler. Eisler has been particularly diligent in instructing her readers not to confuse "femininity" with women, or "masculinity" with men, and to recall that these sexual stereotypes are "socially constructed" rather than corresponding "to any inherent female or male traits." [18] Yet her work is filled with these terms (always carefully enclosed in scare quotes).

The idea that femininity belongs most properly to women, while men are also capable of possessing it, conforms to common usage. (That is, "femininity" is the sum of all those characteristics thought to be descriptive of—and appropriate to—women, but men sometimes evince those traits, and when they do, they are called "feminine" or "effeminate.") It is peculiar though that feminist matriarchalists like Eisler should retain this usage, as it is based on a deep dichotomy between women and men, femininity and masculinity. And arranging the world into dualisms (like feminine and masculine) is said by feminist matriarchalists to be a patriarchal practice. Indeed, some feminist matriarchalists claim that this was the key patriarchal innovation that put an end to the matriarchal way of thinking, which was "wholistic" and "deliberately non-dualistic." [19]

In spite of this, the entire premise of feminist matriarchal myth is dualistic: there was a time in the past, associated with women, when people lived and thought one way; now there is a time, associated with men, when people live and think in another way. Furthermore, matriarchy and patriarchy are not simply two ways of being in the world, existing in a complementary balance (the sort of relationship feminist matriarchalists sometimes envision for women and men, "feminine" and "masculine"); they are polar opposites, one good and the other evil. In feminist matriarchal thought, the goddess, who abjures dualisms, is constantly pitted in direct opposition to the patriarchal god of western cultures, whose primary failing is his penchant for separating "us" from "them," "good" from "bad," "mind" from "body," and, of course, "women" from "men." In a remarkable piece of double-think, Elizabeth Judd tells us that "the recognition of rigid gender distinctions is characteristic of males but not females";[20] and yet here she is, female, marking out rigid gender distinctions upon which her entire theory of human life and history rests.

The hope seems to be that with the one, correct, overarching dualism—whether matriarchy versus patriarchy, partnership versus dominator, goddess versus god—all the other terms will lose their polarizing grip. Eisler says this explicitly: "Through the use of the dominator and partnership models of social organization for the analysis of our present and our potential future, we can . . . begin to transcend the conventional polarities between right and left, capitalism and communism, religion and secularism, and even masculinism and feminism." But in Eisler's work, nothing like this happens. Instead, the oppositional terms proliferate. All manner of human qualities and behaviors are relentlessly assigned to partnership and dominator categories, yielding long lists of dualistic pairs. In *The Partnership Way*, the study resource for *The Chalice and the Blade*, these pairs are presented in table form, with two columns running side by side to help the reader compare and contrast the "two basic alternatives for the organization of human society."[21] There are clear value judgments in this table. No one would have to think too long or hard to decide whether war was preferable to peace, hoarding to sharing, or indoctrination to education.

Where do these differences between female and male, feminine and masculine come from, and how inescapable are they? Feminist matriarchalists differ on this point. We have already seen that biology, primarily the experience of childbirth and the possession of a uterus, plays a role. Feminist matriarchalists are certainly not above employing (and occasionally even admitting to) biological determinism. For example, Jane Alpert proudly proclaims that "*female biology is the basis of women's power* [her emphasis]," that "biology is . . . the source and not the enemy of feminist revolution." References to "female psyche" and "female soul," to "the spirit, the energy, the frequency, the form of women," indicate that gender differences are not a superficial matter for feminist matriarchalists. Gender differences reach far down into realms where even patriarchal religions have hesitated to find them. Thus while feminist matriarchalists wish for harmony between the genders, they rarely express a hope for nondifferentiation.[22]

But biological determinism does not tell the whole story of how feminist matriarchalists understand gender. There is a cultural component as well, particularly in the insistence that the qualities women evidence today are at least in part the product of the social roles they have occupied over the past several millennia, roles assigned to them by male dominant cultures. Some cite the psychological theories of Nancy Chodorow, suggesting that women's closeness to nature and to others comes from having been parented primarily by their mothers, the parent of the same sex—traits that therefore might change if men became more involved in child care (which is indeed what Chodorow recommends).[23]

In fact, the myth of matriarchal prehistory could almost be read to say that gender, at least as we know and experience it, is a cultural invention. One of the greatest strengths of matriarchal myth from a feminist perspective—arguably, one of the main reasons it was created—is that it gives historical rather than biological reasons for the dominance of men.[24] And, at least in theory, matriarchal myth could also give us license to believe that what we think of as femininity and masculinity are not inborn traits but are the cultural constructs of a patriarchal system, and thus are rooted no more deeply than this five-thousand-year-old social organization.

Tellingly, feminist matriarchalists rarely make this move.[25] Sexism is certainly said to be a historical construct, but femininity—however it is understood—is usually taken to be timeless. Women are seen as a class of people who have predictable attitudes, values, and preferences almost regardless of their social context. This class of people experiences fortunes and reversals over the span of prehistoric and historic time, but their fundamental nature does not change. Matriarchal myth was conceived in strong reaction to the thesis that human society has always been patriarchal because of biologically determined sex differences, yet its basic approach has been to accept these biologically determined sex differences, while shrugging off the inevitability of their current arrangement.

THE PITFALLS OF "DIFFERENCE FEMINISM"

With its celebration of the unique capabilities and attributes of females, feminist matriarchal thought places itself firmly in the camp of "difference feminism," a way of thinking about women's liberation that dates back at least as far as the first wave of American feminism in the nineteenth century. The goal of difference feminism is to see that women's special roles and values are accorded adequate respect, a respect equivalent (or perhaps superior) to that accorded to men's. Difference feminism has been defended on two grounds: first, that it is more effective to appeal to sex differences than to "sameness" between the sexes, whatever the reality; and second, that "difference" is in fact a more accurate reflection of reality. Inevitably though, the two positions drift together. As Kwame Anthony Appiah points out in reference to race, "group identity seems to work only—or, at least, to work best—when it is seen by its members as natural, as 'real.'" Certainly in the case of feminist matriarchal thought, that differences exist between the sexes is almost always believed to be the way things really are. Difference feminism is not a position that feminist matriarchalists adopt only for temporary convenience; rather there is a set of defining features about women and men that are expected to continue indefinitely. Given this, say the proponents of difference feminism, it would be folly to behave as though women and men were fundamentally the same. To do so may even constitute sexual violence toward a group (in this case women) "whose difference is effaced." [26]

Difference feminism has some strengths, especially tactical ones, but it also creates—or at least permits—a wide range of problems that feminist matriarchal thought illustrates especially well. These pitfalls sort themselves into three basic groups: the content of the feminine ideal that feminist matriarchalists uphold; the fact that they uphold a feminine ideal at all; and finally, the question of how closely this feminine ideal conforms (or does not) to "naturally" occurring sex differences.

The first thing one notices about the matriarchalist vision of femininity is how very familiar it is: nurturance, relationality, embodiedness, and links to the earth and nature are hardly new connotations for femaleness. Surely it is reasonable to want to rehabilitate activities and values habitually defined as—and denigrated as—feminine. But to do so by keeping these activities and values affixed to women is problematic. For one thing, it is not as though this collection of gender stereotypes has never cast women in a positive light before: it is a staple of right-wing antifeminist rhetoric to stress the nurturing, affiliative qualities of women, along with their undoubted ability to give birth and lactate. The valorization of motherhood—as an ideal type separate from individual women's experiences of it—is a tactic that has served patriarchal cultures very well. Even as women's childbearing and childrearing activities have been named as the seat of a higher and purer morality—on the face of it, a very positive move—women have been bracketed off from historical processes, indeed from the entire project of culture. Romantics have hailed "Woman" as the avatar of "nature" for centuries now, as a being that could rescue us all from "the artificiality of civilization." [27] But such views have typically left women firmly in their traditional places, not significantly disrupting the public, patriarchal world or its policies.

It is hard to believe that staying within a patriarchal culture's lexicon of femininity can provide a hardy alternative to the present order. Falling back into the traditional meanings of these stereotypes will be the path of least resistance. This is particularly worrisome when one takes note of the longevity and cross-cultural prominence of associations between women, the body, and nature. These associations reach back through Western history for millennia, but, as Sherry Ortner notes, they are "hardly an invention of 'Western culture.'" According to Ortner, all cultures seek to negotiate the divide between "what humanity can do" and "that which sets limits upon those possibilities." This divide has frequently been linked to gender, with males representing freedom and females constraint, males "culture" and females "nature." There is a natural human tendency to favor possibility, opportunity, and achievement over impotence, restraint, and stasis, and so long as women are linked with the latter they will be relatively devalued. In Simone de Beauvoir's estimation, a "renewed attempt to pin women down to their traditional role" (which she describes as "woman and her rapport with nature, woman and her maternal instinct, woman and her physical being"), "together with a small effort to meet some of the demands made by women—that's the formula used to try and keep women quiet." [28]

Of course, feminist matriarchalists believe that associations between women, the body, and nature are not theirs to adopt or discard at will, because they believe these associations are rooted in a reality they cannot change. You can't buy, bribe, pretend, or achieve your way out of femaleness, feminist matriarchalists say, and they consider it both foolish and morally reprehensible to try. Indeed, feminist matriarchalists have a lively interest in the phenomenon of "pseudomen": women who adopt roles or attitudes that are thought to be traditionally male. They think such women have been sold a bill of goods: sometimes by "the patriarchy," but more often by other feminists. Feminist matriarchalists cast slurs on these women, extend pity to them, and fear becoming them. They relate conversion narratives in which striving, "male-identified" women come to a crisis in their lives that teaches them how important it is to "get in touch with" their femaleness. In one such cautionary tale of male-identification, Jean Shinoda Bolen relates the story of her friend Freya, who accompanies Bolen on a pilgrimage to goddess sites in an attempt "to be more in touch with her feminine energies." Prior to this, Freya had "lived too much in her head and intellect and had spent most of her time with men." Freya's was no idle quest; she had developed cancer of the uterus, and she saw "a meaningful coincidence" between her uterine cancer and the male environment she had called home. [29]

In *The Heroine's Journey*, Maureen Murdock discusses in more general terms the sad fate of "male-identified women." These women adopt the "stereotypical male heroic journey," seeking worldly success and choosing male mentors and role models. But on the very threshhold of achievement, these women find themselves exhausted, ill, unhappy, and confused. They develop substance abuse problems, or "they are silent until the lump in their breast or cervical cancer makes them come to terms with the fact that the heroic journey did not take into account the limitations of their physical bodies and the yearnings of their spirit." These women, Murdock says, have been "injuring their feminine nature." To heal their feminine nature they take up ceramics, cooking, gardening, or massage; they redirect their energy to "giving birth to creative projects, rediscovering the body, and enjoying the company of other women"; they may abandon their careers and seek marriage and motherhood. Though this may look like "dropping out," Murdock argues that what is really happening is that women are finding their true, feminine selves and coming to understand how reckless it is for women to attempt to live by a male model.[30]

And so feminist matriarchalists set off on a quest for an authentic womanhood which "has been dormant in the underworld—in exile for five thousand years."[31] But in the absence of any sure information regarding what "femininity" is ("into what exactly are we to develop?" asks Kim Chernin, "if we are not . . . taking on masculine attributes, clothes, and qualities?"[32]), feminist matriarchalists typically fall back on the image of femaleness they grew up with: woman as mother, as the tender of children and gardens (and even husbands), as she who lives in the world of emotion and relationships and does not soil herself with the pursuit of money or power. Feminist matriarchalists construct this as an exceptionally strong version of femaleness, a "world-building" one not to be confused with the sentimental Victorian "angel in the house," and yet the two have much in common. In their creation of a "feminist femininity," matriarchalists have done remarkably little to move off the territory of patriarchal femininity.

Even if they did, however, there are difficulties associated with declaring *anything* inherently "feminine." For to the extent that a woman becomes the embodiment of "the feminine," she gains an archetypal identity, but loses a human one. Feminist matriarchalists gaze in at themselves, in the wonder of self-discovery, but what looks back at them is not their individual self, but the eternal feminine. It can be difficult to resist this idealization. As Andrea Dworkin points out, "It is hard for women to refuse the worship of what otherwise is despised: being female."[33] But it is dangerous *not* to refuse it. The practical effect of clinging to a single concept of femaleness—whatever its content—is that it becomes not an ideal type that you naturally express, but one that you must live up to, whether or not it fits with your interests and inclinations. Your only options are to follow the path laid out for you, or to forge off into the underbrush and at best be branded as "inauthentic" and "male-identified," and at worst die of uterine cancer. This is if you happen to belong to the same social classes and ethnic groups as most feminist matriarchalists. If you do not, *your* cultural versions of femaleness are either nothing more than delightful variations on the eternally feminine theme, or they are smokescreens impeding the view of your true femininity. In short, instead of broadening the concept of what women can be, feminist matriarchal thought narrows it, making "femininity" about as inescapable as a pair of leg irons.

Further complicating the matter is that in order to construct femininity, one must construct masculinity too. And dividing human characteristics along gendered lines is an invitation to sexism. Theoretically, it should be possible to make sharp distinctions between classes of people while still valuing each class equally and providing them with equivalent opportunities in life.[34] In practice, this rarely happens (something the U.S. Supreme Court recognized in *Brown v. Board of Education*, when it ruled that "separate but equal" education could never be truly equal). It might not be a pleasant fact about ourselves, but it seems that human beings have a hard time making a clear distinction without at the same time being tempted to make a differentiation in value. This has long been the case with gender, where distinctions between women and men devolve effortlessly into assertions of superiority and inferiority.[35] The doctrine of genetic inferiority—which some feminist matriarchalists happily apply to men—has long been employed as a device to subordinate whole groups of people, including nonwhite races, women, and the working classes.[36] Feminist matriarchalists presently lack the means to marginalize and subordinate men on the basis of men's supposed genetic inferiority. Much more important, they lack the motivation. Feminist matriarchalist visions of a matrifocal, gynocentric future almost always include men as active, respected participants. Nevertheless, their frequently veiled, occasionally explicit embrace of the doctrine of genetic inferiority leaves room—in principle if not in practice—for such abuses.

A strong conception of femininity not only encourages sexism, it also encourages racism and classism. Defining femaleness by a few key biological attributes and their supposed psychological corollaries implicitly trivializes differences across cultures, over time, and between individuals. As Sue Monk Kidd proclaims of women's journeys to discover the goddess and prehistoric matriarchies, "women's differences tend to give way to something more universal . . . we find a deep sameness beneath our dissimilarities. We find we are all women, and down deep we ache for what has been lost to us." With all women thus enfolded within the deep sameness of their femaleness, any other way a woman chooses to (or is forced to) identify herself is arbitrarily rendered secondary by feminist matriarchalists. If, for instance, a working-class woman feels herself to have more in common with working-class men than with upper-class women, she is simply misguided. As with class, so with race.[37]

Perhaps though, gender is just this determinative, overriding all other identities we might have or take on. Perhaps, as feminist matriarchalists sometimes state, femaleness is written on every cell of our being, and any attempt to deny the absolute centrality of our feminine identity is a flight of fancy that we cannot afford to indulge.

These are not conclusions that sex difference research, for all its flaws, supports. Feminist matriarchalists cite sex difference studies occasionally, but they resolutely fail to note their most important finding: that variations between individuals of the same sex are invariably greater than categorical differences between the two sexes.[38] In other words, if the distribution of a particular trait forms a bell-shaped curve within each sex, the two curves overlap, usually by quite a lot.

What does this mean in practical terms? To take an example, one sex difference study reported that among a sample of children, 15 to 20 percent of the boys scored higher on a measure of "rough-and-tumble play" than any of the girls. This is a comparatively large difference, by the standards of sex difference research. But this study also concluded that 80 to 85 percent of the boys were not rougher or more physical in their play than 80 to 85 percent of the girls: an impressive overlap.[39] Or to take a more intuitively obvious example, one can measure the heights of women and men and conclude quite factually that men are on average taller than women. But one cannot reliably predict an individual's sex by height alone: short men are shorter than most women, and tall women are taller than most men. This also means that if you have work that needs to be done by short people, it would be decidedly inefficient for you to ask that only women apply, since many women would not fit the job description, and many men would.

In other words, statistically significant sex differences are achieved long before socially significant ones are. And even statistically significant sex differences are less common than the rhetoric of feminist matriarchalists would suggest.

This is especially impressive when one considers that sex difference research—like feminist matriarchal thought—is strongly biased in favor of positive findings (that sex differences exist) over negative findings (that the sexes are similar in important ways). As neurophysiologist Ruth Bleier remarks sarcastically, "there is . . . no field of 'sex similarities.'" Further undermining the credibility of this research is that it cannot be carried out on fully precultural beings, so whatever sex difference it uncovers is potentially a contribution of culture rather than biology. For example, one study of differential mathematical ability in boys and girls proclaimed that it had found an inherent difference between the sexes. But as some of its critics pointed out, "anyone who thinks that seventh graders are free from environmental influences can hardly be living in the real world." In fact, we know that people treat even infant boys and girls differently, which suggests that culture may play a very dramatic role in constructing gender. Researchers playing videotapes of babies dressed in gender-neutral clothing have found that observers will identify a baby's behavior as an expression of "fear" when they are told the baby is a girl and "anger" when they are told the baby is a boy. Mothers playing with infants variously dressed in "gender-appropriate apparel" and "cross-gender apparel" behaved more physically with the "boys" and "responded with soothing and comforting actions" in response to the "girls." Parents have been shown to encourage their daughters, as early as seven weeks of age, "to smile and vocalize more than their sons." [40]

Discussions about sex difference often degenerate into a fruitless argument between those who see women and men as being dramatically different, for biological reasons, and those who assert that no such differences exist. Both positions are untenable. The former, as just noted, has not been supported by sex difference research, even in an environment where we know sex differences to be exaggerated by cultural forces. The latter, even if it has some deep philosophical truth, will simply not wash for people who can spot women and men at a hundred paces and make an accurate identification 95 percent of the time. But also, and more importantly, even if there are significant biological differences between women and men—differences that affect not only reproductive roles, but also aptitudes, values, and preferences—this does not necessarily entail everything feminist matriarchalists assume.

NEGOTIATING SEX DIFFERENCE

Suppose for a moment that the behavioral differences feminist matriarchalists identify between women and men are real, and are biologically based. Even so—even if "biology is destiny"—there is still a lot of flexibility built into that equation. People frequently react to the suggestion that we choose anything other than what is most "natural" for women and men as though this were heresy: both psychologically dangerous and morally wrong. And yet we make choices "against nature" all the time, every day. We wear clothes, we drive cars, we heat our homes, we cut our hair; we do everything in our power to live as long as we can, far past what "nature" has allotted to us, even supplying ourselves with prosthetic limbs and artificial hearts if we need them. To act as though we would never be so foolish or presumptuous as to tamper with our biological destiny is the purest hypocrisy. We develop a sudden squeamishness about interfering with our "natural" biological destiny when it comes to gender—which is very convenient for systems of male dominance—but clearly what is most "natural" to us as human beings is the use of culture to adapt our bodies and environments to suit our needs, wishes, and values.[41]

Steven Goldberg, author of *The Inevitability of Patriarchy*, notes sarcastically that the differential in male and female strength could be eliminated by making women lift weights and confining men to bed.[42] Though he regards this as a ridiculous proposition, in fact, he is right: this would undoubtedly be an effective means of reversing biological tendencies, making women generally stronger and men generally weaker. There are other ways of negotiating the tendency of men to be physically stronger than women. Separate athletic competitions can be held for women and men in most sports; girls can be given remedial physical fitness training; physical strength can be taken advantage of whether it is women or men who exhibit it; and there is, of course, the middle-class Victorian favorite, its echoes still audible today, of exaggerating a biological differential in women's and men's strength by putting men to work and keeping women in their parlors. There is no *a priori* reason, written on our genes, that forecloses any of these options. Some may be more practical or desirable than others—certainly in feminist terms—but these are decisions of culture, not biology.

Nevertheless, biology continues to hold a mystical attraction for most contemporary westerners. It continues to be seen as bedrock, the firm foundation upon which culture is built. This assumption permeates discussions of feminist matriarchal myth, pro and con. For example, scholar of religion Rita Gross concludes that "biological explanations for male dominance, if accurate, would suggest that efforts to eradicate patriarchy are futile."[43] But if biology is bedrock, it is geologically active, constantly moving and shifting. This is the entire premise behind Darwinian evolution. If humans move to a new environment, their biology gradually adapts, via natural selection. In other words, a cultural choice—to migrate—eventually makes a biological difference. Or to take a classic sociobiological example, if women preferentially select bigger, stronger males as mates—perhaps a sensible choice in a warrior culture, for example—the entire population may gradually become bigger and stronger. Again, culture may be seen to move biology: very slowly, but definitely.

Sociobiologists themselves rarely recognize these as cultural choices. They assume, to take the above example, that human females are biologically programmed to select bigger, stronger males as mates. Yet the enormous variety in how different cultures value different traits would suggest that there is nothing biologically determined about such choices. Genetically altering the human population as a method of producing, say, a gender egalitarian society may not be practicable or morally sound, but it is simply false to insist that our biological makeup is a fixed unchanging essence over which cultural conventions are forever doomed to dance ineffectually.

This leads directly to a logically prior question, however: whether "biology" and "culture" can be productively separated at all, their relative influences pinpointed and quantified. This is a difficult concept to grasp in a world where the nature/nurture game is played out endlessly in books, on radio talk shows, and in the conversation of parents trying to fathom why their children behave as they do. But the point is not just that we can be wrong (as we often have been in the past) about what is irreducible human nature and what is the product of cultural learning. Rather it is that the two don't exist independently of one another. Our biological "essences," if we have them, cannot, by definition, have an arena in which to express themselves that will not also inevitably affect the content of that expression. It is impossible to have an organism without an environment. The idea of a biological "essence" to human nature (or to women and men separately) may be a helpful tool for thought, but its existence and character are only stipulated, never demonstrated.

This calls into question the usefulness of the classic feminist distinction between "sex"—which is biologically foreordained—and "gender": that set of role expectations and stereotypes built upon it. This is true first in practice: though "sex" is supposed to be a set of obvious biological facts, these "facts," as science has described them, have changed dramatically over time, typically shifting in response to changing political needs regarding gender. But it is also true in principle: sex—biological sex—is never "outside or before culture," and thus it cannot be distinguished from gender, which is more usually taken to be the site of cultural practice. As Thomas Laqueur says, the actual existence of sexual dimorphism notwithstanding, "almost everything one wants to *say* about sex . . . already has in it a claim about gender." [44] Rooting sex in biology, then, is not the last word on anything, even though it typically postures as such.

Despite their claims of biological determinism and robust sex difference, feminist matriarchalists recognize the cultural determinants of gender. This is seen most obviously in their frequent exhortation to women that they must *learn* to be women. There is a feminine nature captured within women that is struggling to be free of the cultural doctoring of patriarchy, say feminist matriarchalists, and it is the task of women living now to find out what that nature is. This task can be challenging. As Vicki Noble explains: "Women do not know how to be feminine. We may think we have a corner on the market, since we were born with feminine bodies, but it's just as new to us as if we were men. We have to create the feminine." [45]

What feminist matriarchalists don't tell us is *why* we have to create the feminine. Why can't we just ignore it and see if it goes away? Surely if sex differences are as strongly determined as feminist matriarchalists suggest, they will continue to bubble up regardless of what we do culturally to change them. In the absence of any gendered expectations, presumably men would continue to grow beards; why would women not as easily continue to evince traits of nurturance and relationality, whatever they were taught to the contrary, if this is in fact our biological nature?

The feminist matriarchalist answer to this is undoubtedly that women *do* evince these traits, over and over again, across all cultures, all the way back to prehistoric times. But if this is so, why can't they leave it at that? Let women become who they naturally are, but don't suggest to any individual woman that she's not doing a good job of being female, and that therefore she must learn to be feminine? On the face of it, it is odd that the same people who are most devoted to the "naturalness" of sex differences—from fundamentalist Christians to feminist matriarchalists—also seem to be afraid that these "natural" sex differences will disappear if we don't constantly reinforce them, sometimes by outright coercion. What nightmare do they imagine awaits us if we stop obsessively labeling characteristics as feminine and masculine? Will we fail to recognize who we need to have sex with to make babies and the entire race will come to an end? (I say this with tongue in cheek, but I also believe that our addiction to labeling everything as masculine or feminine is part and parcel of our heterosexism.)

Why is it that feminist matriarchalists continue to cling to the edifice of gender difference, where women have been walled in for millennia? Perhaps the best explanation is that they see no escape. Whether "femininity" is produced by the possession of two X chromosomes or by a lifetime of cultural indoctrination is beside the point. Either way, gender is a reality against which everyone—but particularly women—must contend. Given this reality, maybe the best we can do is to see how the facts of femaleness can be negotiated to serve women's interests . . . which is precisely what the myth of matriarchal prehistory does. Popular culture shows no sign of ceasing to regard sex differences as important. (The *Men Are from Mars, Women Are from Venus* phenomenon is sufficient to prove this.) If anything, the pink and blue blankets have been swaddled ever more tightly over the past ten to fifteen years in reaction to feminist claims for equality. Feminist matriarchalists are not imagining that sex differences exist; they *do* exist, and they legislate life choices with a sometimes frightening force.

This is something that is easy to overlook if one has spent too much time in the rarefied air of gender studies. Currently popular theories about both sex and gender are that they do not exist outside of culture—a point to which I have already given my enthusiastic assent—and that furthermore they are only able to exist through their constant reiteration in acts and symbols. Gender is, these theories say, "not a fact or an essence, but a set of acts that produce the effect or appearance of a coherent substance." Gender is not embodied, they say, but performed, over and over again.[46] Whatever the intent of this analysis, the psychological effect of dwelling on the insubstantiality of gender is to make gender appear ephemeral and therefore powerless. If gender is only able to retain its force because we reinforce it today and then again tomorrow, theoretically it will stop dead in its tracks the minute we announce a sit-down strike.

Gender may in fact be nothing more than the effect of a performance (and I obviously have no wish to suggest that it is the unmediated outcome of biological sex difference), but it still has incredible social power which we ignore at our own risk. Biological, cultural, or performed, gender is very, very real.

The closest available parallel to gender in this sense is probably race. Both gender and race are assigned at birth, and people are then "tagged for life by certain phenotypic markers." Both types of identities are arrayed in hierarchical social systems. And race, like gender, is assumed to make a statement about an individual's true nature that reaches far beyond the "visible morphological characteristics" which are initially used to place an individual in a specific category. Until recently, race was believed to be determinative in exactly the same way as gender: biologically. Though this theory is now in disfavor among biologists and anthropologists (who believe that race "refers to nothing that science should recognize as real"), the fact is that race is still terrifyingly real. As Kwame Anthony Appiah explains, "belief in races"—which has "profound consequences for human social life"—"is real enough to make up for the unreality of races."[47]

The great advantage to difference feminism is that it takes account of this reality where gender is concerned. It meets people where they are, in a world where sex determines quite powerfully and completely. This alone goes far toward explaining the appeal of feminist matriarchal myth. Since "femininity," "femaleness," and "womanhood" are categories against which all women are measured—with or without their consent—it is arguably a stroke of psychological genius to revalue those categories such that they become marks of pride rather than discomfort or shame. Basically, if one has to be a woman, with all that implies in terms of opportunities and expectations (or lack thereof), then imaging femaleness as strong, praiseworthy, beautiful, and possibly superior to maleness would seem to have its merits.

Again, the parallel to race is instructive. Construing race as a positive source of identity—instead of as an imposed insult—has historically been one means of dealing with racism. It is the "difference feminism" of racial politics. But while this approach has a definite payoff in terms of enhanced dignity and self-esteem, it does nothing to escape the straitjacket of race itself. And since the categories of race have been from the beginning tools of racism—since this may indeed be their only raison d'être—there is something discomfiting about accepting race as a positive identity.

All these drawbacks are as present in feminist matriarchal thought as they are in racial politics. Feminist matriarchalists construct femaleness as a positive identity. But both the category of femaleness and its content are to a large degree determined by prior discrimination against the very people who are forced to occupy that category. Difference feminism then, for all its apparent support of women, underwrites the system upon which sexism feeds.

Is there any other option? I like to think that there is, but it is important to appreciate how difficult it is to criticize the way women are perceived and treated and simultaneously insist that there is no such thing as femaleness per se. Obviously there is, or it wouldn't be possible to know who we—the mistreated—are. There is a deep and compelling desire among feminists to have it both ways: we are women, and there are things about femaleness that we treasure and want to celebrate; yet we will not be limited in our choices and actions just because we happen to fall into the category you have labeled "woman." Without femaleness—the category of women—feminism "would be lost for an object, despoiled of a fight"; but with this category firmly in mind, it is too easy to forget that "femaleness" serves sexist interests, was possibly created to do so, and will always threaten to continue to do so.[48]

Fortunately, this dilemma may yield up its own solution. We can begin by acknowledging that within patriarchal cultures, theories of "femaleness" or "femininity," as well as the general division of people into two incommensurate sex categories, serve to rationalize the social domination of one class (women) by another (men). These notions of femininity (and masculinity too) do not correspond to some objective reality, some biological or cultural "really real" gender difference. They are, quite simply, "the mechanism by which women are subordinated to men." Returning to the very overworked language of sex and gender, it is because gender exists—i.e., because the social positions of women and men differ hierarchically—that it becomes worthwhile to take note of biological sex. Gender "naturalizes" male dominance, just as race naturalizes—that is, provides a supposed biological excuse for—racism.[49] As feminist theorist Christine Delphy argues:

> No one is denying the anatomical differences between male and female humans or their different parts in producing babies, any more than . . . that some humans have black and some white skins. But since science has thrown out all "biological explanations" of the oppression of the working class and non-whites, one after another, we might have thought that this type of account of *hierarchies* would have been discredited. . . . Why should we, in trying to explain the division of society into heirarchical groups, attach ourselves to the bodily type of the individuals who compose, or are thought to compose, these groups?[50]

If gender exists only (or primarily) as the means through which oppression is achieved, surely there can be no merit in reifying it, as feminist matriarchalists do. The obvious option seems to be, as feminist scholar Denise Riley suggests, "to stand back and announce that there *aren't any* 'women.' "[51] And yet there are. I meet them on the street every day, and they and I both know that they are women and that that has no small effect on what sort of lives they are able to live.

It seems to me that it is more productive to recognize this reality, to call these people women, just as they have been named in the service of a male dominant ideology, but at the same time to insist that what makes them women is not their genitalia or any sex differences that may or may not follow from their biological sex, but simply their secondary status in a male dominant culture. Women are not then a sex, as we commonly understand the term, or even a gender, but a group of people who have been placed in a sometimes idealized, often despised category. The gendered category in which women have been placed has formed their experience. But they are not the rightful occupiers of this category; they are merely the product of the category's existence. Essentially, this is a stalwart refusal to play the game of gender—which is the game of sexism—while recognizing that its victims (both male and female) are very real. So long as the category exists, and people are placed in it, there will be women, and they will be in need of political action directed toward their liberation.

On the face of it, this approach has the disadvantage of making women seem to be nothing more than their victimization, and of course we are much more than that. But we need not be more than that *as women*; we can simply be more than that, just as all people are arguably more than the categories into which they have been (productively or tragically) placed.

In her book *Women's Mysteries*, Christine Downing discusses her ambivalence regarding female identity: "I want to embrace the word women *and* cast it off," she says. "I would like to say (to myself and others), Choose if you belong and how. Yet I also see that it is not entirely a matter of choice. Even resisting our inclusion in the category seems inevitably to be possible only in the context of having already internalized containment by it."[52] I would put it a bit differently: Whatever you think you are choosing, there are plenty of people out there who have already decided where you fit in the scheme of things, and if you think you are going to convince them that you are not female because you personally "resist inclusion in the category," then you are sadly mistaken.

This was brought home to me several years ago when I was being interviewed for an academic job. In the course of this interview, there was a rather heated exchange about sex difference. One of the interviewers responded to a remark of mine with the comment, "If it were appropriate for me to say so, which it isn't, I would tell you that yours is a very male way of thinking." Did this mean I was in some sense a man? Could I decide that I felt more comfortable thinking in this male way, and as a result, would people recognize that I was "really" a man? This question was answered rather forcefully when I left the interview and walked out into a dark and deserted downtown area in my dress-for-success suit and high heels. Certainly none of the men I encountered on my very nervous walk back to my hotel recognized that I had opted out of femaleness by choosing to think like a man. They saw a woman, and, as I concluded from their stares and catcalls, they saw a target.

This is, I suggest, what femaleness *is*—the experience of being perceived to be a woman and being treated as women are treated (however it is they are treated in any particular cultural context, whether it is to their personal detriment, or benefit, as it sometimes can be). Femaleness can be other things, of course; it can be defined by the experience of bearing and nurturing children, the claim to a close connection to nature, the cozy community of the kitchen after a family dinner—wherever female individuals or groups find it to be, feminist matriarchalists included. But none of these is femaleness *per se*, nor should they be confused with it. They are pockets of femaleness, experiences of subgroups of women. The only femaleness that is characteristic of all women as a class is the experience of having the label "woman" affixed to one's being.

On the positive side, this understanding of who women are has the potential to enable women to work together across other lines of social difference. Sexism comes at women in very different guises depending on race, class, and other measures, and these different sexisms must be approached individually. But if the fact of sexism applies to women of many different sorts, this provides an opportunity for making common cause, for building coalitions with one another.

Defining women by the sexism that labels them also does not rule out the possibility of rehabilitating values traditionally dismissed as "feminine." We can work to make the world a place that practices compassion and nurturance, that values relationships and the natural world. In doing so, we can note that these qualities have been attributed to women in recent Western history, and perhaps elsewhere as well. We can even suggest that more women than men embody these values today, since having been given these identities, women to some extent have become them. Insights like these can play a valuable role in the broader context of a feminist movement. They can provide useful political perspective and increased self-esteem (as they do for proponents of feminist matriarchal myth). But this must not degenerate into universal claims about who "women" really are, what traits they will (or ought to) evidence as a result of their biological sex. These stereotypes can ricochet back on us in potentially disastrous ways. In the inimitable words of Millicent Fawcett, a nineteenth-century British feminist: "We talk about 'women' and 'women's suffrage,' we do not talk about Woman with a capital W. That we leave to our enemies." [53]

CHAPTER 5

Finding Gender in Prehistory

Matriarchal myth is problematic on feminist grounds. By organizing itself around "the feminine"—an ideologically strong but politically regressive foundation—feminist matriarchal myth cannot recommend itself to us as a remedy for male dominance. We still have to confront the possibility though that prehistory happened just as matriarchal myth says it did. And if matriarchal utopia and patriarchal revolution are our true heritage, we must find ways to encompass that, even if our understanding of sex and gender and our goals for feminism differ from those of feminist matriarchalists.

As it happens though, matriarchal myth fails completely on historical grounds. Evidence from prehistoric times is comparatively sparse, and hard to interpret conclusively. However, even taking these difficulties into account, what evidence we do have does not support the thesis that prehistory was matriarchal and goddess-worshipping, or even that it was sexually egalitarian.

Probably the greatest challenge for the myth of matriarchal prehistory is, of course, the fact that matriarchies are said to have occurred *pre*historically, before written records of any kind. Thus one very important source for reconstructing the human past—texts—is absent.[1] Feminist matriarchalists sometimes claim this is no handicap: they regard the nonliterate record as so rich and deep that written texts are simply not necessary to establish important truths about prehistory. Certainly it is important not to overvalue written texts, or to rely on them to the exclusion of other sorts of evidence. Written sources, just like material sources, must be interpreted, and can be misinterpreted.[2] But even if the availability of written documents is not considered a watershed in our ability to know the past, it adds dramatically to the sheer volume of evidence at our disposal. Still, a variety of resources can be brought to bear on the task of discovering what gender relations were like in prehistoric times and whether or not they fit the model of peaceful, woman-honoring theacracies that feminist matriarchalists envision.

CULTURAL ANTHROPOLOGY AND GENDER

Cultural anthropology's contribution to reconstructing prehistory is its documentation, via ethnography, of other cultures. Information about contemporary and historical tribal groups is used both to help interpret the material remains that archaeologists uncover and to speculate about prehistory in the absence of material evidence from the past. The assumption here is that the ethnographic record, as compiled over the past few hundred years, provides data that allows us to observe important correlations in human social life (say, between communal ownership of property and nonhierarchical social relationships); illustrate specific phenomena that may have been relevant in the past (for example, that hunting is generally a male preoccupation); or, most grandly, serve up full-bodied exemplars, living untainted by modernity in remote parts of the globe, of what past human societies "must have been like."

When early anthropologists (and colonialists and missionaries) first encountered other cultures, they used this method extensively. They placed the cultures they documented on a continuum from most primitive to relatively more advanced. This continuum doubled as a timeline, recording the stages of human progress. Primitive peoples—encountered not only in South Sea isles, but even in urban ghettoes and among peasant farmers—were "living fossils": they represented "the history and experience of our own remote ancestors when in corresponding conditions." It was further thought that the social practices of prehistory could be inferred from vestiges of those practices incorporated into contemporary cultures: this was the so-called doctrine of "survivals."[3]

These postulates have been roundly criticized by twentieth-century anthropologists. First, even the most "primitive" peoples we know of have been on earth as long as the rest of us "civilized" folk and so have had ample time to develop in a variety of directions away from our shared deep prehistory. Second, the choice of which cultural characteristics are to count as "survivals" of a prehistoric past and which are more recent inventions is quite arbitrary, based mainly on what one hopes, in advance, to confirm for prehistory.[4] Most cultural anthropologists today forswear the tendency to draw easy equivalences between the practices of living peoples and our prehistoric ancestors. Even attempts to compare a wide swath of living cultures in search of their common features are increasingly out of fashion among anthropologists.

Still, anthropologists continue to speculate about prehistory through the use of ethnographic material. It is very tempting to do so, and besides, it makes good sense. Without going to the extreme of suggesting that all human societies are blindly marching through a predetermined historical trajectory (with some—conveniently for prehistorians—getting stuck in the early stages), it is still reasonable to hypothesize that there may be certain regularities in human social relations, ones we can uncover by looking at as many different societies as we can. Granted that tribal groups are not fossils from the Stone Age, they nevertheless have more in common with how we believe our prehistoric ancestors lived (namely, in small groups, subsisting by hunting and gathering or horticulture) than we do.[5] When feminist matriarchalists attempt to make their case for a gynocentric prehistory through ethnographic analogy then, it is not their basic premise that is flawed.

Actually, these days the greatest limitation of ethnographic analogy as a means of reconstructing prehistory is probably not its sloppy application to prehistoric questions, but how the ethnographic record was and is constructed. Though on the face of it, it might seem a straightforward matter to go live with the natives, learn their language, and report on their customs, it is notoriously difficult to give accurate, informative portrayals of human cultures. What is seen has a great deal to do with who is seeing it, and with who is giving the "insider" accounts that ethnographers so often rely upon. Ethnographers face the further problem of choosing between the evidence of their observations and the reports of informants. These do not always agree, even on the most basic matters. For example, I have heard fundamentalist Christians assert that the man is the undisputed head of the household and then watched as fundamentalist women transparently bulldozed their preferences into family policy. Clearly, both the assertion and the behavior are important, but they are just as clearly contradictory, and for ethnographers eager to be responsible mouthpieces for the people among whom they have lived, navigating their way between these two can be tricky.

These difficulties are only compounded when the attempt is made to gather together these various partial and biased ethnographies in order to hazard guesses about what counts as a general rule of human social life. Existing ethnographies have been composed with a huge variety of agendas in mind, including everything from converting the primitive heathens to Western values to learning from the wise natives how to reform corrupt Western culture. Some groups (unfortunately, many groups) are now gone, and therefore we must rely on whatever existing records we have, no matter how poor, if we wish to learn anything at all from them. But even investigations undertaken now, presumably with a heightened methodological sophistication, must be carried out by many people. No one person could do the fieldwork necessary to have a firsthand appreciation of a large number of peoples. So if the quest is to reconstruct prehistory, armchair anthropology is a necessity. We have to be prepared then to work around its shortcomings.

One attempt to correct its shortcomings has involved setting down in advance what cultural features ethnographers should document. This greatly eases the task of comparison. But collecting data on some predetermined item like cross-cultural religious practices assumes that there is something like "religion," as the researcher defines it, among the people under observation. Looking for religion is a near guarantee that one will find it, even if it's not there. The opposite holds true as well: walking into another society with the expectation that the people there may think about everything from ontology on up in a way completely foreign to you is likely to produce an ethnography full of fascinating exotica accompanied by reflections on the irreducible uniqueness of human cultures and thought systems. Finally, even relatively valid generalizations are likely to fall victim to the Kamchatka syndrome: that there is some place in the world—say, Kamchatka—where the rule doesn't hold.[6]

This only becomes more complicated once the sensitive topic of gender is tossed into the mix. For quite some time, it was thought that a full and accurate picture of a group's gender roles could be attained as soon as there were enough female ethnographers in the field, dutifully quizzing female informants. Early male ethnographers rarely asked about women's roles, and when they observed women in other lands, what they saw was influenced by their biases and expectations. On the one hand, if native women seemed to have freedoms that women in their own homeland lacked, the tendency was to give an exaggerated estimation of their autonomy, simply because it appeared unusual by Western standards. On the other hand, many assumed that males were always dominant, foreclosing in advance the possibility of discovering less obvious forms of women's social power.

But the introduction of female fieldworkers into the discipline did not, as expected, suddenly throw a great light upon women's lives. If anything, the opposite occurred. The more cultural anthropologists looked at gender, the less, it seems, they were able to see . . . or at least to agree upon. It turned out to be surprisingly difficult to determine just what women's status was in any one group, not to mention across many cultures.[7] Perhaps this should not be surprising, when one stops to consider how differently people view the status of women in contemporary American cultures. Feminists are virtually unanimous in believing that women's status is always worse than men's, differing only in how dreadful they assess the situation to be. But there are others who think that women are better off than men, experiencing less pressure to achieve success in the world of work, savoring the deep satisfactions of bearing and caring for children, having emotional lives and networks of support that are far more rewarding than men's, and so forth. Just how women are faring in the United States is not an idle question, for if we are unable to come up with any standard to evaluate women's status at home, what makes us think we can do so abroad, or in the past?

Indeed, the same range of perceptions of women's status that we see in the United States arises when observing cultures not our own. Two ethnographers reporting on the same group can—and sometimes have—come back saying opposite things.[8] Often it seems to come down to the attitude of the observer: does she want the glass to be half full, or half empty? If half full, she will return with reports of women's separate rituals, the significant amount of productive work women do, and informants' own statements that relations between the sexes are as they should be. She will tell a story about a savvy woman who worked around formal sex inequality to assure that she got her own way. If half empty, she will return with reports of women's exclusion from male rituals, the undervaluation of their work, and anecdotes of culturally approved beatings of wives by their husbands. She will tell a story about a girl baby left to die during a food shortage while a boy born at the same time was tended carefully.

The greatest divide in ethnographies of gender seems to be between those anthropologists who focus on official ideology and those who are more attuned to behavioral variation and face-to-face interactions. Those anthropologists who have come to the conclusion that women are everywhere subordinate to men are usually looking at ideology, while those who see women as at times equal or dominant are generally drawing their conclusions from behavior. This makes sense: presumably women's power is always there, if you trouble yourself to look for it and aren't too picky about what form it takes. As Sherry Ortner notes, "whatever the hegemonic order of gender relations may be—whether 'egalitarian,' or 'male dominant,' or something else—it never exhausts what is going on"; for "every society/culture has some axes of male prestige and some of female, some of gender equality, and some (sometimes many) axes of prestige that have nothing to do with gender at all." [9]

Whether out of loyalty to their informants or fear of ethnocentrism, many feminist anthropologists have been loath to see and name sexism in other cultures in places where they would find it in their own. Or conversely, they emphasize women's status and autonomy in other cultures in forms they would not recognize as such on their own turf. Anthropologist Alice Schlegel assures us, for example, that corn-grinding by Hopi women is not "the onerous and time-consuming task it would appear to be" since "women sing corn-grinding songs as they work to lighten the task and express its life-giving contribution." [10] Perhaps we should not automatically assume that this is an instance of sexism, but it should at least raise a red flag in our minds. American slaves sang songs too (much to the satisfaction of their masters, who interpreted this as a sign of contentment), but this cannot justify the conclusion that slavery was not really an oppressive institution. Even if we had reports from slaves themselves in which they swore that they considered themselves fortunate in their lot, we would have to regard those reports with suspicion. Similarly, we should regard with suspicion women's statements from ethnographic contexts that appearances of sexism notwithstanding, they find their lives to their liking. This does not mean that these women are being dishonest; individuals can enjoy and appreciate their lives while still being in structurally disadvantaged positions relative to others.

Given the frustrations inherent in attempting to pin down the status of women, many feminist anthropologists have abandoned the task as such. Some go so far as to argue that women and men do not exist anywhere except as cultures create these categories. Therefore the responsible anthropologist will not even assume that there *are* women and men in a given culture until she has been shown that these are relevant social categories for the groups under study. Au courant goals in the anthropology of gender are to "favor specific histories, debunk essentializing categories" and turn attention to "the subtleties, complexities, contradictions, and ambiguities of gender relations in different contexts."[11]

Again, this is not the level at which the myth of matriarchal prehistory operates. It is a very general story, based on generalizing premises. One could, of course, reject the story on that basis alone, and many anthropologists (feminist and otherwise) do. But it seems more fruitful to give feminist matriarchalists the benefit of the doubt, and ask if the ethnographic record, mixed and contradictory as it is, lends support to their claims.

ARCHAEOLOGY AND GENDER

Archaeologists look first and foremost at the actual remains of prehistoric cultures: those things that can be dug up out of the ground, held in one's hands, and seen with one's eyes. Material evidence like this could provide an impressive amount of information about prehistory if our ancestors planted their remains to send us a message about their cultures: a sort of time capsule. But what we actually find—"the accidentally surviving durable remnants of material culture"[12]—is more of a scattershot affair and, unfortunately, most remains are not detectably gendered.

This has not stopped archaeologists from reading gender into material evidence from the past, however. Particularly over the past fifteen years, archaeologists have been eagerly playing catch-up, bringing thirty years of academic and political debate on the topics of sex and gender into their discipline. For a variety of reasons, archaeologists came late to this debate. Inherent difficulties with attributing gender to prehistoric material culture combined with a naïve sexism to produce an archaeology that was rarely explicit about gender, ruling it out as a conceptual category while all the time smuggling it in in the form of unquestioned assumptions. The situation has changed altogether since then, as unprecedented archaeological attention is given over to questions of gender, among not only self-described feminists, but archaeologists of all stripes. Great hope is held out that archaeologists can shed light on such questions as "the universality of gender ideologies and gender divisions of labor, how and why gender relations vary, how and why they evolved, whether or not truly egalitarian societies have existed, and the origins of gender inequalities" [13] —questions of obvious interest to feminist matriarchalists.

Though almost everyone seems game to find gender in the archaeological record, no one is quite sure how it should be done, or even if it *can* be done. Skeletons can be sexed as male or female (within a margin of error), and then examined in order to draw tentative conclusions about women's and men's diet, life expectancy, and patterns of work based on bone degeneration, tooth wear, and mineral content in the bones themselves. Grave goods, if they differ between female and male skeletons, may also offer clues to prehistoric gender, and some paintings and sculptures give clear evidence of sex. But beyond this, it is impossible (at least without historical or ethnohistorical support) to know which artifacts go with which sexes. Even the most basic questions—who makes those weapons? who uses those grinding stones?—cannot be answered definitively through the preliterate material record alone. And so archaeologists typically rely on ethnographic analogies to other cultures to help them interpret the gendered significance of their material finds. For example, spear points are generally attributed to men, since in most human societies we know of, men are responsible for hunting.

Attributions like this are inevitably controversial. Recently it has even become difficult to make arguments about prehistoric gender based on sexed skeletons, for there is concern that a biological female may have been a social man (or vice versa), or that other gendered categories beyond the standard two existed. These would be impossible to detect if it were unproblematically assumed that female skeletons are the remains of women, and male skeletons the remains of men. Even this is not the end of the potential ambiguities of prehistoric sex and gender, for as we now know, biological sex itself is not set on a simple male/female switch, but may be composed of a variety of chromosomal and morphological anomalies.[14]

This difficulty with identifying prehistoric women is probably exaggerated. Ethnographic evidence supports the notion that gender is a cross-cultural phenomenon of impressive universality, and the vast majority of individuals can be—and are—easily differentiated into sex classes on the basis of their genitalia.[15] Nevertheless, the fact that most archaeologists of gender are taken by the possibility of "third genders" has a decisive impact on the questions they ask of their material evidence, and indeed how they view the entire enterprise of discussing prehistoric gender. Catherine Roberts has distinguished between "the archaeology of gender," which asks that questions of gender be added to the archaeological agenda, and "gendered archaeology," which has the broader ambition of reframing archaeological inquiry altogether. Most feminist archaeologists have been rather contemptuous of "the archaeology of gender," referring to it as the "add gender and stir" approach. "Gendered archaeology" is still developing, but it rests on two basic assumptions: that gender was a pronounced category in prehistory and that it was characterized by "variability, permeability, changeability, and ambiguity," that it was "dynamic and historically specific."[16] This is something quite different than what feminist matriarchalists imagine for the past, for where feminist archaeologists expect variety, feminist matriarchalists expect uniformity.

Indeed, feminist archaeologists have relatively little in common with feminist matriarchalists, in spite of their shared interest in the role of women in prehistory. They operate out of entirely different assumptions, owing mainly to the fact that feminist matriarchalists are greatly indebted to the work of Marija Gimbutas. Gimbutas, for all her research on gendered symbols in prehistory, never entered the gender and archaeology discussion. She began her work much earlier than most feminist archaeologists, and like other archaeologists of her generation—especially European archaeologists—Gimbutas was a grand theorist. She was not interested in reconstructing one possible account of one particular archaeological site; rather she was intent on telling *the* historical truth about a huge swath of human prehistory.

Gimbutas's defenders have suggested that her work has been dismissed by archaeologists because she portrayed prehistory as goddess-worshipping and matricentric.[17] And yet earlier archaeologists made extensive claims for prehistoric goddess worship—and even for a female priesthood—while retaining a high standing in their field. More likely, Gimbutas's status in archaeology was peripheral because she represented a way of approaching prehistory that her colleagues had repudiated: she was considered passé, embarrassingly so. Like someone's eccentric uncle Henry, Gimbutas was infrequently criticized, and more often stolidly ignored by her archaeological colleagues, who did not wish to disown her but, on the other hand, didn't want to be publicly associated with her. As archaeologist Bernard Wailes reports, "Most of us tend to say, oh my God, here goes Marija again."[18]

It would be relatively easy to pit the arguments of feminist matriarchalists against, say, the claims of the archaeological establishment today, but this is ultimately unfair to all parties involved. There is no archaeological consensus, and if there were one, we would still have to question whether or not it were correct. Feminist matriarchalists are seeking a matriarchy in the past, which undoubtedly colors what they find there. But other prehistorians are also "seeking validation in the past" for their own scholarly and political agendas.[19] No prehistorian can abstract herself away from the sorts of passions—sometimes explicitly political passions—that drive her to study prehistory.

Some feminist matriarchalists have explicitly defended the investigation of prehistory as a political exercise. Eschewing "objectivity" as neither possible nor desirable, they wish to work their "life experiences, histories, values, judgments, and interests" into their research as legitimate interpretive tools. This is not a view limited to feminist matriarchalists. Other prehistorians have enunciated it too, with somewhat different emphases. For example, in *Reading the Past*, archaeologist Ian Hodder notes that each generation asks their own questions of the past, viewing new or altered evidence in novel ways. With these constantly shifting agendas and methods, Hodder claims that "the ultimate aim" of archaeology "can only be self-knowledge. In projecting ourselves into the past, critically, we come to know ourselves better."[20]

On the one hand, to say this is merely to state the obvious: history (and prehistory) is authored in the present by human beings, each of whom has interests and is situated within a particular world of meaning. But it is an entirely different thing to suggest that because the past can be known only imperfectly, through the agency of biased individuals, that therefore one account of the past is as good or bad as another. There are dangers associated with this idea, dangers that feminist matriarchalists have no trouble recognizing. Feminist matriarchalists do not wish to claim that all accounts of prehistory are relative, that there is no basis for choosing among competing accounts apart from individual preference and political usefulness, because then they would have to admit that androcratic interpretations of prehistory that stress the inevitability and universality of patriarchy are as valid as their own.

All prehistorians are interested in establishing the plausibility of the stories they tell about prehistory; all want to offer coherent accounts based on the available data. What is required then is some way of adjudicating competing truth claims about prehistory, a way of building rigor into accounts of prehistory. In judging the adequacy of feminist matriarchalist accounts of prehistory I will be working from a few simple standards that are not specific to particular archaeological, anthropological, or historical methodologies, but are inherent in all of them. First, an adequate account of the past must offer data in its support. Second, it must seek to interpret all the data, and not merely that which is convenient to or supportive of the theory. Third, it must strive to have conclusions follow evidence, rather than the other way around. And finally, it must be possible to show that an account is wrong or implausible: in other words, it must be falsifiable. This last standard of adequacy for an account of human prehistory is the most important one, and to a large extent subsumes the others. A theory may be interesting and provocative, even true; but if there is no way to tell whether or not it is true—that is, no way to disprove it—it can only be a conversation piece. It is no more likely to be accurate than any of dozens of imaginative and even compelling stories told about prehistory, stories that draw their persuasive power not from what we see in the prehistoric record but from our own culturally limited notions of what we wish or believe prehistory to have been like.[21]

In light of these basic standards, I will examine those prehistoric materials that archaeologists, cultural anthropologists, and feminist matriarchalists have relied upon in reconstructing prehistory, particularly those of late Paleolithic and early Neolithic Europe and the Near East, asking if the evidence feminist matriarchalists cite truly supports the story they tell, and if the evidence they *don't* cite tells another story.

CHAPTER 6

The Case Against
Prehistoric Matriarchies I:
Other Societies, Early Societies

There are many claims that feminist matriarchalists make for prehistoric societies that can be tested against the ethnographic and archaeological records. For convenience, they can be collected into
four broad categories: reproduction and kinship, goddess worship,
women's economic roles, and interpersonal violence. The question of
whether or not prehistoric cultures practiced extensive goddess worship will be examined in the next chapter, when we turn to prehistoric art and architecture. Here, confining ourselves to ethnographies
from contemporary and historical societies and nonrepresentational
material evidence from prehistoric societies, we will judge the plausibility of such central feminist matriarchalist claims as men's ignorance
of their role in conception, the correlation between goddess worship
and women's social status, women's invention of agriculture, and the
peacefulness of prehistoric societies.

REPRODUCTION AND KINSHIP

According to feminist matriarchalists, the miracle of childbirth—especially miraculous when no male role in conception was recognized—caused all women to be viewed with respect and honor.
Strong links between mothers and their children led to matrilineal
kinship systems and matrilocal residence patterns which placed
women in positions of social power.

The idea that prehistoric peoples might not have recognized paternity was first proposed in the nineteenth century. From the comfort of their armchairs, several anthropologists speculated that "prim-
itives" either were so promiscuous that fatherhood could not be

determined or that they were ignorant of the connection between sexual intercourse and conception. This speculation received some grounding in ethnographic evidence when reports filtered back from Australia and Melanesia that certain aboriginal peoples denied that sexual intercourse had anything to do with pregnancy. One of the earliest of these reports came from W. E. Roth in 1903, who said the Tully River Blacks of North Central Queensland believed pregnancy resulted from a woman roasting black bream over a fire, catching a bullfrog, responding to a man's verbal instruction to become pregnant, or dreaming of having a child placed in her womb. Bronislaw Malinowski's reports from the Trobriand Islands engendered even more excitement back home in Europe. As Malinowski stated categorically in 1927, "The views about the process of procreation entertained by these natives . . . affirm, without doubt or limitation for the native mind, that the child is of the same substance as its mother, and that between the father and the child there is no bond of union whatever." [1]

Most contemporary anthropologists agree that these "proofs" of the ignorance of paternity were actually errors in ethnography. In the Trobriands, even Malinowski's own findings left room for suspicion: he reported that Trobrianders believed sexual intercourse was necessary for pregnancy (a woman's womb had to be "opened" so that a spirit child could enter); that children were thought to resemble their fathers as a result of the father's continued sexual intercourse with the mother; that the children of unmarried women were deemed illegitimate; and that pigs were thought to be conceived through their sexual intercourse with one another. Later ethnographers of the Trobriand Islanders came back with reports that differed from Malinowski's. For example, H. A. Powell was told that conception was a result of semen "coagulating" menstrual blood, clearly indicating the necessity of sexual intercourse. When Powell told his informants that this was different from what Malinowski had been told, they maintained that Trobriand beliefs had not changed, but rather that Malinowski had been listening to "men's talk," reserved for formal situations, whereas "women's and children's talk"—intended to convey helpful information to youngsters—had always maintained a connection between sexual intercourse and pregnancy.[2]

Later ethnographers also cast doubt on the theory that Australian aborigines did not recognize physiological paternity. They noted that Roth did not spend more than a month among the Tully River Blacks (who even at the time told him that sexual intercourse was the cause of conception in animals), and that Roth neglected the fact that there was a word in their language meaning "to be the male progenitor of," connecting a particular act of copulation to conception. In all cases, it seems that anthropologist Edmund Leach is correct in concluding that these peoples were saying, albeit in different language and with different metaphors, the same things that many contemporary Westerners say about reproduction: that "conception is not predictable in advance but is recognized by certain physiological signs after the event"; that "sex relations are a necessary preliminary to this condition"; and that "the foetal embryo has a soul." [3]

Indeed, what seems to be more often in doubt across the ethnographic record—even in the interesting cases of Australia and the Trobriands—is how or whether *mothers* are related to their own children. Peoples are of course everywhere acquainted with the fact that babies emerge from women's bodies, but in the absence of an avowed role for insemination, women were not thought to reproduce parthenogenetically, magically creating children out of their own substance (the scenario most often envisioned by feminist matriarchalists for prehistoric peoples). Instead it was thought that women were impregnated by "spirit children" and that thereafter the mother "was merely the incubator of a spirit-child." [4]

This should be a familiar theory to Westerners, since it was articulated by no less a light than Aristotle. Aristotle claimed that the form and essence of a child are given by the father and remain uncontaminated by the woman, who merely supplies the material substance for the child and contains it during pregnancy. We tend to think of the equal contribution of mother and father to their children's biological makeup as the truth of the ages, but it is a very recent discovery. The way in which we now understand physiological reproduction—as the result of the joining of ovum and sperm—was not even in place at the time when nineteenth-century anthropologists first began speculating about the ignorance of paternity among prehistoric peoples. Anthropologist Carol Delaney has shown that in present-day Turkey, Aristotelian beliefs about reproduction continue to flourish. As one villager explained, "If you plant wheat, you get wheat. If you plant

barley, you get barley. It is the seed which determines the kind of
plant which will grow, while the field nourishes the plant but does not
determine the kind. The man gives the seed, and the woman is like
the field." Or as one Albanian informant explained the facts of reproduction to ethnographer René Grémaux, "The woman is a sack for
carrying."[5]

The ethnographic record—like the history of the West—displays
varied and contested ideas about human reproduction. The sheer
quantity of these ideas suggests that it is possible that people did not
always recognize a connection between sexual intercourse and conception. But a notable commonality among all this variety is the insistence that there is a necessary relationship between sexual intercourse
and conception. Other events may also be necessary—such as the entrance of a spirit child through the top of the head (in the case of the
Trobriand Islanders), or the entrance of a soul into a fertilized egg (in
the case of Roman Catholics)—but it is simply not believed that
women bear children without any male participation whatsoever. It
is also doubtful on commonsense grounds that human beings would
be wholly ignorant of paternity. As Edmund Leach points out, "human beings, wherever we meet them, display an almost obsessional
interest in matters of sex and kinship," and "presumably this has always been the case." Even evidence from the material record suggests
that prehistoric peoples were aware of the relationship between sexual intercourse and conception. Paleolithic cave paintings depict animals mating, pregnant, and giving birth in such a way that these
events seem connected. And a plaque from Çatalhöyük carved in gray
schist shows "two figures in an embrace on the left and a mother and
child on the right," an artifact which some—including some feminist
matriarchalists—read as a visual text on the results of copulation.[6]

It seems quite likely then that prehistoric peoples were aware of
the male role in reproduction. Some feminist matriarchalists could
agree to this quite readily, saying that prehistoric peoples were aware
of biological paternity but simply chose not to grant it much significance. This is a hypothesis that cannot be disproven, but there is no
ethnographic evidence for it whatsoever. Wherever we have encountered human groups, we have found individual men forming paternal
relationships with the children of their wives or other female partners. Additional relationships between particular men and children
definitely occur, but that between fathers and their children seems

primary.[7] Suggesting that there was a time when this was not so raises the thorny question of why men were content to ignore their physiological relationships to particular children (apparently taking a passive, benign interest in children in general) for hundreds of thousands of years, only to begin to care very much about this issue around 3000 BCE.[8]

It is important to recognize that the feminist matriarchalist devaluing of paternity is at the same time a construction of motherhood. As we have seen, feminist matriarchalists routinely imagine childbirth as an occasion for awe, and motherhood as a role and relationship to which men habitually deferred. Why this would have been true prehistorically and not equally true today is not clear. If it is possible for us and for many generations of our ancestors to systematically disadvantage women in spite of (or perhaps *because of*) their unique and essential mothering capabilities, why should it not have been equally possible for our prehistoric ancestors to do the same? In fact, ethnographic evidence suggests that childbirth does not regularly work to women's advantage. Anthropologist Sherry Ortner has noted that women tend to lose rather than gain status when placed in reproductive roles, and to be permitted greater liberties and occupy more powerful public positions when virginal or menopausal.[9] This is difficult to accept in light of examples we are familiar with in which motherhood is elevated to a divine calling, but as anthropologist Alice Schlegel points out, "a highly valued role will [not] necessarily grant prestige to one who holds it. Motherhood, open only to women, may be highly valued by both men and women without women necessarily receiving prestige as mothers." [10]

Anyway, given what we know of human nature, it would seem doubtful that childbirth would cause men to revere or even respect women in any pure or uncomplicated manner. When one group of people has a monopoly on a much-valued resource, the reaction of the have-not group is not typically one of worshipful awe. More often, the reaction is one of jealousy and resentment, and a wish to gain their own access to the coveted resource. Some feminist matriarchalists acknowledge this, and describe relationships between men and women as being driven first and foremost by men's "womb envy," by men's desire to participate in or control women's childbearing powers.[11]

There is in fact some ethnographic evidence of men trying

to gain some share of women's childbearing and other reproductive functions through ritual efforts, a practice that might be understood as womb envy. L. R. Hiatt describes what he calls "pseudo-procreation" rituals among Australian aboriginal men, rituals used to assert men's "supernatural contribution" to conception, and to "rebirth" boys from men (to symbolically supersede their birth from women) as a part of their initiation into manhood. Similarly, Anna Meigs reports that Hua males (from New Guinea) engage in "rituals of imitation, adulation, and control of female reproductive power" in the confines of the men's house by mimicking menstruation and consuming foods thought to be related to women's fertility. Other customs have sometimes been said to testify to a desire on the part of males to take some part in women's reproductive roles. One of these is couvade, in which fathers act out the pain of childbirth and follow the same postpartum taboos as their wives who have just given birth. Another is a ritual in which the underside of the penis is cut open and allowed to bleed, apparently in imitation of menstruation.[12]

Significantly, however, none of these ethnographic examples of male imitation of female reproductive powers is accompanied by any rise in women's status. Hiatt reports that the Australian aboriginal men who imitate childbirth regard themselves as superior to women and children; Meigs says that Hua women have no political voice and cannot own land or control the products of their own labor. In both these cases women are excluded from the female-imitating rituals themselves, sometimes on pain of death.[13] Feminist matriarchalists typically work around these reports by insisting that such rituals and practices date from a time during or after the patriarchal revolution, when men became intent on coopting women's childbearing powers. But again there is no explanation for why men did not experience womb envy as a source of pain and frustration before then. And going on these particular ethnographic examples, it would seem that if prehistoric men *did* envy women's reproductive abilities, it would have worked to women's detriment.

One also has to ask how much prehistoric peoples valued reproduction. If it were extremely difficult to propagate, if tribes were in constant danger of dying out, it might be the case that fertility and childbirth would be highly valued. But it is doubtful that children were such a scarce commodity in prehistoric times. Prior to the

Neolithic revolution, we have every reason to believe that prehistoric peoples, like contemporary hunting and gathering peoples, were more interested in restricting their fertility than enhancing it. Contraception, abortion, and infanticide are all practiced in hunting and gathering groups, and in horticultural societies as well, with infanticide rates ranging from 15 to 50 percent.[14] Skeletal evidence suggests that childbirth was dangerous for mothers and children alike. Infant mortality rates were high at Çatalhöyük, for example, and women there and elsewhere died very young by our standards (on average in their late twenties, earlier than men) in part because of high maternal mortality.[15] It seems unlikely under these conditions that pregnancy and childbirth were invariably regarded as miraculous and welcomed as the gift of a munificent goddess.

Feminist matriarchalists also argue that motherhood structured social relations, making women the hub of society, the power center around which all others revolved. The most tangible forms this centrality is thought to have taken are matriliny—in which family status, clan membership, and sometimes property are passed through the mother's line—and matrilocality, in which husbands come to live with their wives or their wives' families upon marriage.

The matricentrism of prehistoric societies is said by feminist matriarchalists to be apparent in their "sensitive and careful burial of the dead, irrespective of sex, with a relatively uniform grave wealth." This evidence, if accurate, does not support assertions of matriarchy or even of sex egalitarianism. In their introductory archaeological textbook, Kenneth Feder and Michael Alan Park suggest that "if some future archaeologist were to walk into a twentieth-century graveyard, he or she would almost certainly be provided with some insight into our perspective on life, social system, religion, and, of course, death." [16] But what insight would this future archaeologist get about, say, gender relations in the contemporary United States? I am told by several cemetery directors that it is rare to see any distinctions between male and female burials apart from the type of clothing placed on the corpses. And while it is still common to bury a woman under her husband's name, a future archaeologist who could not decipher our mortuary inscriptions would not be aware of this patronymical custom. Even signs of variations in wealth in U.S. cemeteries—principally in casket materials and plot size and position—are not terribly

large. On the basis of contemporary U.S. cemeteries, we might conclude that twenty-first-century Americans lived in a sexually egalitarian society where there were only minor distinctions of wealth.

Some feminist matriarchalists have ventured to find evidence of
matrilineal and matrilocal social structure in the overall layout of prehistoric graveyards. This has been especially true of Çatalhöyük. The
people of Çatalhöyük seem to have practiced excarnation, a mortuary practice in which the bodies of the dead were exposed to insects
and birds of prey outside the settlement. Once their flesh had been
stripped, the skeletons were recovered for burial in the houses under
"sleeping platforms." According to James Mellaart, the site's first excavator, men were buried under a small platform whose location was
variable, while women were buried under a large platform that was always in a fixed spot in the room. Children were sometimes buried
with women under the large platform or under additional platforms,
but never with men.[17]

Feminist matriarchalists have suggested that the woman under the
large platform was the head of the household, while the man under
the small platform was her brother or son.[18] But there are other
equally valid ways of interpreting the burial pattern at Çatalhöyük. If
these were sleeping platforms, perhaps women's platforms were larger
because women were expected to share their beds with more people
(say, their children). Or maybe the dead were not placed under the
spot where they customarily slept. Perhaps the large, fixed platforms
belonged to the men, and they buried their wives and children under
them to feel close to their deceased family members, or even to
underscore the fact that in death—as in life—these people were considered their property. In actuality, very few skeletons recovered from
Çatalhöyük were found complete, and it is possible that individual
skeletons were not buried in a single location, but split up and "shared
out among various buildings or platforms within a building,"[19] just as
some people are cremated today and have their ashes spread in several
different locations.

Further complicating the matter is the fact that the evidence from
Çatalhöyük is apparently not as Mellaart presented it. Though adult
men and women do seem to be buried in separate areas, it is now clear
that children were sometimes buried with men and that women were
buried in other locations besides under the large platform Mellaart

identified as theirs. The current excavators of Çatalhöyük are speculating that burials in any one room were those of extended family
members, and that buildings were abandoned upon the death of the
senior member of that family. Based on the one room that has been
fully excavated as part of the new work at Çatalhöyük, principal in-
vestigator Ian Hodder concludes that this senior member was probably a man.[20]

Another matter of interest pertaining to the graves at Çatalhöyük
is the disproportionately high percentage of female skeletons. Some
feminist matriarchalists have explained this by saying that men, who
were less important to the life of the community, did not always merit
burial within the inner sanctum of the home. Archaeologist Naomi
Hamilton has made the veiled matriarchalist suggestion that there
were fewer men among the skeletons because women were killing
male babies to oppose "an ideology of women as mothers and carers
[sic] of males" and to create "their own majority" during a time when
women's "social power was being eroded."[21] This is a highly implausible scenario without any known ethnographic parallel, and one
which presupposes that something detrimental was happening to
women's status at Çatalhöyük—something that hadn't already happened under earlier conditions. A rather obvious explanation for the
disproportionate number of female skeletons is that men were not
dying at home, but elsewhere, and that no one thought to (or was
available to) bring their bodies back to the village. We know that the
people of Çatalhöyük engaged in long-distance trade,[22] and if men
dominated this activity—as men have tended to do in the ethnographic contexts of which we are aware—they had plenty of opportunities to die away from their small sleeping platforms. The evidence
of grave patterning does not, by itself, allow us to determine what
gender relations the people of Çatalhöyük had in mind when they
buried their dead as they did.

Matriliny and matrilocality certainly could have occurred prehistorically, if not at Çatalhöyük, then elsewhere. These kinship and residence patterns are attested ethnographically (though considerably
less often than patriliny and patrilocality). However, they are associated with only "modest benefits for women," if any at all.[23] Indeed, in
most societies we know of, matricentric and patricentric customs are
mixed together. For example, the matrilineal Nairs "worship only

male ancestors"; the patrilineal Mundurucú settle matrilocally, while the matrilineal Trobrianders settle patrilocally; in Wogeo, New Guinea, potential marriage partners are selected matrilineally, but succession of political office and inheritance of property are patrilineal. We also have reports of adjoining groups who practice different means of reckoning kinship and yet are virtually identical in all other relevant respects (such as religion, means of subsistence, form of habitation, and—significantly—relative gender status). Impressively, kinship can even be matrilineal in groups that insist that women are only passive carriers of men's seed, and patrilineal in groups that swear that men have no procreative role. We also know that matrilineal kinship has been practiced at times simply because it is politically or personally inexpedient to acknowledge paternity (for example, in the slaveholding United States, slave owners imposed a rule of matriliny on the slave community so that the children of slave mothers and white fathers would be counted as slaves). And finally, the feminist matriarchalist assertion that matriliny and matrilocality are the "original" forms of human kinship, dominant all over the world before the patriarchal revolution, is belied by the fact that matrilineal kinship systems are found at all levels of social complexity, not just in groups judged to be most like the social model we conjecture for prehistoric times.[24]

Marriage is another matter of interest to feminist matriarchalists, if only by omission. Some feminist matriarchalists like to imagine that marriage did not exist prehistorically, but some form of marriage is so consistently found cross-culturally that it is extremely likely that prehistoric peoples practiced it. And if the ethnographic record is any guide, marriage was probably not especially beneficial for women. One of the few things we can say with confidence about marriage cross-culturally is that it is overwhelmingly a heterosexual institution. Same-sex marriages have been found in many cultures, but they are rare compared to heterosexual unions, and often (though not always) mimic them. It is within the institution of marriage, then, that women are most clearly defined as women, in opposition to men. For example, among the African Mbuti, terms of address and reference rarely distinguish between male and female. But there is an important exception when discussing partners in a reproductively active marriage: terms for these partners are consistently gendered.[25]

As feminist matriarchalists are quick to point out, distinguishing between the genders does not necessarily mean discriminating against either one, and it may mean discriminating in favor of women. What is key to the feminist matriarchalist vision of prehistoric marriage is not its heterosexuality or lack thereof, but that marriage (if the institution existed) did not restrain women's autonomy, sexually or otherwise. However, one of the things marriage seems to do most efficiently—cross-culturally speaking—is to restrict women's choice in sexual partners (and men's too, though generally to a lesser extent). Within marriage, the demand for female sexual fidelity is quite common, as is the belief that a wife is the sexual property of her husband, who can use or transfer his rights in her as he sees fit. These characteristics are true of both societies that are "sex positive" (which legitimate and promote human sexuality) and "sex negative" (which regard sexuality as sinful or polluting).[26] If one agrees that the ethnographic record provides clues to prehistoric life, we have to assume that marriage in prehistoric societies did not routinely enhance women's sexual freedom.

GODDESS WORSHIP AS EVIDENCE OF MATRIARCHY

More even than the ignorance of paternity or the centrality of motherhood in prehistoric cultures, feminist matriarchalists feel that the prevalence of goddess worship in prehistory confirms the gynocentric nature of these societies. As Judy Mann puts it, "if the goddess is female, then females are goddesses."[27]

Several facts confound this interpretation of prehistoric goddess worship. The first is that feminist matriarchalists almost always posit a form of goddess monotheism for prehistory—though it is rarely called that[28]—and what evidence we have seems to cut the other way. Goddess monotheism has not been documented any place on the globe. Historical religions, from classical antiquity to the present day, are home to many different goddesses if they include female deities at all. In classical Greece, for example, the various goddesses had diverse roles and functions. The Greeks did not regard them as "aspects of a unitary goddess."[29]

Another troubling fact about goddesses as we know them ethnographically and historically is that they do not always resemble the image that feminist matriarchalists stipulate for prehistoric cultures:

the loving mother, the giver and taker of life, the embodiment of the natural world. Some goddesses are incredibly violent—and not in a way that suggests the benevolent function of watching over the natural cycles of death and rebirth. For example, an Ugaritic text from 1400 BCE Canaan says of the goddess Anat: "She is filled with joy as she plunges her knees in the blood of heroes." The Sumerian Inanna is also a goddess of war, and, significantly, neither she nor Anat is portrayed as a mother. Shitala, worshipped today in Bengal, "tempts fallible persons, and especially mischievous children, with irresistible delicacies, which then break out on their bodies as horrifying and fatal poxes." [30]

More troublesome than these deviations from the feminist matriarchalist ideal is the fact that goddesses are often known to support patriarchal social customs. Goddesses may have nothing whatsoever to do with women's religious needs, representing instead men's fantasies of "the Eternal Mother, the devoted mate, the loving mistress," or even the fearful nature of women's power (should it be allowed to wriggle out from under strict male control).[31] Goddesses may be strongly, if ambivalently, distinguished from human women, and the differences between the two repeatedly emphasized: that is, goddesses "accentuate what womanhood is *not*" as often as they reflect a culture's notion of what women are. In her research on goddess worship in India, Cynthia Humes has noted that devotees see important commonalities between goddesses and human women, especially related to their "natural maternal instincts." But devotees also report that there is "an unbridgeable chasm between goddesses and human women, since female bodies are irremediably permeated by evil and pollution." As one male pilgrim told Humes, "the difference between the Goddess and women is like the difference between the stone you worship and the rock on which you defecate." [32] Goddess worship has been reported for societies rife with misogyny, and at times goddesses even seem to provide justification for beliefs and practices that are antiwoman. Contrariwise, the worship of male gods can coincide with relatively greater power for women.[33] There is simply no one-to-one relationship between goddess worship and high status for women.

Feminist matriarchalists do not deny the phenomenon of patriarchal goddess worship; they suggest that it was pioneered by the Kurgan invaders. But what they are proposing for prehistory is something different: goddess worship that is culturewide, exclusive, and consistently supportive of women's power and independence. They thereby put themselves in the very difficult position of arguing for a type of goddess worship that has never been seen, either historically or ethnographically.

The fallback option for feminist matriarchalists is to insist that all the historic and ethnographic knowledge we have cannot tell us for certain what prehistory was like. If a worldwide patriarchal revolution occurred before scribes or ethnographers could (or would) accurately record what preceded it, then prehistory could be a world unto itself, not interpretable in terms of the cultures that followed. This is, however, a very drastic thesis. And as calamitous as the patriarchal revolution is taken to be by feminist matriarchalists, it is rarely seen in terms this grandiose. So the usual tack is to simply keep insisting that there is an important equation between the worship of goddesses and an enhanced status for women, evidence to the contrary notwithstanding.

Feminist matriarchalists are basically going on instinct in believing goddesses to be positively related to the status of women—and instinct, in this case, does not prove to be a very good guide. They note that male dominance is correlated in recent history with the veneration of a male god or gods and assume that the obverse must also be true because it "seems logical." They imaginatively place themselves in cultures that worship goddesses and cannot believe that "with such a powerful role-model," girls and women would not "naturally consider it their right and duty to fully participate in society and to take the lead in government and religion." Their own experience suggests that this must be true, since they have themselves been empowered by the presence of the goddess in their lives. As Sue Monk Kidd enthuses about the goddess, "believe me, there is no way *this* word, this symbol, can be used to hush women up or get them back in line [her emphasis]."[34]

In fact, so passionate is the desire to believe that goddess worship benefits women that feminist matriarchalists frequently see such benefits in unlikely places. For example, though Jennifer and Roger Woolger admit that for women in Athens "there was little choice between being a homebound matron, a hetaera or high-class prostitute, or a slave," they nevertheless argue that "the mere existence of the various cults to goddesses as individual as Aphrodite, Artemis, Demeter, and Athena provided many rich possibilities for women's psychic and spiritual life, many more than were later retained in Christianity or Judaism." Likewise, Gerda Lerner argues that "no matter how degraded and commodified the reproductive and sexual power of women was in real life, her essential equality could not be banished from thought and feeling as long as the goddesses lived and were believed to rule human life." This is a peculiar way of assessing women's status. Women's self-esteem, secured through the worship of something female, may be a valuable commodity under harsh patriarchal conditions, but this is not remotely akin to the amelioration of those conditions via goddess worship. "Free" women in classical Greece were lifelong legal minors who were mostly forbidden to leave their homes and who were not even their husbands' preferred sexual partners. What exactly is the point of celebrating this ancient culture's goddess worship and contrasting it to our own culture's lack of the feminine divine?[35]

Feminist matriarchalists sometimes retreat to the argument that such societies were "*less* male-centered than those which worshipped . . . an omnipotent male deity, exclusively," even if they were not absolutely female-centered.[36] But some scholars of religion argue precisely the opposite of this thesis. Indeed, this is what a Marxist analysis of religion would predict: goddess worship would compensate women for what they lack in real economic and social power and would serve to keep women from rebelling against their actual low status. In examining the veneration of the Virgin of Guadalupe in Mexico, Ena Campbell notes that although Guadalupe "has eclipsed all other male and female religious figures in Mexico," she is worshipped more by men than women and is used in recompense for women's "actual position in the social scheme." Comparing data from Roman Catholicism, Hinduism, and Buddhism, Campbell concludes that "mother goddess worship seems to stand in inverse relationship with high secular female status."[37] Thus, far from being a sign of special respect accorded to women, goddess worship would, in the absence of other evidence, be expected to correlate with a poor state of affairs for women.

It seems more likely that goddess worship can coexist with various degrees of status for women, high or low. Certainly, ethnography has not uncovered a consistent pattern. In *The Status of Women in Pre-industrial Societies*, anthropologist Martin King Whyte attempted to uncover the determinants of women's status. Of the items he investigates having to do with religion, only one of them—equally elaborate funerals for women and men, as opposed to women having none or less elaborate ones than men—is shown to correlate with women's status at all, and that only weakly. The others, including "sex of gods and spirits," "sex of mythical founders," "sex of shamans," "sex of witches," and "religious ceremony participation" all vary independently of other markers of the status of women (such as menstrual taboos, husbands' authority over wives, and property ownership).[38] It seems that people can worship gods or goddesses, have priests or priestesses, remember ancestresses or ancestors, without it having any particular effect on how ordinary women are treated. There is no warrant for the feminist matriarchalist assumption that prehistoric goddess worship, insofar as it existed, conferred greater respect upon women or insulated them from misogyny or subordination to men.

WORK AND THE STATUS OF WOMEN

Feminist matriarchalists often suggest that woman-favoring social systems arose prehistorically partly in response to women's important economic roles. In foraging societies, they say, men do all or most of the hunting, but it is women's gathering work that usually provides most of the group's diet. And once agriculture was invented—by women—their added labor is said to have enhanced women's status further, giving them control over the group's produce and property. It is not until men seized control of agriculture by making more intensive use of land through plows and draft animals that feminist matriarchalists see women's economic power decreasing dramatically.

Virtually all societies of which we are aware do stipulate different work for individuals based on their sex or gender, usually along the lines that feminist matriarchalists note: in foraging societies, men hunt and women gather; in horticultural societies, men continue to hunt or fish, but also clear and prepare land for farming, while women tend fields, carry wood and water, and care for children; in more intensive agricultural economies, the same pattern continues, with men doing proportionately more farm work and less hunting and fishing.

Children are typically inducted into their gender-specific roles at a young age.[39] In all these different types of economies, women tend to work closer to home, performing tasks that have to be done daily, while men are more inclined to travel and perform tasks that vary. Grave goods provide some support for the notion that these same divisions existed prehistorically. Generalizing for the Middle Neolithic in Europe (Gimbutas's "Old Europe"), Sarunas Milisauskas describes the contents of men's graves as "flint tools, weapons, animal bones, and copper tools" while women's included mostly pottery and jewelry.[40]

A notable fact about the sexed division of labor is that it is fairly arbitrary. Broad patterns aside, there is considerable variation in how different groups assign different tasks by sex: women's work is not everywhere the same, nor is men's, and cultures do not hold to preassigned roles with equal rigidity. One culture may demand that men make pottery, while another says that only women can do so. But even the general patterns can be regarded as arbitrary from the point of view of physiological capability. As James Faris notes, "even game hunting . . . depends far more on organization than on superordinate strength"; likewise, gathering, cooking, and child care (after weaning) are not dependent on female-specific attributes. Yet these patterns recur frequently, and anthropologists typically explain them in terms of what they say is a nearly universal desire to have women's work be compatible with caring for small children: women should perform only "tasks that are not dangerous, do not require distant travel, and are interruptible."[41]

Another notable fact about the sexed division of labor among humans is that it is always characterized by some degree of reciprocity: the sexes perform different tasks and then engage in exchange with one another. One might expect that this mutual dependence would lead to mutual respect.[42] This is the hope upon which feminist matriarchalists hang their vision of prehistory, for they almost never challenge the idea that women in matriarchal societies were gatherers and horticulturalists who provisioned men with vegetable foods while in turn accepting the products of men's labor. But the ethnographic record shows that the vital labor women provide in foraging and horticultural economies does not usually give them social power comparable to men's.

Foraging societies are often said by cultural anthropologists to be "egalitarian," so this looks like a hopeful place for feminist matriarchalists to begin. However, anthropologists mean something by the term egalitarianism that turns out, oddly enough, to be compatible with the most virulent misogyny and sexism. Egalitarian societies are defined by anthropologists as small groups which lack any elaborate political hierarchy. Individuals are free to come and go as they please; they have immediate access to resources and can exert influence over other individuals in their group. There are pecking orders in egalitarian societies, but they depend "more upon personal qualities and skills than upon inherited wealth or status at birth." But among the "personal qualities" most frequently used to determine status in so-called egalitarian societies are "age, sex, and personal characteristics." Now age and sex are not earned. An individual's age changes, inexorably, and in this sense can be regarded as a kind of achieved status. But this is not so for sex, which is "ascribed for life." Thus arises the irony of speaking of societies which systematically discriminate against one sex in preference to the other as "egalitarian." [43] Such discrimination can be relatively minor, as it is among the Mbuti and San of Africa, where men are slightly more likely to participate in collective decision-making, but there are also many glaring examples of male authority, dominance, and disproportionate prestige in foraging societies. Even in societies that lack class systems or political leadership, one can find fathers giving away their daughters, husbands beating their wives or having legitimate control over them sexually, men raping women without penalty, and men claiming a monopoly on the most significant forms of ritual power. [44]

Foraging peoples do rely more, calorically speaking, on women's gathering than on men's hunting, with foods contributed by women typically making up 60 to 80 percent of the group's diet. Women in horticultural societies also frequently contribute a greater share to the group's subsistence and spend more hours at their appointed tasks than men do at theirs. But whatever women's work is, however valuable—even crucial—it may be to the local economy, there is simply no correlation between the type, value, or quantity of women's work and women's social status. [45]

We do not need to look beyond ethnographic analogies to our own history to suspect that this would be the case. Who provided the labor that made the economic engine of the antebellum South run? Enslaved Africans. Did social power, authority, and respect accrue to them as a result? Hardly. Prehistoric economies were drastically different from the antebellum South, of course. Social groups were much smaller and economies aimed to produce little more than what subsistence required. But the basic relationship does seem to hold for horticultural societies just as it does for later slave societies: those who hold power make others work for them. Economically speaking, the quickest index to social power would seem to be who is working least, not who is working most.[46] The fact that women work harder in horticultural societies should, if anything, arouse our suspicion that these cultures are dominated by men.

Furthermore, men's work—whatever it is—tends to be more valued than that of women in foraging and horticultural societies. Hunting, for example, is generally a high-prestige activity. Men also tend to win greater prestige even when they engage in work identical to women's. For example, among the Trobriand Islanders, both men and women cultivate yams, but only men's yams are used as an object of exchange. In other words, while the content of men's work can vary, it seems to carry with it a characteristically male level of prestige. Women's work, in contrast, is more often viewed as routine and pedestrian.[47] This is not to say that women's work is never a source of prestige, or that men's always is; the ethnographic record is nothing if not variable on this point. But it is at least clear that the vision feminist matriarchalists paint of hard-working women standing as the economic pillars of their communities, respected as tribal mothers by all, is not very plausible in light of what we know of contemporary foraging and horticultural societies.

Some cultural anthropologists have suggested that the crucial question is not what kind of work—or how much of it—women do, but whether or not women can own or control the distribution of resources. Women, especially in horticultural societies, often own land. In these societies, however, this is rarely a significant category of wealth. Land is quickly exhausted, and new land must be cleared. Thus the sense in which we tend to think of land—as valuable, transferrable property—has little to do with how most horticulturalists think of it: as a temporarily useful commodity, "owned"—for whatever it's worth, which isn't much—by those who cultivate it. Even female control over a group's principal economic resources does not correlate with a high social status for women. Among the Mundurucú of the Amazonian jungle, the principal horticultural product, farinha, is entirely under women's control; moreover, men give all the game they kill to women, who then decide to whom it will be distributed. And yet this is a group with gender relations that no feminist in her right mind could either envy or endure: women are expected to keep their eyes lowered and their mouths covered when in the company of men; they cannot venture outside the village alone without consenting—in effect—to being raped; decisions affecting the community are made in the men's house with no women present; men hold the monopoly on religious ritual, and any invasion of their domain is punished by gang rape (as are other infractions); and the dominant ideology is that women must be subordinate.[48]

In feminist matriarchal myth it is said that women enhanced their already high status in prehistoric times even further by inventing agriculture in the first place, extending their knowledge of plants to the deliberate cultivation of them.[49] There is no way to prove that women invented agriculture, and as speculative arguments go, this one is relatively weak. Men in foraging societies gather too—in order to feed themselves when on long hunting expeditions, if not on a more regular basis—so it seems likely that men had as much opportunity to familiarize themselves with plant life cycles as women did. And given that women and men in small foraging societies interact with each other a great deal, it seems unlikely that women would not have shared with men any potentially helpful information about securing food sources as soon as it arose. More likely, the sexes worked together to introduce and perfect this technology.[50] Indeed, agriculture has never been the preserve of women to the extent that hunting has been the preserve of men.

When the technology of deliberate cultivation arose, its effect on women seems to have been variable. The severity and location of degenerative joint disease (arthritis) among Native Americans as agricultural technologies were adopted tells us something of women's and men's differential work patterns. These patterns vary from site to site, with women showing the scars of a heavier workload in some locations, while at others, men appear to have borne the brunt of the new technology.[51] In terms of raw measures of skeletal health, the

change to agriculture was sometimes beneficial for women and sometimes not.

The move to intensive agriculture (as opposed to horticulture)
was an enormous transition for human societies, one that is generally
said to have been unfavorable for women. Intensive agriculture made
unprecedented population densities possible. In hunting and gathering societies, population density is generally quite low, and local
groups are rarely much larger than baboon troops. With the introduction of agriculture, babies could be weaned earlier (to be fed with agricultural foodstuffs), so women could conceive again more quickly.
And once babies no longer needed to be carried from place to place, it
was possible for women to care for more young children at one time.
Under these conditions, human societies have been known to increase very quickly, as fast as 3 percent each year (which yields a dou-
bling of the population in only twenty-three years).[52]

With the increased population density made possible by intensive
agriculture came greater levels of social stratification. Unlike "egalitarian" societies, divided on lines of age and sex, these "complex" societies could be divided along class lines too: aristocrats and slaves,
royalty and commoners, natives and foreigners, and so on. Given that
one of the most common axes of inequality in so-called egalitarian
societies is sex, one might expect that it would persist, and perhaps become exaggerated, under conditions of heightened stratification,
such as that experienced with the rise of state-level societies. However, the effect of social stratification on women is not all negative; or
rather, it is not negative for all women, since one of the groups state-
level societies stratify is women. Although a woman may not outrank
a man of her class, she may—and frequently does—outrank men in
lower classes.[53] It becomes increasingly difficult under such conditions to talk about *the* status of women (and it was never easy, as we
have seen). Women of the upper classes may have access to economic
and political power that would have been unimaginable to men in
simpler societies; on the other hand, women of the lower classes may
be subordinated more completely than they ever could have been in
"egalitarian" societies.

What, then, does the ethnographic evidence tell us about women's
status in relation to the economies and technologies that we can safely
assume applied in prehistoric times? It tells us most basically that there

is no reliable connection between forms of subsistence and women's status.[54] If there is one broad pattern regarding women's status, it is that it is lower than men's, whatever the prevailing economy or women's specific place in it. Within this generalization, however, there is a staggering amount of variation, from vague nuances of differential personal autonomy or authority to unmistakable sexual slavery. If ethnographic reports are any indication, then women's status prehistorically was variable, not uniform; in some places it was probably very good, while in other places it was probably horrific.

WAR AND PEACE

Feminist matriarchalists also claim that prehistoric human societies were peaceful, a claim that is doubtful on both ethnographic and archaeological grounds. Warfare is common in ethnographic contexts at all levels of technological sophistication. And violent death—probably not the result of accident—is archaeologically attested for many prehistoric populations dating to the purported matriarchal era. For example, Steven J. Mithen notes that numerous skeletons from Mesolithic cemeteries dating thousands of years earlier than any proposed patriarchal revolution "have injuries caused by projectile points." Brian Hayden reports on mass graves from the European Neolithic containing as many as seven hundred skeletons, some with arrowheads embedded in their bones. Some archaeologists have even theorized that certain skeletal features from Minoan Crete indicate human sacrifice.[55]

Weapons have been discovered in many Paleolithic and Neolithic graves in Europe and the Near East, particularly in those of men. Gimbutas repeatedly insists that "no weapons except implements for hunting are found among [the] grave goods" in Old European burials; at times she goes further to say that "there were no weapons produced at all" by Old Europeans, or at least no "lethal weapons." But if the technology exists to hunt deer and pigs—and to slaughter domesticated sheep, goats, and cattle—then the technology exists to kill human beings, who are merely large mammals like the rest. In addition, maces are present among Neolithic grave goods from Çatalhöyük to the Balkans, which, according to archaeologist David Anthony, are specialized "anti-personnel" weapons, of little use in hunting or splitting wood, but very effective at bashing in the skulls of other human beings.[56] Finds of daggers and arrowheads are not as conclusive in proving the presence of warfare as armor or shields might be, but the latter are made of metal, and metallurgic technologies did not exist in most of the times and places feminist matriarchalists deem matriarchal. This raises the possibility that Old Europeans and other putatively matriarchal peoples had forms of weaponry and other technologies of warfare that have not survived in the material record. The Nantucket Whaling Museum in Massachusetts has an exhibition of weapons of war from the South Pacific, clearly identified as such by the people who brought them back to the United States. They are mostly enormous wooden clubs which would rot away in the earth long before we could dig them up. Some are inlaid with rows of sharks' teeth to better inflict injury. Such a weapon could well end up hundreds of years later as nothing more than a handful of sharks' teeth, which the unwitting archaeologist might interpret as jewelry or as a means of exchange.

Larger settlement patterns also point to greater interpersonal and intertribal violence than feminist matriarchalists imagine for prehistory. Feminist matriarchalists often claim that Neolithic villages in Europe had no defensive fortifications. For example, Gimbutas argues that the "occasional V-shaped ditches and retaining walls" surrounding Old European villages were "structurally necessary." But other archaeologists, looking at the same or additional evidence, are quite certain that many of these settlements were designed to fend off attack from outside. David Anthony reports the use of deep ditches in Neolithic Europe, "backed by multiple lines of palisade walls with elaborate gate-like constructions," and dismisses the argument that they were "peaceful flood-control devices." Indeed, some of these ditches are filled with mass graves.[57]

Even if there were no evidence of fortifications in Old Europe, this would not mean there was no war. Defensive fortifications would not have been necessary for groups that conducted their warfare on other people's territory. Marvin Harris suggests that Minoan Crete, for example, may have been warlike, but if "military activities were focused on naval encounters"—which one might expect for an island society—there would be little material evidence of warfare on their home territory. A New World example helps make this clear. The Mayas, whose cities were completely unfortified, were long thought

to be "an unusually gentle, peaceful people living in a relatively benign theocracy." But as the Mayan writing system began to be deciphered and as new excavations were undertaken, a different picture
emerged. Archaeologists found depictions of severed heads and
bound captives and unearthed dismembered skeletons of sacrificial
victims under public buildings. As archaeologist Arthur Demarest
concludes on the basis of this new evidence, "the Maya were one of
the most violent state-level societies in the New World." [58]

Of course, feminist matriarchalists are in a difficult position when
confronting ethnographic and archaeological evidence. What they
most want to find in prehistory is the absence of things with which we
are all too familiar—sexism, warfare, and environmental degradation, among others—and it is much harder to prove the absence of
something than its presence. If feminist matriarchalists were in search
of the dominating power of women, one could imagine archaeological finds that might validate this: for example, burials with murdered
men interred beside a richly equipped female,[59] or wealthy grave
goods allocated to women and poor ones to men. But sexual egalitarianism, peace, and harmony with nature—the qualities most feminist
matriarchalists seek—are more elusive. Digging up comfortable
homes, material prosperity, even bodies free of disease or spared untimely death (all things we might reasonably want) still does not mean
that we have excavated a society free of sexual oppression. What then
(other than texts, which are not available for this period) might speak
of matriarchy, as feminist matriarchalists envision it? To this, feminist
matriarchalists have a ready answer: pictures . . . which, as the old
adage goes, are worth a thousand words.

CHAPTER 7

The Case Against Prehistoric Matriarchies II:

Prehistoric Art and Architecture

The promise representational art holds forth is to tell us how prehistoric peoples saw themselves and their world. Our own representational art is often said to fulfill this function, graphically displaying who we are and what we value. For example, Christian iconography is rich in symbolic portrayals of Christian theology and ethics; images in advertising are thought to speak volumes about who Americans want to be. In theory, prehistoric art is similarly a window onto the subjective experiences of our ancestors, one not provided by the amount of strontium in their fossilized bones or the varying shapes of their flint blades.

What we lack for prehistory, however, is a trained observer, an insider who could translate prehistoric art for us. We effortlessly and accurately read most of the images we stumble across in everyday life, but we may forget how much we had to learn to attain this interpretive mastery. Years of enculturation lie behind our ability to decipher the visual images we encounter. When images are divorced from most other markers of culture (such as language and behavior), as they are for prehistoric societies, accurate interpretation becomes extremely difficult.

If we know anything about artistic conventions, it is that they are *conventions*, and as such they may have only an oblique link to "real life." Some things rarely experienced are frequently imaged, and vice versa. As André Leroi-Gourhan has noted, European heraldry is full of lions and eagles, though in the ordinary run of their lives, Europeans were vastly more likely to encounter cows and pigs; likewise, if women's magazines were my sole record of American culture, I might conclude that there were no fat people in twenty-first-century America. Cultures may neglect to represent all kinds of quotidian realities for a variety of reasons: they may consider these realities too banal to be worth portraying in art; they may wish to deny certain unpleasant realities about their lives and cultures; or they may think some matters too special or sacred to commit to a visual symbol. And even things that are routinely represented are open to misinterpretation by observers who lack the relevant knowledge to read it correctly. Carl Jung tells the story of a man who returned to India after a visit to England and told his friends that the English worshipped animals, because he had seen eagles, lions, and oxen portrayed in churches.[1]

One of the central problems in interpreting prehistoric images is that the material itself—pictures and statues of human beings and animals—looks disarmingly familiar, so it often seems that inferences about the meaning of this art have more to do with an individual observer's imaginative, empathic, and intuitive abilities than with any archaeological credentials. A person who "sits in the ruins and catches the vibes," as Philip Davis disparagingly puts it, may feel herself to know as much about prehistoric peoples as those who work with spades, sieves, and brushes. No one is immune to the powerful reactions that this art can elicit, from the archaeologist who digs it up to the casual consumer of glossy reproductions of artifacts on the other side of the coffee table. Patricia Reis, author of *Through the Goddess*, remembers stumbling across pictures of Paleolithic Venus figurines in an art book at a university library. As she recalls, "My body became electrified. . . . These objects held a haunting mystery filled with sacredness."[2] It is hard to believe that any reaction that comes with such force and conviction could be simply mistaken, at least for the person experiencing it (strength of passion being notoriously easy to confuse with acuity of insight). This misplaced confidence has plagued both archaeological and feminist matriarchalist interpretations of prehistoric art.

The conflicting interpretations offered for prehistoric visual images gives us sufficient reason to be suspicious of anyone's claim to have finally decoded them. The tendency among archaeologists today is to feel that, if anything, prehistoric art is *less* illuminating and more open to misinterpretation than other forms of prehistoric material evidence, particularly when it comes to the sensitive issues of gender and religion.[3] Feminist matriarchalists, in contrast, believe they have a method which provides consistent, reliable, and indeed rather obvious interpretations of prehistoric art. To resist these interpretations, they often suggest, requires a willful blindness.

READING SYMBOLS

In interpreting prehistoric art, feminist matriarchalists make liberal use of the assumption that a relatively stable set of cross-cultural meanings are attached to femaleness, and in turn to the symbols thought to represent it. This symbolic approach to prehistoric art allows feminist matriarchalists to accomplish two important tasks: first, they are able to extract broad, clear meanings from long-dead societies; and second, they have a warrant not only to construe female anthropomorphic figurines[4]—the prime suspects for "goddesses" in prehistoric art—but also everything from wavy lines to crosses as "a kind of universal female symbolism."[5]

This symbolic code leads feminist matriarchalists to speak as though there were no relevant differences between the essential focus of religion in Siberia in 27,000 BCE and Crete in 1500 BCE. They usually treat all of prehistoric Europe and the Near East as if it were a single cultural complex, viewing cultural variations as an epiphany of the multiplicity of the goddess rather than as evidence of distinctive religious beliefs or systems of social organization.[6] This is a very long time and a very large area for a single religion to dominate. The repetition of a few symbols in the imagery of these different cultures cannot by itself support the notion that these cultures progressively, and in concert with one another, developed an iconography of a single deity. In fact, the cultures from which feminist matriarchalists draw their symbolic examples of goddess religion do not overlap either chronologically or geographically. The material evidence itself illustrates this. There is a dramatic difference, for example, between "the figurine and clay-rich archaeological record of Neolithic Southeast Europe" and the several millennia during which the British Neolithic apparently failed to produce a single female figurine.[7]

Feminist matriarchalists are usually forthcoming with explanations, however questionable, for why everything they list qualifies as a goddess symbol, in spite of the geographic and chronological distance that sometimes separates them. Some symbols are chosen for their supposed analogy to portions of the female anatomy: the chalice, as a container, is said to stand for the womb; the mouth of a cave for the goddess's vagina. Others, such as lions, are determined to be goddess symbols because they are repeatedly (or sometimes only once) seen partnered with female figures in prehistoric art.[8] The list of symbols that are supposed to make us suspect "that a matristic consciousness was operative in a culture if they are found in that people's relics"[9] is alarmingly long. It includes:

bears	phalli	zigzags
lions	women	spirals
bulls	eggs	parallel lines
bison	trees	meanders
deer	lush vegetation	tri-lines
horses	pomegranates	Xs
goats	apples	Vs
pigs	the moon	hooks
dogs	the sun	crosses
hedgehogs	stones	chevrons
birds (hawks, owls)	shells	swastikas
snakes	caves	lozenges
toads	storehouses	halved lozenges
turtles	pillars	hooked lozenges
fish	labyrinths	ovals
bees	wells	triangles
butterflies	cauldrons	circles
snails	chalices	dots[10]
eyes	nets	
hands	rings	

This proliferation of purported goddess symbols makes it possible to find evidence of goddess worship in virtually every scrap of prehistoric art. Even the simplest of signs can shout "goddess." Gimbutas, for example, relishes the fact that the stamp seals of Old Europe are "almost all . . . engraved with either straight lines, wavy lines or zigzags," which she interprets as a water and rain symbolism attributable to goddess religion. Reaching even farther, Rachel Pollack claims that "the oldest carefully marked object," an ox rib found in France dating to 200,000 to 300,000 BCE, about six inches long and incised with "a pair of curved parallel lines" (visible under a microscope), is "precisely that image" that appears repeatedly in "later Goddess art."[11]

But if straight lines and wavy lines are both symbols of the goddess, is it possible to draw a line another way, or to use it to mean something else? Rachel Pollack notes that there are goddess images "that are almost universal, such as the cross or the spiral,"[12] but she never points out the obvious: that these are very simple images to draw. They may mean nothing—prehistoric doodles—or they may mean very different things in different cultures. Even more importantly, symbols may have no analogical link at all to that which they are supposed to symbolize, just as the numeral 7 means seven, though there is nothing in the shape of the numeral itself to suggest the number seven. In some cases, we cannot even be sure what the symbols we find in prehistoric art are supposed to be (if anything), let alone what meanings they may carry. For example, Anne Baring and Jules Cashford display a series of "Neolithic images of the moon" in their chapter on "the Neolithic Great Goddess of Sky, Earth and Waters."[13] None look like what I see up in the sky on a clear night, though several bear a powerful resemblance to snowflakes (see Fig. 7.1).

How then do feminist matriarchalists know that every animal and geometrical symbol found in prehistoric art is a representation of the goddess or one of her qualities? Only by believing, before they look, that the art is religious art, and in particular, an iconography of a prehistoric goddess. Though I will not attempt the exercise here, I feel certain that if I were looking for evidence of the prehistoric worship of "the masculine principle," I could find it as readily as feminist matriarchalists uncover goddess symbology. Perhaps I could also "discover" that the implements of war are present in cleverly disguised—symbolized—form. In the absence of a prehistoric Rosetta stone translating prehistoric symbols into some language we can understand today, we are of course welcome to pore over the art of prehistoric cultures looking for internal patterns, just as Gimbutas has done. We may find things of interest, but none that can stand as the conclusive interpretation of these images.

Paleolithic Cave Art
Apart from Gimbutas's detailed work on symbols from the Neolithic period in Old Europe, the most elaborated argument for goddess

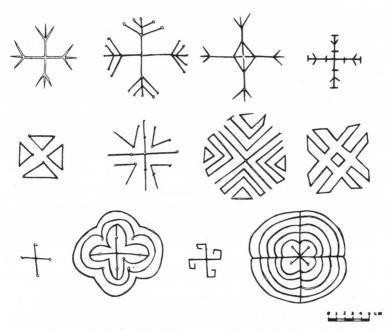

FIG. 7.1   Images incised on Neolithic pottery from sites in Bohemia, from the end of the sixth to the early fifth millennium BCE, interpreted as "Neolithic images of the moon."

symbology is that offered for Paleolithic cave art. Cave art is restricted to a few neighboring locations in southern France and northern Spain (though caves that are seemingly equally suitable for painting are available elsewhere on the continent) and dates from roughly 30,000 to 10,000 BCE, with the majority being produced after 20,000 BCE.[14] Archaeologists theorize that the Franco-Cantabrian caves were preferred as sites for art because they were in the most southerly region of open tundra during the last glaciation. Animals were plentiful, and as a result, so were humans: tribes may have gathered together to hunt there during seasonal migrations. The subjects of the paintings are almost exclusively animals, both species that were routinely hunted, such as reindeer and mammoth, and ones that were not, such as wolf and lion. Representations of humans are comparatively rare, though present. Men and women never appear in proximity to one another.

Men are typically portrayed as simple stick figures, whether painted or engraved, while women are always engraved and rendered in significantly more detail. Men may be active or passive, while women are always inactive; men tend to be portrayed alone, while women appear most often in groups. Numerous schematic designs, including dots, circles, triangles, rectangles, and imprints of human hands, also appear. These various design motifs, as well as the animal and human representations, are frequently superimposed on one another.[15]

Feminist matriarchalists are comparatively uninterested in the animal representations in Paleolithic cave art, and even in the engraved female figures. What draws their attention instead are the schematic designs, which they interpret as "vulva symbols." Feminist matriarchalists are not the first to advance this theory. In 1910, the Abbé Breuil, a French priest who began interpreting Paleolithic art at the age of fourteen, was asked to comment on the meaning of some engraved marks on two limestone blocks recovered from the site of Abri Blanchard in southern France. He immediately labeled them "pudendum muliebre." Indeed, an early observer, L. Didon, describes Breuil as having "recognized vulvas without hesitation," operating "with the completely unique skill in deciphering prehistoric mysteries characteristic of him." Most archaeologists in the twentieth century followed Breuil's lead, finding vulvas everywhere in Paleolithic art. This vulva-finding expedition at times went to rather remarkable extremes. Not only were triangular or horseshoe-shaped designs termed vulvas; so were a myriad of other shapes, denoted by terms like "squared vulva," "bell-shaped vulva," "broken, double vulva," and "atypical vulva." Vulvas have even been discovered in a single straight line ("an isolated vulvar cleft"), and at least one excavator, convinced that some symbols must have been intended to be vulvas, felt free to occasionally draw in the "missing" lines.[16]

An even more ambitious reading of these "vulva" symbols has been offered by French archaeologist André Leroi-Gourhan, who divided up the totality of the schematic markings found in Paleolithic caves into "male" and "female" symbols, so classified because of their putative resemblance to human genitalia. The "male" symbols are straight lines, barbed lines, and rows of dots (the "narrow signs"); the "female" symbols are triangles, ovals, shields, and rectangles (the "wide signs"). While Leroi-Gourhan admits that many of these sym-

	OVAL	RECTANGLE	KEY SHAPE		HOOK	BARB	DOT
NORMAL							
SIMPLIFIED							
DERIVED							

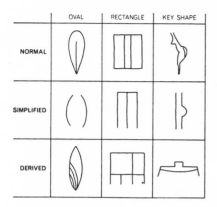
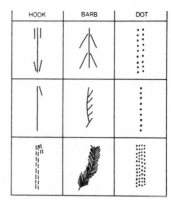

FIG. 7.2   "Wide" and "narrow" signs in Upper Paleolithic cave art, said by Leroi-Gourhan to "have evolved from earlier depictions of female and male figures or sexual organs."

bols are "extremely stylized," he nevertheless insists that most of the wide signs "are quite realistic depictions of the female sexual organ" (see Fig. 7.2). These wide signs turn up in some odd places—for example, in the wounds on animals and in the guts spilling from a disemboweled bison—but Leroi-Gourhan does not hesitate to identify them everywhere as vulvas.[17]

Feminist matriarchalists have enthusiastically embraced the interpretive scheme that sees the walls of Paleolithic caves plastered with disembodied vulvas. For feminist matriarchalists, "the vulva is preeminently a symbol of birth, representing beginnings, fertility, the gateway to life itself," and its presence in cave art indicates that Paleolithic peoples valued birth, death, and rebirth.[18] Yet as some observers note, there is an undoubted resemblance between the vulvas in Paleolithic cave art (that feminist matriarchalists celebrate as the sign of the goddess) and those that "would be right at home in any contemporary men's room."[19] For feminist matriarchalist purposes, Paleolithic vulva images must not be pornographic, for then they are by definition objectifying and oppressive to women. But they must be sexual, for sex is good in matriarchalist terms: it is part of what worship of the goddess entails, part of what separates goddess religion from its wicked stepsons (Judaism, Islam, and Christianity).[20] The solution to

this conundrum is typically to assert the sexuality of Paleolithic images, but to insist that they are completely unlike pornography. "In
fact," says Riane Eisler, "the contrast between these two kinds of sexual images is so striking they almost seem to come from different
planets." Yet how different can two inverted triangles with median
lines be? The only thing that could possibly distinguish them is context. When high school boys spray paint vulvas on her front steps,
novelist Barbara Kingsolver is confident that "their thoughts were oh
so far from God," but when confronted with the same images from
prehistoric Europe, she knows them to be an expression of "awe" for
"female power."[21] How do we know that the caves of Paleolithic Europe were not more like Barbara Kingsolver's front steps?

Moreover, the distinct possibility remains that these "wide signs"
of Paleolithic cave art were not meant to represent vulvas at all. The
symbols purported to be vulvas are extremely variable (see Fig. 7.3)—
Sarah Milledge Nelson says that many of them look more like molar
teeth than anything else—and few are truly triangular, which is the
shape that characterizes all the female genitalia found in context in
Paleolithic art (that is, on full female figures).[22] However, feminist
matriarchalists have something much better than engraved "vulvas"
from the Paleolithic (and wavy lines from the Neolithic) upon which
to stake their claim that femaleness was revered in prehistoric Europe
and the Near East. For these peoples produced a huge number of anthropomorphic figurines, many of them clearly female.

DECODING ANTHROPOMORPHIC ART

Before becoming too enthusiastic about these anthropomorphic
figurines, it is important to recognize that many of the figurines that
feminist matriarchalists declare to be representations of the goddess
are not obviously divine, female, or, in some instances, even human.
For example, Marija Gimbutas titles a figure from Starčevo "an early
loom-weight in the form of the Goddess" (see Fig. 7.4). This object
has no arms, legs, or neck, and only dashes for eyes, a hole for a mouth,
and a pinched nose: its face could belong to either gender or to a wide
range of nonhuman animals. Similarly, Buffie Johnson discusses an
"amulet of the buttocks silhouette" recovered from Paleolithic Germany (see Fig. 7.5). Though this 1¾ inch sculpture has no head and
no arms, Johnson asserts that wherever "an arc and a straight line"

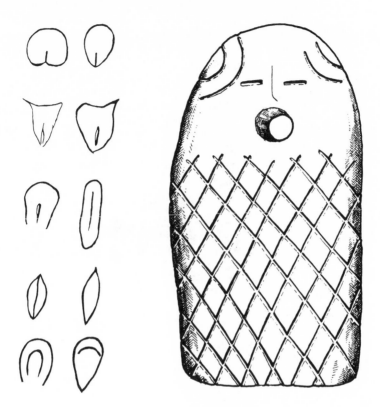

FIG. 7.3 (left)   Incised and carved images from Upper Paleolithic cave art, said to be "vulvae."

FIG. 7.4 (right)   Carved figure from Starčevo, Bulgaria, 5800–5600 BCE (height: 8.8 cm), identified by Marija Gimbutas as a "loom weight in the form of the Goddess."

combine to form a "P shape," one is viewing the "exaggerated egg-shaped buttocks" of the goddess.[23] It is easy to see a human female in these objects if one is told that that is what is there. But if these figures were captioned differently, it would be as easy to see something else. A Paleolithic engraving which Johnson describes as "a female figure with Cosmic Egg in rump" does look like a highly schematized drawing of a seated person's profile with a circle in its middle, at least when you come across it in the pages of *Lady of the Beasts: Ancient*

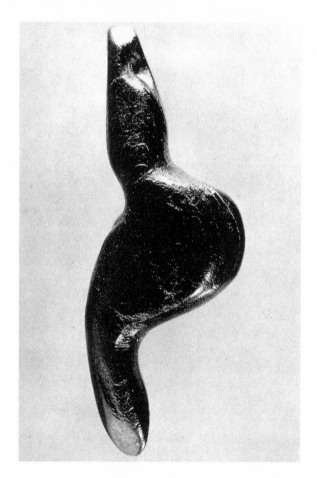

FIG. 7.5   Figure carved in polished coal from Petersfels, Germany, c. 15,000 BCE, called a "buttocks silhouette."

Images of the Great Goddess and her Sacred Animals. But had I seen this same drawing in a book titled, say, *Paleolithic Landscapes,* captioned as "Vézère River showing central island and direction of current," then I would find this an equally plausible description of this engraving (see Fig. 7.6).

Even more questionable than the assignment of humanity to abstract line drawings or sculptures is the classification of virtually all anthropomorphic images as female. Feminist matriarchalists have

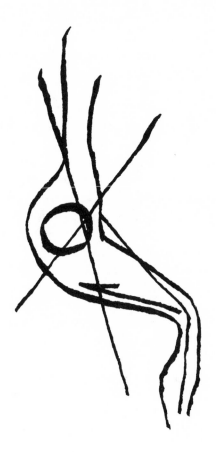

FIG. 7.6   Incised drawing from the Fontalès cave in France, c. 10,000 BCE, described by Buffie Johnson as a "female figure with Cosmic Egg in rump."

been anticipated in this by archaeologists, who have also frequently been inclined to make female the default sex of ambiguous anthropo-morphic images. There are comparatively few images in Paleolithic and Neolithic Europe that are definitely male (possessing a penis) and many that are definitely female (possessing either swollen breasts or a "clear female sexual triangle or vulva"). But what is generally not recognized in feminist matriarchalist studies of prehistoric art is that there is another class of images, varying in size depending on the era or site in question, which have no clear sexual characteristics. If one were to assume that these were all intended to be male, this would generally yield a distribution by sex that is roughly fifty/fifty. These "sexless" images may have been intended to represent females, as feminist matriarchalists suggest, or men, or they may have been intentionally sexless, representing children, "or some generalized idea of the human being." [24]

It is reasonable to attempt to discern stylistic conventions that indicate sex apart from obvious sexual characteristics, but it is a tricky undertaking. Such conventions may or may not exist, and where they do exist, they may be misread. In *The Goddesses and Gods of Old Europe*, Marija Gimbutas juxtaposes two figurines from the Neolithic site of Vinča in Yugoslavia. She describes both as images of the "Bird Goddess." The figurines are clearly of the same basic type, in spite of minor differences in shape and incised markings. One has small breasts, the other none at all (see Fig. 7.7). Gimbutas seems to regard the presence or absence of breasts as yet another minor stylistic difference in the two figures,[25] but the presence or absence of breasts may have been the defining feature of the sex of these figurines: the one with breasts being female, and the one without being male.

There are also prehistoric images that appear to purposefully combine male and female sexual characteristics, including Neolithic figurines said to have a "tall, phallic neck and head," which are described by feminist matriarchalists as "phallic goddesses." Feminist matriarchalists are quite careful to state that the presence of phallic features—or even, in some cases, a phallus itself—does not detract from the overwhelming femaleness of prehistoric anthropomorphic images. As Gimbutas explains, these images "do not represent a fusion of two sexes but rather an enhancement of the female with the mysterious life force inherent in the phallus."[26] Impressively then, even what one might think to be the most obvious signifier of maleness—the penis—is assimilated to femaleness in some feminist matriarchalists' interpretation of prehistoric anthropomorphic images.

The most dramatic example of this assimilation is the feminist matriarchalist reading of Paleolithic "batons." The most popular of these batons has an honored place in feminist matriarchalist iconography, turning up frequently in the first pages or slides devoted to Paleo-

FIG. 7.7   Terracotta figurines from Vinča, Yugoslavia, c. 4800 BCE
(height: 16 and 15 cm), named "Bird Goddesses" by Marija Gimbutas.

lithic images of the goddess. In spite of its striking resemblance to a
phallus, feminist matriarchalists label the Dolní Věstonice baton an
"abstract female with breasts," "shaft with breasts," or "ivory rod with
breasts," and describe it as a "portable shrine," an image of "nurturance reduced to its stylized essence" (see Fig. 7.8). But as archaeologist
Timothy Taylor declares, "it seems disingenuous to avoid the most
obvious and straightforward interpretation" that these are "phallic
objects." [27] Indeed, some of them, at a length of six to eight inches, are
hard to mistake for anything else (see Fig. 7.9).

Feminist matriarchalists also routinely take note of the existence
of "breast pendants" or "breast beads" from Paleolithic Europe.
Gimbutas describes these as an "abstract rendering of the female principle," composed solely of "two breasts at the base of a conical neck."
This has long been the standard archaeological reading of these images, but archaeologist Alice Kehoe points out that the back of the
pendant "exhibits a carefully carved projection through which is a

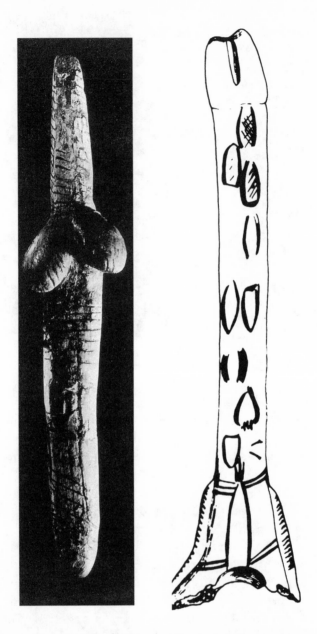

FIG. 7.8   Ivory carving, Dolní Věstonice, Czechoslovakia, c. 25,000 BCE, described as "abstract female with breasts."

FIG. 7.9   Paleolithic "baton," Bruniquel, France, c. 15,000 BCE.

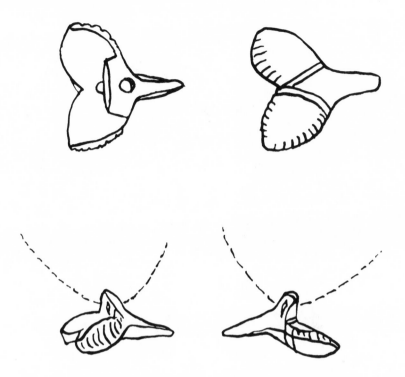

FIG. 7.10   Ivory pendant from Dolní Věstonice, Czechoslovakia, c. 25,000 BCE. Gimbutas and other feminist matriarchalists interpret this artifact as a woman's neck and breasts; viewed at the angle pictured here, it resembles a penis and testicles.

hole," which Kehoe suspects "was designed for a suspension string." When hung on a string the "breast pendant" seems instead "to be an erect human penis and testicles" (see Fig. 7.10). Other objects are similarly ambiguous, their interpretation largely dependent on the angle from which they are viewed. For example, a "seated figure" from Late Neolithic Cyprus viewed from the back appears strikingly phallic. But the top view could be read as a vulva, and from the front or side, it resembles a seated figure with bent knees and tiny feet. Its sexual ambiguity could be an intentional statement of its artist, or, quite plausibly, it may be an artificial penis, equipped with a convenient handle (see Fig. 7.11).[28]

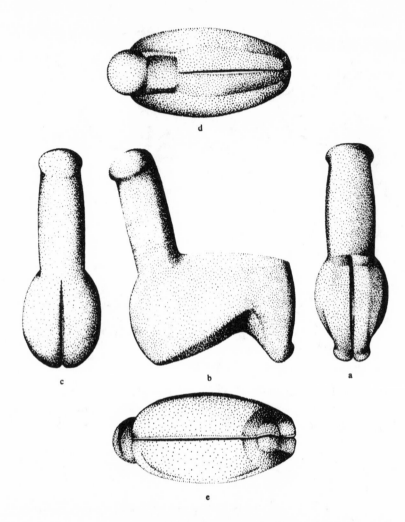

FIG. 7.11   Limestone figure from Sotira Arkolies, Cyprus, c. 2600 BCE, viewed from five different angles (height: 16 cm). View *a* and *b* (front and side views) resemble a seated figure; view *c* (rear view) appears phallic; views *d* and *e* (top and bottom views) resemble a vulva. Surface find.

Feminist matriarchalists would object to this interpretation not so much because they find a prehistoric image of a phallus difficult to incorporate into their picture of goddess-oriented prehistory (we have seen that this is not the case), but because a dildo is not immediately apprehended as a sacred object. And for feminist matriarchalists, everything in prehistoric art—and indeed all of prehistoric life—is sacred, practically by definition. Feminist matriarchalists assert again and again that contemporary archaeologists fail to understand the meaning of prehistoric art because they cannot comprehend its religious nature. Were our ancestors so steeped in the sacred that every image they produced could not help but reveal their deepest values, the objects of their greatest reverence? Gimbutas, who seems to view every cup as a ritual vessel for pouring libations to the goddess, would probably say yes.[29] But there is evidence to the contrary. Contemporary groups, known to us through the work of ethnographers, create decorative art, producing images that they insist have no sacred or ritual intent. In a particularly interesting case from the island of Madagascar, ethnographers tried for years to decipher the deep symbolic meaning of the low reliefs of geometrical patterns which the Zafimaniry people carve into the wooden shutters and posts of their homes. When asked, informants proved refractory, insisting that "they were pictures of nothing," that they were merely making "the wood beautiful."[30] It hardly seems warranted then to name all the prehistoric images we have retrieved as remnants of a vast, multilayered religion of the goddess, or of a religion of any sort. Yet they are surely remnants of *something*, and particularly in the case of definite female images, it seems at least possible that they were intended to portray goddesses.

Paleolithic Venus Figurines

Intriguingly, the first representational art we have knowledge of consists of small statues of females. Those who first excavated these statues named them "Venuses" because they vaguely resembled the classical Venus di Milo with her missing arms. The Venuses have been found across a very wide geographical belt running from southern France to Siberia, but are concentrated in a few sites in France, the former Czechoslovakia, and the former Soviet Union. Many cannot be dated with any great precision, but increasingly scholars are coming to believe that the majority of the figurines were created within a few thousand years, possibly from 23,000 to 21,000 BCE.[31]

Though they are customarily classed together, the Venuses are not all alike. Some are clothed, others naked; they are carved in a variety of materials, including bone, stone, and mammoth ivory; and though generally small, they vary in size from 3.7 centimeters to as much as 40 centimeters. From the time they were first discovered, Paleolithic Venuses were classified as "fertility fetishes" or "goddess figurines." This basic interpretation of Paleolithic Venuses—that they are religious in character and concerned with fertility—has been remarkably persistent among archaeologists, though it has been losing ground over the past few decades as feminist archaeologists have critiqued it.[32] At the same time, however, feminist matriarchalists have taken up the fertility and mother goddess interpretations of Paleolithic Venuses (feminist matriarchalists resist the theory that the Venuses are fertility "fetishes," but still tend to interpret them as being fundamentally concerned with fertility). For example, descriptions of the Venus of Willendorf in feminist matriarchalist books and articles typically refer to her "great nourishing breasts" and "her sacred triangle" (see Fig. 7.12).[33]

The most conspicuous problem with regarding the Paleolithic Venuses as symbols of fertility is that they rarely show signs of pregnancy, childbirth, or lactation. If Paleolithic artists were interested in representing the fertility of women, there are obvious ways in which to do this—such as making female figures that are indisputably pregnant, giving birth, or holding an infant—yet these images have not been found in Paleolithic art. Some, both archaeologists and feminist matriarchalists, insist that the Venuses *are* pregnant, but many of them appear to be fat rather than pregnant, and others are quite thin.[34] Pregnant or not, the very size of some of the Paleolithic Venuses is read by feminist matriarchalists as an expression of fertility. For example, Gimbutas refers routinely to the goddess's "regenerative buttocks," as though buttocks were somehow actively involved in pregnancy and childbirth. Others let the connection to fertility drop and emphasize instead the apparent sacrality attaching to female fatness in Paleolithic times. As Starhawk remarks of the Venus of Lespugue, "whoever carved this figure evidently saw flesh as good, and the female form as worthy of veneration" (see Fig. 7.13).[35]

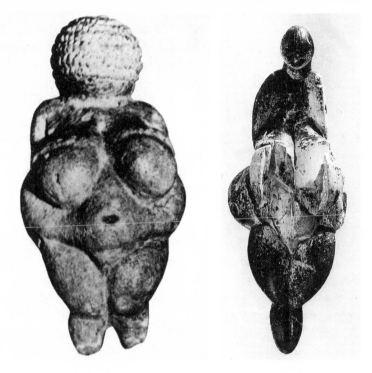

FIG. 7.12   Limestone figure, Willendorf, Germany, c. 30,000–25,000 BCE (height: 11 cm).

FIG. 7.13   Ivory figure, Lespugue, France, c. 23,000 BCE (height: 14.7 cm).

The fatness of the Paleolithic Venuses has been long commented upon. They are "monstrously exuberant and overabundant"; they are characterized by "pendulous breasts, broad hips, rotund buttocks and excessive corpulency." Prehistorians have sought to explain the fatness of these figurines in a variety of ways. Some speculate that it is a reflection of "the community's concern about hunger"; others say that the Venuses are merely straightforward depictions of the women of the time, who happened to be fat. Still others suggest that the Venus is a "Pleistocene pinup or centerfold girl." Some have rejected this notion on the grounds that the Venus of Willendorf could only be attractive "to perverse tastes," but others beg to differ. There is no accounting for taste, they say, and Paleolithic men obviously liked fat women. Björn Kurtén notes that "the female figures often appear in sexually inviting attitudes" and suggests that "there is a straight line from Ice Age art to Rodin, to Zorn's Dalecarlian women, and to the Playboy bunnies of later days."[36] He illustrates his argument by comparing the female torsos of Paleolithic art to contemporary pornographic images (see Fig. 7.14). As with Paleolithic cave art, feminist matriarchalists flatly deny that Paleolithic Venuses are pornographic, primarily because they do not themselves experience this art that way. They deem it "truly pathetic when a woman cannot perceive the difference between the powerful Paleolithic figures and current pornographic portrayals of women as coy, vulnerable toys."[37]

Just what the Paleolithic Venuses signified to those who created them is an irresolvable question. But the idea that they had a religious or magical function is relatively well supported. One of the more notable features of the Venuses is that they tend to have carefully worked torsos compared to their heads, arms, and feet, which are either absent or modeled very simply. Such inattention to faces, usually considered the most individual, recognizable part of a person, seems to indicate that these figurines were intended to symbolize some more general fact of physical, social, or religious life. That so many of the figurines appear unfinished is another indication that they may have fulfilled some religious or magical function, with the act of producing the figurine perhaps being more important than the appearance of the end result.[38] It would seem that these female images were standing for something, just what we cannot tell. The Paleolithic Venuses, relatively few in number and tens of thousands of years old, provide us with few clues to their use or meaning. We have more to go on in the Neolithic era. Many of the archaeological sites are richer and more carefully excavated, and attention to figurine production in ethnographically documented cultures has also suggested some plausible interpretations of the Neolithic evidence.

Neolithic and Cross-Cultural Figurines
As pottery technologies began to be developed during the Neolithic, figurines started to be made out of clay. These have survived in great numbers (though many are broken), especially from sites in the Near East and southeastern Europe. There is considerable stylistic variabil-

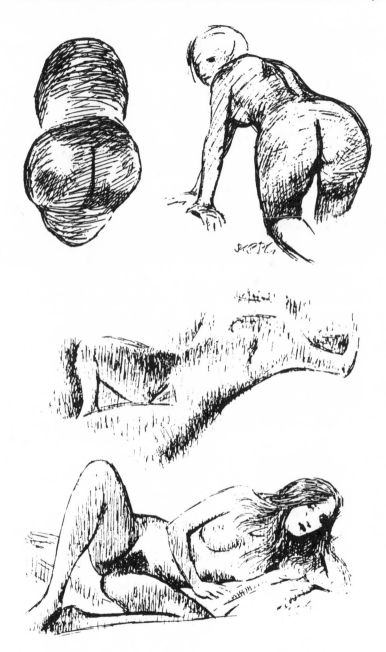

FIG. 7.14   Drawings by Hubert Pepper intended to illustrate a resemblance between Paleolithic figures (both in-the-round and in relief) and contemporary pornographic images of women.

ity among these figurines, both within each site and across many. They are clothed or naked, seated or standing, fat or thin, adorned or plain. Their faces are rarely elaborated, though it is possible that they were decorated with paint or seeds that have not survived. Some figurines are of animals, but more are anthropomorphic, and most are either female or lack any distinguishing sexual characteristics.[39]

The thought that these figurines, like the Paleolithic Venuses, were intended to represent a goddess was well rooted among archaeologists before feminist matriarchalists ever arrived on the scene. But recently the fertility and mother goddess interpretations of these figurines have come in for criticism by archaeologists on the same grounds as the fertility interpretation of Paleolithic figurines, namely that female figurines associated with infants or children are rare. Neolithic figurines are rarely obviously pregnant either, though they, like the Paleolithic figurines, are sometimes quite fat.[40] Certainly it is possible that many figurines which we do not recognize as being pregnant were seen to be so by their creators and users. We know that artistic conventions for depicting pregnancy need not be literal. For example, Our Lady of Guadalupe is said by some to be pregnant because she wears a tassel around her waist that was, for the Spanish, known as a "maternity band."[41]

When feminist matriarchalists speak of Neolithic female figurines as representations of fertility, however, they are not restricting themselves to human reproduction. It is thought that especially with the beginnings of agriculture in the Neolithic era, people would have extended their earlier concern with human and animal fertility to the fertility of the land, which would then also be within the goddess's provenance. However, evidence from historical times does not suggest that this is a particularly likely explanation for female figurines. Though agricultural societies have an active, understandable concern for the fertility of their land and sometimes invoke goddesses in this regard, we have no record of a group that assigns the sole power for agricultural fertility to females or goddesses. Indeed, the goddesses at the head of fertility cults in classical times—such as Ceres and Proserpina in Rome—were believed to bestow human rather than agricultural fertility.[42]

Ethnographic analogies suggest a number of possible alternative functions for Neolithic female figurines. Female figurines have at times played a role in curing or healing rituals. For example, among the Chocó of Colombia, shamans will surround their patient with anthropomorphic figurines (sometimes as many as twenty of them) who represent the shaman's spirit-helpers. Since new figurines must be made for every curing ritual and old ones are disposed of unceremoniously, such a theory, if it were true for the Neolithic, would explain why so many figurines are found in garbage middens. It would also explain the continuum between rough, unfinished pieces and more polished ones, since, among the Chocó, figurines will be made very quickly in an emergency, while they will be constructed far more carefully in the case of a lingering illness when time is not such an issue. Female figurines have also been assigned protective or magical functions in some cultures. Among the Seneca around the time of European contact, female figurines were buried with children, apparently to protect them in death. Female figurines have also performed teaching functions in various ethnographic contexts. They are sometimes associated with the initiation of boys, in addition to (or even exclusive of) girls. Elsewhere, anthropomorphic figurines have been used as dolls or children's toys. Actually, the Neolithic figurines fit many of the features seen in dolls cross-culturally: nudity, small size, sturdiness, and a disproportionate number of female and sexless figures.[43]

Another interpretation of Neolithic female figurines is the feminist matriarchalist one, that they were sacred icons of a goddess or goddesses. Certainly we are aware of numerous cross-cultural instances of goddess worship accompanied by widespread use of icons in the form of figurines, so this is one of the most likely explanations of the Neolithic figurine assemblages. Especially persuasive is the fact that goddess figurines—and larger-scale goddess images as well—exist in later cultures in the same geographic area. But there are some obstacles to this interpretation. To begin with, how would we know these figurines to be divine? Several critics have noted that there is an inconsistency in viewing female images as representations of goddesses while interpreting male or animal images similarly placed as being merely men or animals.[44] The fundamental problem of interpreting images that have been lifted from their original contexts particularly affects attributions of divinity. For example, a sixteenth-century print by Hans Brosamer shows a nude woman with luxurious

FIG. 7.15   Hans Brosamer, *A Whore Venerated by a Fool*, c. 1530. Woodcut print.

hair and a possibly pregnant abdomen holding a lamp and a mirror while a man lies at her feet, gazing up at her with apparent awe (see Fig. 7.15). Those unaware of the image's context could well take it to be a representation of a beautiful, magisterial fertility goddess appearing to a man who responds in an attitude of thunderstruck adoration. However, the work's title, *A Whore Venerated by a Fool*, tells us that that it was intended to warn men against being taken in by women's sexuality.

We know also from historical examples that images of women, even ones that recur over and over again in an apparently symbolic mode, need not be images of goddesses. Disproportionate imaging of females is a widespread (though not universal) phenomenon, in our Western cultures as well as others, and we know that it can coexist with male dominance. We also know, significantly, that extensive female imagery can be found in cultures with male monotheistic religions. Furthermore, deities are not always represented; in fact they can be completely—or largely—invisible, as is the case with the putatively male god of the major Western religions.[45]

Indeed, the worship of relatively invisible male deities accompanied by more visible female deities is a pattern found frequently in ancient times. The iconography of Mycenaean Greek religion is "overwhelmingly feminine," but written tablets reveal that a host of additional deities—significantly, male deities—were also worshipped. Similarly, ancient Mesopotamian art is rife with depictions of Ishtar, who is comparatively rare in texts, while numerous male deities discussed in texts have no "visual counterparts."[46] Excavations from Iron Age Israel (in the eighth century BCE) have revealed a proliferation of female figurines of a specific type: they have a "pillar" base, breasts, and molded head, sometimes with arms and sometimes without. Scholars have termed these the *Dea Nutrix* or "nourishing deity," but we know that the religion of that place and era was adamantly monotheistic.[47] Feminist matriarchalists, presented with this evidence, would fit it into their theories by saying that the pillar figurines indicated the continued household practice of the ancient goddess religion in the face of an official takeover by the patriarchal Semites.[48] But without the textual evidence confirming male monotheism, feminist matriarchalists would probably conclude the obvious: that these people worshipped a goddess, an immanent deity of birth and regeneration. Eighth-century BCE Israelites would fall as easily on the matriarchal side of the ledger as they now fall on the patriarchal side.

In sum, though we cannot know just what Neolithic figurines signified, it is plausible that they are the material remains of goddess worship. The problem is that we don't know whether or not any such potential goddess worship was accompanied by worship of gods, or whether goddess worship, if it was practiced, worked to women's benefit. The female figurines dating to Neolithic times are in no position to enlighten us on these questions.

THE ART OF "MATRIARCHAL" CULTURES

Up until now, we have been looking at particular art forms across several millennia and many hundreds or thousands of miles, a practice I have criticized among feminist matriarchalists. So now let us examine the art of three specific cultures, ones heralded by feminist matriarchalists as matricentric, and see what their artistic production as a whole might say.

Çatalhöyük

The art of Çatalhöyük has been an object of fascination from the time it was first excavated. James Mellaart, the site's first excavator in the 1960s, interpreted the art as evidence of goddess worship, and by 1980, feminist matriarchalists were concluding that the site provided "conclusive evidence for women's preeminence in the Middle Eastern Neolithic." In 1993, when excavations resumed under the direction of Ian Hodder, feminist matriarchalists mobilized to gain access to new archaeological data, and they are now a frequent presence at the site as they arrive on "goddess tours" and work to establish a "Goddess Guest House" in a nearby village.[49]

The art of Çatalhöyük consists of plaster wall reliefs, wall paintings, and figurines either carved in stone or modeled from clay, radiocarbon dated to between 6500 and 5700 BCE. The walls at Çatalhöyük were painted repeatedly, being covered with whitewash in between. Going up the ten to twelve levels of habitation at Çatalhöyük uncovered in the $\frac{1}{32}^{nd}$ of the mound excavated by Mellaart, one can see definite changes in the artwork. Plaster reliefs are present from the beginning, though at first they only include animal heads. They later come to incorporate anthropomorphic figures and "breasts" (conical plaster reliefs usually molded around the skulls of small animals), but by the last levels of habitation, these reliefs fell out of use entirely. Wall paintings include depictions of animals and people; some are hunting scenes. Though females are occasionally present, it is always males who are actively involved in the hunt. One rather famous wall painting is of seven enormous vultures "making a feast of six small headless human beings," a scene which Mellaart relates to the burial practice of excarnation at Çatalhöyük.[50]

Figurines, both zoomorphic and anthropomorphic, have been found at every habitation level, though it is not always clear to which level they "belong." Being made of durable materials, they could have had a use life far exceeding the era in which they were first produced. These figurines range in size from five to thirty centimeters tall. About half are zoomorphic, and of the remainder some are anthropomorphic while others are hard to identify: some call them "humanoid," but others believe they are ducks or other animals. Definitely female figurines have been recovered from houses, grain bins, and, most commonly, rubbish heaps. Some of these figurines are very schematic, with "pointed legs, a stalk-like body, and a beaked head"; others are more naturalistically rendered. One particular figurine, "Goddess with Leopards," is a special favorite among feminist matriarchalists. She is said to sit on a throne flanked by two leopards, as "from between her legs, life emerges" (see Fig. 7.16). The figurine is slightly over four inches tall, and was recovered, headless, from a grain bin. Female figurines are typically found at later levels of habitation, and earlier styles of figurines, both animal and "humanoid," do not persist to the latest levels. If the female figurines are representations of the goddess, one must assume that the earlier inhabitants of Çatalhöyük either did not worship her, or did not make icons of her. This in itself casts some doubt on the matriarchalist interpretation of the art of Çatalhöyük, since this site was in theory goddess-worshipping from the beginning. Mellaart believed he found male figurines as well, though fewer in number. With admirable consistency, he described them as representations of "a male deity."[51] No mention of such a god is made by feminist matriarchalists.

The other major source of putatively female imagery is found in the plaster reliefs that decorate many of the rooms at Çatalhöyük. A familiar image is of a splayed figure with hands and feet pointing upward, sometimes with a slightly swollen belly that is emphasized by concentric rings drawn around the navel (see Fig. 7.17). Mellaart suggests that this figure is pregnant—though it is not decisively so—and that its position "is indicative of childbirth." While it is true that

FIG. 7.16   Seated female figure from Çatalhöyük, Turkey, c. 5800 BCE, called "Goddess with Leopards" or "the Mother Goddess of Çatalhöyük."

women give birth in a variety of positions, this one is particularly odd, since the woman would either be lying down spread-eagled or standing upright, balanced on her heels. Increasingly, archaeologists are interpreting these figures as being of indeterminate sex. Ian Hodder points out that many of the plaster relief figures have "short stumpy arms and legs" which make them "look more animal than human." Recent excavations at other Neolithic sites in Turkey have revealed similar splayed figures, but these have tails and serpentlike teeth, strengthening the case for interpreting these figures as something other than human females.[52]

Bucrania, or bulls' heads, are frequently found in the plaster reliefs at Çatalhöyük, usually consisting of cattle horns incorporated into plaster heads (see Fig. 7.18). These have traditionally been regarded as

FIG. 7.17   Spread-eagled plaster reliefs, Çatalhöyük, Turkey, c. 6200 BCE.

FIG. 7.18   Room with multiple bucrania and cattle horns, Çatalhöyük, Turkey, c. 5800 BCE.

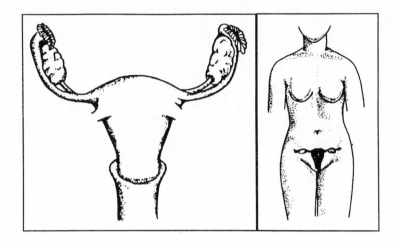

FIG. 7.19 Female reproductive organs, as customarily pictured in medical texts.

"an epiphany of male fertility," signifying "the qualities of male potency and strength." Some feminist matriarchalists have responded to this apparently obvious evocation of masculinity by viewing it as evidence of the complementary balancing of the sexes in Neolithic times, or by conceptualizing the bull as the son of the goddess, mystically symbolizing "the regenerative power of the female."[53] More recently though, matriarchalists have said that bulls have a central place in the imagery of Çatalhöyük because of an "accidental similarity" between a bull's head and the female reproductive organs. This idea was first proposed by Dorothy Cameron, an artist working on Mellaart's archaeological team who was puzzled by the appearance of so many bucrania—as opposed to complete bulls—represented at Çatalhöyük. Consulting medical textbooks, she noticed that these bucrania were shaped like a human uterus, with the horns positioned like fallopian tubes (see Fig. 7.19). The response of feminist matriarchalists to this insight has been enthusiastic. In *The Civilization of the Goddess*, Marija Gimbutas describes the purported similarity of female internal reproductive organs and bucrania as "a plausible if esoteric explanation for the importance of this motif in the symbolism of Old Europe, Anatolia, and the Near East." But what on page 244 is simply an interesting theory becomes on page 246 a certain fact, as

Gimbutas writes, "Bull heads, that is, uteri. . . ." Feminist matriarchalists now routinely argue that bucrania are meant to emphasize not "the bull itself but the female reproductive system it invokes."[54] However, the similarity between the head of a bull and a woman's internal reproductive organs is not striking to those not already prepared to see it. Fallopian tubes "are barely visible upon dissection"— they certainly do not call to mind the size and sweep of the horns of cattle—and bulls' horns lack any indication of ovaries.[55]

Another common motif in the plaster reliefs of Çatalhöyük are the many "breasts" modeled around the skulls of vultures, foxes, and weasels, with "the teeth, tusks or beaks of the animals" protruding "where the nipples should be." A standard matriarchalist interpretation of these images is that they "represent both the nurturing and devouring nature of the Mother Goddess, in that all of her children eventually return to her." The suggestion that these are intended to represent breasts seems far-fetched. These objects frequently appear alone or in rows; when they are paired, they are sometimes stacked one on top of the other in a column rather than side-by-side (as one might expect if these were depictions of female breasts). Furthermore, the shape of a breast is the natural form a small animal skull would take on if plaster were molded around it. This plaster encasing may have been simply a convenient way for the people of Çatalhöyük to attach animal skulls to their walls, or a means of emphasizing teeth and beaks.[56]

Amid all this disputed evidence about the art of Çatalhöyük, a few points do seem clear: most of the images feminist matriarchalists regard as female (plaster reliefs, bucrania, "breasts" around animal skulls) are not definitely or even probably female; the images that *are* unequivocal representations of femaleness do not persist over the entire life of the settlement, suggesting that any goddess worship associated with female figurines was not a stable and enduring feature of Çatalhöyük's religion; hunting continued to be an important activity, in symbol if not in practice, and was strongly linked to men; and death was a prominent theme. None fit the picture feminist matriarchalists paint for prehistory.

Malta
The "goddess" of Malta and the natural beauty of her Mediterranean environs feature prominently in current tellings of matriarchal myth.

Malta falls rather late in the chronology of matriarchal prehistory, flourishing between roughly 4000 and 2500 BCE. It is said by feminist matriarchalists to have survived in the face of patriarchal threats to its existence because of its enviable island locale. Early archaeological interpretations tended to assume that fourth and third millennium BCE Malta was goddess-worshipping, but interestingly, even early observers predisposed to the mother goddess theory didn't quite know what to make of Malta's enormous anthropomorphic statues (fifteen feet tall, unprecedented for that era).[57] The Maltese megalithic "goddesses" betray exceptionally little information about their sex. They could easily be female, or they could be male, like the icons of the Buddha to which Gertrude Rachel Levy likened them many years ago (see Fig. 7.20). They could even, as some have argued, be intended to represent eunuchs.[58] There are some obviously female figurines from Malta, such as the so-called "Sleeping Goddess," but the ones of special interest to feminist matriarchalists are the megalithic figures upon whom the floor plans of the temples are supposedly based.

It has long been thought that these megalithic temples, described by one archaeologist as "a group of chambers centering about a central spine composed of courts and corridors") are a later derivative of the earlier Maltese tombs, which were cut out of rock in ovoid shapes during the fifth millennium BCE. Feminist matriarchalists claim that the floor plans of these temples replicate the body of the large stone statues. The multiple chambers are thought to form the goddess's head, arms, and legs (or, alternatively, her head, breasts, and hips), with entry through "the open legs of the Goddess."[59] This interpretation has become very popular among feminist matriarchalists. "Just as a Christian worshipper enters a cathedral which represents the living body of the crucified Christ," writes Cristina Biaggi, "to enter a Maltese temple is to enter the living body of the Great Goddess."[60] Or as Monica Sjöö puts it in poetic form:

> . . . Through the vaginal gateways of the temples
> one enters into Her body to die and to be reborn.[61]

Certain of the Maltese temples, such as those at Ggantija, Gozo, or Mnajdra, have a floor plan that is a fair model of the human body as it is elsewhere portrayed in Maltese art and architecture (see Fig. 7.21). But other temples require a tremendous excess of interpretation to be regarded as anything remotely like a human body. The Ha-

FIG. 7.20   Headless standing statue carved in limestone, Malta, c. 3600–3000
BCE (height: 48.6 cm), termed "the Maltese Goddess" by Cristina Biaggi.

gar Qim temple, if it is the body of the goddess, has an extra append-
age, with entrance through, perhaps, the goddess's foot (see Fig. 7.22);
the Tarxien temple has one "goddess body" with entrance to what
appears to be a four-tiered snowman from one of her arms (or
breasts). Apart from the temples, Cristina Biaggi has described a rock
formation common in this era in Malta—an inverted trapezoid, as tall
as 1.5 meters—as a "pubic triangle," [62] but the resemblance is invisible
to anyone not looking for vulvas in virtually every geometric shape.
In sum, the evidence for widespread goddess worship on Malta in the
fourth and third millennia BCE is practically nonexistent.

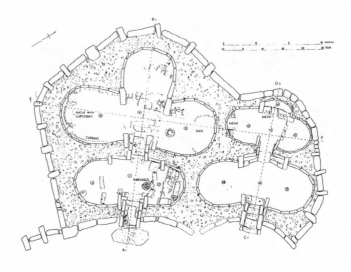

FIG. 7.21   Floor plan of temple at Ggantija, Malta, c. 3600–3000 BCE.

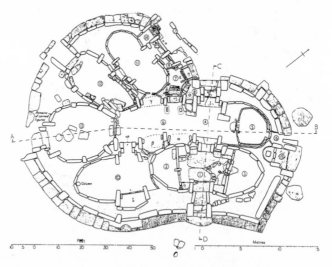

FIG. 7.22   Floor plan of temple at Hagar Qim, Malta, c. 4000–3500 BCE.

Minoan Crete

Minoan Crete has been an integral part of matriarchal myth for several generations now. Like Çatalhöyük, Minoan Crete was originally excavated by an archaeologist (Sir Arthur Evans) sympathetic to the idea of prehistoric goddess worship, and this has colored interpretation of its artwork ever since.

Prose has a tendency to wax and soar when the topic is Minoan Crete, a fact nearly as true of archaeologists' writing as it is of feminist matriarchalists'. There is something about the image of graceful palaces spilling across the rocky hills overlooking a sapphire sea, beautiful women in flounced skirts, and athletic young people leaping over bulls that brings out the poet in just about everyone. Minoan art is attractive to twentieth-century aesthetic sensibilities in a way that much earlier Neolithic and Paleolithic art simply is not. Even feminist matriarchalists frequently comment that they have had to learn to appreciate the beauty and power of earlier artifacts; not so with those of Minoan Crete. As Adele Getty writes, "The brightly coloured pottery and frescoes [of Minoan Crete] depict in free and elegant line both complex ceremonial practices and the beauties of Nature, expressing an inherent joy in the mystery of existence which surely reflects the harmonious relationship to life that the people experienced in their everyday activities." D. H. Trump, author of *The Prehistory of the Mediterranean*, attempts greater detachment, though he too is finally captivated: "True, we are seeing here only the wealthier and more powerful segment of society, to the exclusion of the humbler majority on whose labours this civilization depended, yet it is difficult to escape the impression of a happy people, their eyes open to nature, to foreign lands, to the good things of life, supported by a stable society and economy."[63]

Feminist matriarchalists sometimes say that the palaces of Minoan Crete, like the temples of Malta, replicate the body of the goddess on a grand scale. The palaces are "sited on a north–south axis facing a conical hill and beyond that a horned mountain containing a cave." According to Mimi Lobell, "the valley was her encircling arms; the conical hill, her breast or nurturing function; the horned mountain, her 'lap' or cleft vulva, the Earth's active power, and the cave sanctuary, her birth-giving womb."[64] The resemblance is something less than striking: breasts typically come in pairs and horned

FIG. 7.23   The "grandstand" fresco from Knossos, Crete, c. 1600 BCE, showing a group of women in conversation.

mountains sound more phallic than vaginal, the caves notwithstanding.

The frescoes give us what appears to be our clearest picture of Minoan gender relations. We here have the advantage of seeing relatively naturalistic portrayals of groups of people, male and female, interacting in what appear to be the normal (if festive) situations of Minoan cultural life (see Fig. 7.23). A further advantage in interpreting this art is that there was a convention in Minoan art—though one occasionally broken—of painting women white and men red. This can be used to sort out gender in questionable cases, especially since women and men are otherwise depicted with a similar body type: waspishly thin waists combined with "exaggeratedly curved chests." The frescoes often portray women and men as "partners in relationship," say feminist matriarchalists, with women, like men, "strenuously engaged as boxers, bull-leapers, acrobats, charioteers, and hunters." From the testimony of these frescoes, women appear to have been active "in every sphere of Minoan society." [65]

The evidence of the Minoan frescoes concerning the free interaction of the sexes is indeed impressive, though part of the reason for this is the background against which this art is typically viewed: namely, what we know to have been the relations between women

FIG. 7.24   "Master of Animals" sealstones from Minoan Crete, c. 1500 BCE.

and men in classical Greek times. Still, art is art, and life is life, and there may be no clear resemblance between the two. As classicist C. G. Thomas comments, "If the Procession Fresco were our only evidence for the position of Minoan women, we could give no answer. The subject is similar to that of the Parthenon frieze where Athenian maidens play a conspicuous role, and fifth century Athens was definitely not a matriarchal society."[66]

Scholars generally agree that many of the female images in Minoan sealstones and statuary represent goddesses, probably because they are reading back from classical times when this was a common meaning of female images. However, no female figurines have been recovered from "a definitely ritual context" or from graves; most have been found, as earlier, in garbage heaps. Females represented in sealstones, if goddesses, are notable mostly for their relationship to animals, with whom they are generally portrayed. Other "adorants," when present, are mostly women, leading classicist Nanno Marinatos to conclude that the Minoan goddess was "primarily the protectress of her own sex." Females do predominate in Minoan art. But there are considerably more males depicted in Minoan Crete than in Paleolithic and Neolithic European art more generally. Interestingly, these males appear in characteristically different roles than females. The most common male image is of a "god" whom classical archaeologists sometimes name "Master of Animals," for he "holds two wild animals in a position of submission or subjugation" (see Fig. 7.24). In

FIG. 7.25   Faience female figures from Knossos, Crete, c. 1600 BCE. The figure holding the snakes in front of her is 34 cm tall; the one holding the snakes in the air is 20 cm tall without her head. Neither was found intact, and both were reconstructed under the supervision of Sir Arthur Evans, the site's first excavator.

other pictures, males "hunt wild beasts" or engage in combat, unlike comparable females, who are typically shown "feeding or tending animals."[67]

What captures feminist matriarchalists' imagination more than all else, however, is elegantly-crafted figurines of the Minoan "snake goddess": a bare-breasted woman holding snakes in each of her hands (see Fig. 7.25). Feminist matriarchalists have devoted extensive attention to interpreting this figurine (which is unmatched in number of modern reproductions by any save the Venus of Willendorf), as can be seen in this passage from Anne Baring and Jules Cashford's *The Myth of the Goddess*:

> The open bodice with the bared breasts is eloquent of the gift of nurture, while the caduceus-like image of intertwined snakes on the belly suggests that the goddess whose womb gives forth and takes back life is experienced as a unity. . . . The trance-like, almost mask-like expression . . . composes a meditation upon this theme of regeneration. . . . The net pattern on her skirt, which gathers significance from its Palaeolithic and Neolithic ancestry, suggests she is the weaver of the web of life, which is perpetually woven from her womb. Her skirt has seven layers, the number of the days of the moon's four quarters, which divide into two the waxing and waning halves of the cycle. . . . Although seven was also the number of the visible "planets," this is probably a lunar notation of series and measure, so that sitting in the lap of the goddess, as the overlapping panel of her gown invites, would be to experience time supported by eternity, and eternity clothed in time. For the goddess, by virtue of holding the two snakes, is herself beyond their opposition; or rather, she is the one who contains the two poles of dualism and so prevents them falling apart into the kind of opposition that our modern consciousness assumes as inevitable.[68]

Whatever their meaning, it is clear that the "snake goddesses" have been given a symbolic role out of proportion to their very modest number. Though this has been described as "a deity very popular in Minoan times," there are actually only two such figurines from the entire palace period in Crete, both uncovered from the same pit in the palace at Knossos. As Nanno Marinatos writes, one may as well "speak of a Lily, Goat, Lion, or Griffin Goddess."[69]

The art of Minoan Crete is certainly beautiful, but the divinity of the figures pictured is uncertain, and again we must ask what effect any Minoan goddess worship might have had on human women. The evidence of sealstones indicates that hunting and combat were thought of as male activities, which is not suggestive of a peaceful cultural ethos. And though the frescoes show an unprecedented intermingling of the sexes and significant freedoms for women, they are no more than what we are accustomed to in our own culture, one which, according to feminist matriarchalists, is patriarchal.

It is unfortunate that prehistoric art cannot tell us more about how women were regarded in prehistoric societies, or how they lived their lives, but the evidence of prehistoric art is simply inconclusive. It tells us that women existed, and that people in prehistoric societies chose to represent them, usually in stylized or abstract forms. It tells us that then, as now, women seemed to be depicted more often than men. But beyond that, we are given precious little information about the status of either divine or human women in prehistory; it shows us nothing that would contradict the alternative hypothesis that male dominance flourished throughout the prehistoric times from which these works survive.

CHAPTER 8

Was There a Patriarchal Revolution?

If the vision of a prehistoric matriarchal utopia cannot stand against cultural anthropological and archaeological evidence, the possibility remains that there was nevertheless a decisive change in social organization around 3000 BCE (at least in southeastern Europe and the Near East) that propelled human civilization in a more patriarchal, hierarchical, and warlike direction.

Previous chapters have cast doubt on explanations for the rise of patriarchy that attribute it to internal developments within matriarchal cultures. The connection between sexual intercourse and conception was probably well known long before 3000 BCE; it seems doubtful that male "womb envy," insofar as it exists, would take a sudden and nefarious turn five thousand years before our time; intensive agriculture has been found historically and ethnographically to correlate with class-stratified societies and male dominance, but horticultural and foraging societies tend to be male-dominated as well; and animal husbandry, far from being a patriarchal invention, was already being practiced in Çatalhöyük and Old Europe, cultures which feminist matriarchalists claim were goddess-worshipping and matricentric. We are left then with the leading external explanation for patriarchal revolution: that armed invaders imposed their male-dominant, male-god-worshipping cultures on formerly peaceful goddess-worshippers. Since Semitic invasions are mentioned by feminist matriarchalists but rarely discussed at any length, we will confine our attention here to their favored invaders: the horse-riding, nomadic Kurgans.

In reconstructing the era in which the Kurgans supposedly descended on the goddess-worshipping lands to the south, we have access to resources not available in earlier eras: the evidence of comparative linguistics, which, together with archaeological evidence, can help trace probable prehistoric population movements; genetic studies on contemporary populations which may also document migrations; and written texts that may provide clues to past events that were still living in human memory when they were recorded. Together these sources speak to the question of whether or not there was a patriarchal revolution in southeastern Europe and the Near East on the very eve of the historical era.

PREHISTORIC MIGRATIONS
There is much disagreement among prehistorians as to whether or not the invasions—or, more neutrally, migrations—described by feminist matriarchalists occurred during the late Neolithic in the areas under question. For most of the twentieth century, archaeologists have tended to assume that changes in the material record were due to shifts in population. So, for example, when a certain type of pottery known as a "bell beaker" turned up in, say, Holland, the assumption was that the "bell beaker people" had immigrated to Holland from wherever they had been before. This assumption is now out of favor. Archaeologists are currently much more prone to envision stable, sedentary Neolithic populations that adopted the pottery styles of their neighbors without ever relocating themselves from one spot to another.[1]

This accounts, in part, for the chilly reception of Marija Gimbutas's work among other archaeologists. From the 1970s on, she continued to postulate large-scale migrations at a time when archaeological fashion had turned in the opposite direction. But on the face of it, it seems as dubious to suggest that prehistoric populations virtually never moved as it is to say that they were constantly picking up their bell beakers and traveling hundreds and thousands of miles with no apparent provocation. Certainly taking the long view of human history, back to the beginnings of the hominid line and forward to our own times, migration has been the rule rather than the exception. There are groups who sit on the same plot of land, cultivating or hunting within an established range for many generations. But there are also groups who are highly mobile. And even in sedentary groups, there may be a number of mobile individuals trading, exploring, colonizing, or immigrating.[2] Large-scale prehistoric migrations, such as those that feminist matriarchalists propose for the Kurgans, cannot be ruled out in advance.

The Evidence from Linguistics

The spread of Indo-European languages throughout Europe, the Near East, and southern Asia is a key piece of evidence for feminist matriarchalists. The reach of the patriarchal revolution can be charted very simply, they suggest, by noting when and where Indo-European languages appear.

Today Indo-European languages blanket Europe and much of southwest Asia, and owing to colonial expansion, the Americas and Africa as well. In the eighteenth century, when European linguists began to trace connections between these languages, there were dozens of Indo-European languages and very little record of any non–Indo-European languages having been spoken in Europe. Indo-European languages were first written down in the nineteenth century BCE; by this time, there were already several such languages.[3] However, the usual postulate for linguists—and for feminist matriarchalists too—is that at some time earlier than this, prehistorically, there was a group of people who spoke a language which, for convenience, is called "proto-Indo-European." It is further assumed that this group must have lived somewhere in Europe or Asia in such a position that their language could have, by whatever means, proliferated outwards to fill the territory that the languages derived from it eventually came to inhabit.

By searching through the most widely separated Indo-European languages for vocabulary they share in common, linguists believe that they can reconstruct a small portion of the proto-Indo-European language. This bank of words, the protolexicon, is an extremely important tool in efforts to locate when and where proto-Indo-European may have been spoken, and what sort of economy and society its speakers might have had. For example, the English word *birch* is found in a similar form in German, Lithuanian, Old Slavonic, and Sanskrit, which is taken as an indication that *bhergh*—a parent word for birch, reconstructed and assigned to the proto-Indo-European lexicon— grew in the landscape where the proto-Indo-Europeans lived.[4]

It has been a longstanding tradition among linguists to think of the proto-Indo-Europeans as nomadic herders, since there is a fairly rich vocabulary in the protolexicon for the herding and breeding of domesticated animals (including dogs, sheep, goats, pigs, horses, and especially cows), while there is a comparatively sparse vocabulary for agriculture (although it is definitely present in words like "wheat" and "barley"). It is certainly possible that the proto-Indo-Europeans had a thriving farming economy, but that for whatever reason it was words related to herding that successfully propagated themselves down the many lineages of Indo-European languages. (Perhaps the people who adopted Indo-European languages used their native words for farming, but Indo-European ones for herding.) This caveat notwithstanding, it is clear that the proto-Indo-Europeans practiced animal husbandry and that they were familiar with horses, both important factors in the matriarchalist thesis. The case for the proto-Indo-Europeans having been nomads, as feminist matriarchalists suggest, is not as strong: they apparently built their houses of wood, which is not easily transportable, and they did in fact have terms for a more intensive and sedentary form of agriculture, namely plowing.[5]

There is not much argument among linguists regarding the basic social system of the proto-Indo-Europeans: it was patriarchal. It has been more or less established that kinship was reckoned patrilineally, that a woman went to live with her husband or his family upon marriage, and that the term "husband" had roots meaning "master" or "lord of the house."[6] There are also indications that it was a class-based society, since the basic tripartite scheme of the top levels of the caste system in India—priests, warriors, and herders-cultivators—is seen in other ancient societies in which Indo-European languages were spoken.[7] Most linguists believe proto-Indo-Europeans owned slaves and practiced warfare, though terms for slavery are unknown and terms for weapons are extremely limited. There are terms for "sword" and "bow and arrow," but they are not widely attested, being found in only two Indo-European languages each. Little is known about proto-Indo-European religion. There is a generic term for "god," but only one name for a specific god survives in known Indo-European languages: the Greek Zeus or Latin Jupiter, whose name is related to the word "day." Feminist matriarchalists have suggested that the god of the proto-Indo-Europeans was a sky or sun god, and indeed there are intriguing phrases that surface in several Indo-European languages: "the wheel of the sun" and the expression, in reference to the sun, "he who spies upon gods and men."[8]

Just where the proto-Indo-Europeans called home—the *Urheimat*, or homeland—has probably been the subject of the most intense debate among Indo-European linguists. Many candidates have been proposed, based either on the reconstructed protolexicon, on archaeological and historical evidence for migrations, or both. Today the contenders have been more or less narrowed down to two: Anatolia (present-day Turkey) and the Russian-Ukranian steppes.[9] The case for an Anatolian homeland is relatively weak. Anatolia is nowhere near the first known geographical center of Indo-European linguistic dominance; Indo-European languages are not the only or even the most common languages of the region. Nor do these languages seem to resemble their Semitic neighbors, as one might expect if they had been in close contact with one another for several millennia.[10]

The argument in favor of the Russian-Ukranian hypothesis is, in contrast, quite good. Geographically speaking, the steppes provide "a corridor for constant movement and migration." Central Europe is accessible via the Danube; northern Europe can be reached by heading north of the Carpathian mountains, through Poland; the Near East and western Asia lie directly below the steppes. Certainly in later eras (later than those Gimbutas posits for the patriarchal invasions) there is excellent evidence that the steppes were home to nomadic, horse-riding pastoralists: the Cimerians, Scythians, Sarmatians, Alans, Huns, Magyars, Bulgars, and Mongols, among others. And though words from the protolexicon can be used to argue for an enormous variety of potential homelands for proto-Indo-European, terms for trees and animals do seem to suit the flora and fauna of the steppes.[11]

A best guess for when Indo-European languages began to disperse can also be derived from the protolexicon. Since there are terms for things like "milk" and "wool" in the protolexicon, associated with what is known as the "secondary products revolution" (when domesticated animals began to be used not only for meat, but also for transportation, clothing, dairy products, and the like), we can be fairly certain that the languages did not disperse before 4000 BCE. There is also a term for "copper" in the protolexicon, but none for metals which came into use later, and this too points to a dispersal beginning in the fourth or fifth millennium BCE.[12] Putting these together, most linguists provisionally date the dispersal of the proto-Indo-Europeans to 4500 to 2500 BCE, a time span that matches feminist matriarchalists' claims perfectly—which should not be surprising when one remembers that this time frame was adopted directly from Indo-European linguists, especially Gimbutas.

What information from the Indo-European protolexicon cannot tell us is if the people who spoke proto-Indo-European moved to a new area, or if the people previously living in that area merely adopted their neighbors' language (to facilitate trade, for example). It cannot tell us if the transmission of the language was friendly or hostile, or how much of proto-Indo-European was grafted onto preexisting languages. It cannot tell us with certainty which words were shared because they existed in the parent language, and which were invented much later and then traded between neighboring languages (as words like "television" and "telephone" are shared between many otherwise unrelated languages today). Linguists examine the spread and differentiation of *languages*, not of cultures or peoples. Any connections to be drawn between the two must be done carefully—usually with the help of other sorts of evidence, primarily archaeological.[13]

The Evidence from Archaeology

Prehistoric pastoralists of the Russian-Ukranian steppes are known to us—though not terribly well—through archaeological excavations. The Sredny Stog culture, dated to 4500–3500 BCE, is located near the Dnieper River in southern Ukraine, and its material remains indicate that the people of this culture were cattle herders who also farmed, hunted, and fished. Excavations have unearthed "cheekpieces," which may indicate that they rode horses. Following the Sredny Stog culture, and apparently growing out of it, is the Yamnaya or "Pit Grave" culture that Gimbutas has named "Kurgan." Covering a much broader swath than the Sredny Stog culture (from the headwaters of the Danube across to the Volga River and beyond) and dated from 3600 to 2200 BCE, the basic signature of the Yamnaya culture is, predictably, its style of burial: the body was placed in a deep pit, lying on its back with the knees drawn up. A mound was placed over the top of the grave after it was filled in. Sometimes wagon wheels marked the corners of these pit graves. Feminist matriarchalists regard these burials as novel in two ways: first, they were not communal, but individual, which they take to suggest a possible weakening of community ties, and second, some of the graves contain greater wealth than was typical of the burial practices of earlier societies.[14]

Similar burials—graves for a single individual, covered by a mound—emerged around 3000 BCE across northern and western Europe, along with a distinctive style of pottery called "Corded Ware." This "culture complex" has often been thought to have been related to the Yamnaya culture of the steppes. If the Yamnaya people spoke an Indo-European language, as many suggest, then the Corded Ware people may have as well, forming another center from which Indo-European languages could then have spread (see Fig. 8.1). What is thought to have facilitated these migrations is the mobility made possible by the domestication of the horse (for riding) and the introduction of wheeled vehicles. Both innovations appear to have taken place on the Russian steppes, with domestication of the horse occurring in the fifth millennium, and the invention of wheeled vehicles in the fourth millennium.[15]

To reiterate though, the spread of archaeological artifacts, such as pottery types, or even of new technologies and practices such as wheeled transportation or the domestication of the horse, does not necessarily reflect the spread of either people or languages. There is no shortage of examples of military and linguistic dominance coinciding (as in the European conquest of the Americas), and it is difficult to throw off the image of warlike, horse-riding invaders imposing political rule and linguistic change upon subject peoples. But there is also no shortage of examples of the peaceful transfer of languages, or of military conquests that bring about no linguistic changes.[16] And the existing evidence for the Indo-European case can be explained in other ways.

The most common criticism of the theory of horse-riding nomadic invaders from the steppes is that articulated by archaeologist Colin Renfrew, who asks, "Why on earth should hordes of mounted warriors have moved west at the end of the Neolithic, subjugating the inhabitants of Europe and imposing proto-Indo-European language on them? What enormous upsurge of population on the steppes

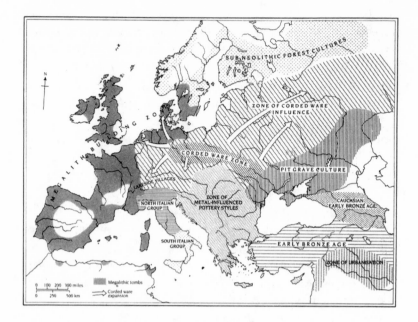

FIG. 8.1 Map of late Neolithic, Chalcolithic, and early Bronze Age Europe, 3500–2500 BCE, as derived from archaeological findings. The Pit Grave culture is that which Gimbutas calls Kurgan and which feminist matriarchalists claim is the source of Indo-European language, horse-riding, war, male-dominated religion, and patriarchy. Some archaeologists have suggested that the Corded Ware culture is related to the Pit Grave culture and that Indo-European languages were spoken in both.

could have been responsible?" When people migrate, Renfrew implies, it is because conditions where they are have become unsatisfactory: either the environment has changed or the population has expanded beyond what the environment can comfortably carry. There is no archaeological evidence of either of these events occuring on the Russian steppes in the fifth and fourth millennia BCE.[17] We are left, then, with the general sentiment behind matriarchal myth: that the peoples of the steppes—the proto-Indo-Europeans, the Kurgans—were cruel and greedy, and, presented with an opportunity to rape and pillage, they took it, although they already had everything they needed at home.

To my cynical mind, this is not an outrageous hypothesis, but it doesn't sit well with many archaeologists.[18] And indeed there are other potential explanations for the social disintegration that is apparent in the archaeological record around the time of the purported patriarchal revolution, at least in southeastern Europe. The best evidence for incursions from the steppes comes "long after the stable villages of the Copper Age had disappeared" because of deforestation and environmental degradation. As J. P. Mallory summarizes, "almost all of the arguments for invasion and cultural transformations are far better explained without reference to Kurgan expansions."[19]

The Evidence from Genetics
Scientists' increasing ability to detect relationships between peoples based on genetic material found in their blood and bones is providing another means for reconstructing prehistoric migrations in Europe and western Asia. To date, genetic research has been conducted on living Europeans—not their ancestors. And the way genetic material is distributed in Europe today is the result of so many overlapping population movements that it is by no means trivial to separate and identify them.[20] Nevertheless, genetic studies have yielded some interesting data that informs speculation about prehistoric migrations.

Pioneering work in this area was first carried out by Italian geneticist Luigi Luca Cavalli-Sforza and his collaborators in the 1970s. Sampling blood from modern European populations and tracking key genetic differences across these populations (beginning, most simply, with blood type), Cavalli-Sforza was able to detect statistically significant differences that could be mapped directly onto the European landscape. He sorted these differences into "principal components." That which accounted for the largest portion of the total genetic information (27 percent)—the first principal component—was centered in the Near East and gradually thinned out in radiating arcs as it pushed across the European continent. Cavalli-Sforza and others have interpreted this first principal component—the oldest—to be consistent with a gradual movement of farming populations from Anatolia throughout Europe. But Cavalli-Sforza uncovered other principal components in the genetic material of modern Europeans, ones that mapped quite differently. The second principal component, accounting for 18 percent of the genetic similarity, indicated a movement of population from northern Europe southwards, and was theorized to be "due to a genetic adaptation to the climate difference between north and south Europe" or to the southward movement of speakers of Uralic languages. The third principal component (accounting for 12 percent of the genetic similarity), uncovered something far more exciting to feminist matriarchalists: a trend centered in Poland, the Ukraine, and southern Russia, extending out into Europe proper. The fit between this third principal component and Gimbutas's theory did not go unnoticed even by Cavalli-Sforza, who wrote as early as 1984 that one possible explanation of this genetic phenomenon "would be the expansion of Indo-European speaking people whose homeland has been placed in the region to the north of the Black Sea on the basis of linguistic considerations."[21]

Feminist matriarchalists have welcomed this as proof that Gimbutas was correct in postulating a series of invasions from the Russian steppes,[22] but this is not exactly how Cavalli-Sforza and certain anthropologists view the matter. Cavalli-Sforza has noted that the center of the third principal component of his gene mapping project does not have "precise contours," and that the genetic effect it represents could be due to much later invasions, even as recent as the end of the Roman Empire. Others have suggested that the third principal component dates to significantly earlier times (around 7000 BCE), before any purported patriarchal revolution, with the expansion of a Mesolithic hunting and gathering population. Furthermore, tests how well Cavalli-Sforza's third principal component conforms to Gimbutas's archaeologically derived maps are "currently still at the borderline of statistical significance."[23] It simply cannot be said, on the basis of the available data, that genetic evidence proves that there were Indo-European invasions in the fifth and fourth millennia BCE, or indeed migrations of any sort from the Russian steppe to southeast Europe and the Near East at this time. In short, the case for the spread of Indo-European speakers from the Russian steppes is merely suggestive, and the argument that this spread occurred via military conquest is completely speculative—though not entirely implausible.

READING BACK FROM THE LITERATE PAST

Another avenue back into the era of putative patriarchal revolution is written texts. Since feminist matriarchalists believe that the patriarchal revolution coincided with the development of written language, or else lived within the memory (or oral history) of the earliest writers, they believe that that conflagration is recorded in very early histories and myths.

The earliest texts of the West, when they trouble themselves to speak about women, seem to indicate that male dominance, in one form or another, was already the norm. Cuneiform texts from ancient Sumer (beginning around 2500 BCE) record widespread goddess worship, with female religious functionaries being more common than male ones. Women of the upper classes were able to own slaves and other property, to transact business, and to retain control over their dowries (though inheritance went first to sons, if there were any). Royal women in particular had considerable power, founding dynasties, managing large temple estates, and even ruling city-states. But farther down in the class structure, legal texts show that women could be sold by their husbands, put to death for adultery, divorced if barren, or drowned for refusing to bear children. Since most girls were wed by age eleven or twelve, marriage was the state in which they lived most of their lives. Women's children were regarded as the property of their fathers, who were permitted by law to decide whether they should be exposed, married, or sold as slaves. The lot of female slaves was of course worse: in addition to being "subject to the master's sexual whims," female slaves received about half as much food as their male counterparts, and many died at a young age owing to the harsh conditions under which they labored.[24]

Minoan Crete also had a written script—Linear A, an apparently non-Greek language developed around the eighteenth century BCE. Some scholars have found what they believe to be the names of individual deities in Linear A texts, though their gender is not clear. But since Minoan texts remain undeciphered, written records in the Mediterranean cannot be used to determine the status of women in ancient times until the emergence of Linear B (a syllabic script, representing an early Greek language, with a visual appearance similar to Linear A) on both Crete and the Greek mainland in roughly the fourteenth century BCE. Deciphered Linear B documents indicate that there was a king (male) in Mycenaean Greece and that there were numerous female workers who had possibly been taken captive in raids and were either slaves or servants in the palaces. Male workers also appear in Linear B texts, rearing sheep and managing groups of female laborers whose tasks were more menial than those of men (apart from weaving, which was a skilled occupation restricted to women). Linear B tablets also record offerings made to goddesses and gods, with women most often serving female deities, and men male ones.[25] Thus Linear B texts, like cuneiform ones, suggest that women had roles as religious functionaries, but also portray a society stratified by class in which women—at least those of the lower classes—had fewer advantages and harder lives than the men of their own class.

A picture of early Greek life begins to emerge in the works of Homer, which, though they date to the eighth or ninth century BCE, offer accounts of earlier events and are believed to be the codification of a preexisting oral tradition. The window which the *Iliad* and the *Odyssey* open on the position of women in Bronze Age Greece must be regarded with some suspicion, given the intervening time and the poet's agenda (which was not the dispassionate recording of historical fact). Homer's central female characters are aristocratic women, some of whom evidence considerable power within their families. The only other women he mentions are slaves. Homer's aristocratic female characters are free to walk the streets (accompanied by an escort) and can sit in the public rooms of their homes with male guests, unlike women in later Greek societies. But a Homeric woman's principal tasks were, as classicist Eva Cantarella details them, to be beautiful, to take care of domestic tasks, and to "above all be obedient." Female slaves had fewer freedoms and possessions, and like aristocratic wives, were required to be sexually faithful to their master alone.[26]

Later Greek literature paints a picture that is not at all favorable to women. Aristotle, writing in the fourth century BCE, put it unequivocally: "The male is by nature superior, and the female inferior; and the one rules and the other is ruled." Greek poetry, drama, and myth are full of the "problem" of women. The eighth-century BCE poet Hesiod describes woman as a drone who "sits within the house and reaps the fruits of others' toil to fill her belly," saying that even a "good wife" will bring misfortune upon a man. Indeed, the myth of Pandora suggests that women were regarded as a breed apart, not truly human. Pandora, the first woman, is created as a punishment to men. And though Greek literature recognizes it as an (unfortunate) fact that women are involved in reproducing all human beings, Pandora is named only as the origin of "the race of women."[27]

The misogyny evident in Greek literature permeated Greek society. Women in classical Athens were under the guardianship of one male or another for their entire lives. Married free-born women were confined to their houses—actually to one portion of the house designated for women, the *gynaecaeum*. Fathers had the right to expose their newborn children, and more girls than boys were left to die in this manner. Heterosexual sex was understood as "an unequal transaction by which woman steals man's substance," and so men were better advised to have sexual relations with one another. As Eva Keuls sums up classical Athens: "In the case of a society dominated by men who sequester their wives and daughters, denigrate the female role in reproduction, erect monuments to male genitalia, have sex with the sons of their peers, sponsor public whorehouses, create a mythology of rape, and engage in rampant saber-rattling, it is not inappropriate to refer to a reign of the phallus."[28]

Nothing in this picture is particularly congenial to the matriarchal thesis, unless one interprets the zeal with which women were oppressed in antiquity to the newness of the practice. Many feminist matriarchalists draw exactly this conclusion, and they believe it to be documented—albeit in carefully encoded ways—in one type of ancient text, namely myth.

Finding Matriarchy in Ancient Myth

Gender was fascinating to the ancient cultures of the West, as it is to us, and their myths are full of references to conflicts between the sexes at both the individual and communal levels, among humans and also, strikingly, among the gods and goddesses. A subset of these myths is particularly fascinating to feminist matriarchalists: first, those that involve the triumph of gods over goddesses; second, those that tell a story of women's former dominance and its overthrow; and third, those that describe a past golden age. The first two types are taken to be documentation of a patriarchal revolution, while the third is seen as a memory of matriarchal times.

One of the most dramatic ways gods triumph over goddesses in ancient myths, according to feminist matriarchalists, is by murdering them. The narrative that is most often cited in this regard is the Babylonian myth of Tiamat and Marduk, in which Marduk conquers the chaotic forces of nature by subduing the primeval mother goddess Tiamat. Tiamat fights Marduk with serpents, dragons, water snakes, and other ferocious animals, but Marduk eventually dismembers her, then uses the pieces of her sundered body to create the earth and the sky. Feminist matriarchalists argue that all serpents and dragons are symbols of prehistoric goddess religion, and that therefore myths of serpent murder (like Marduk's of Tiamat and her reptilian creatures), found from India to Israel to Ireland, are records of patriarchal revolution.[29]

The new gods sometimes achieve the same ends without actually killing the old goddesses, feminist matriarchalists say. For example, the rape of Persephone by Hades and the consequent rupture of her heretofore exclusive relationship with her mother Demeter is thought to be another allegory of patriarchal revolution. So too is the myth of Athena's birth. Feminist matriarchalists say that when Zeus swallowed Athena's mother Metis and produced Athena from his head, he in effect "swallowed the ancient matrilineal line and gave birth to Athena . . . the first daughter of the patriarchy."[30]

One of the most fully elaborated myths involving a transition from the power of the goddess to the power of the gods is found in Hesiod's *Theogony*. As a compilation of preexisting Greek myths about the gods and goddesses, the *Theogony*, dating to roughly 700 BCE, sought to put these disparate myths in a logical order. The resulting narrative progresses from the physical—embodied in Gaia and her parthenogenetic children, Sky, Mountains, and Sea—to the anthropocentric: Zeus and the rest of the Olympian pantheon. This is also, says translator and editor Norman O. Brown, an evolution "from the primacy of the female to the primacy of the male."[31]

Two other ancient Greek narratives are repeatedly cited by feminist matriarchalists as evidence of the patriarchal revolution, and both tell a more transparent story of women's loss of power, on the secular rather than the divine level. The first is the *Oresteia* by Aeschylus; the second is the myth of the naming of Athens (taken from Varro and appearing in Augustine's *City of God*). Aeschylus's tragedy was based on a legend told by Homer in the *Odyssey* (and later retold in different versions by the Greek poets Stesichorus and Pindar). The basic plot of the *Oresteia* revolves around a series of murders within the "house" or family of the king of Mycenae, Agamemnon. Agamemnon sacrifices his daughter Iphigenia to the gods to calm the winds so that his ships may safely sail off to war; Clytemnestra, Iphigenia's mother, kills

Agamemnon upon his return in revenge for his having killed their daughter; and finally Orestes, their son, avenges Agamemnon's death by killing his mother, Clytemnestra. This is quite enough action for even the triology of plays that form the *Oresteia*, and this seems to be where the earliest versions of the legend end. But in Aeschylus's version, the drama is just beginning: Orestes finds himself pursued by his mother's avenging furies (*erinyes*) who wish to punish him for his act of matricide. His case comes before a tribunal in Athens, over which Athena presides. Orestes's defense is offered by Apollo, who claims: "The mother is not the true parent of the child / Which is called hers. She is a nurse who tends the growth / Of young seed planted by its true parent, the male." To underscore his argument, Apollo points to Athena: "Present, as proof, the daughter of Olympian Zeus: / One never nursed in the dark cradle of the womb." The tribunal—composed of Athenian citizens—votes on whether to convict or acquit Orestes in the murder of his mother, and the vote is tied. Athena breaks the tie by voting to acquit, stating, "No mother gave me birth. Therefore the father's claim / And male supremacy in all things . . . wins my whole heart's loyalty." Although no earlier matriarchal period is explicitly invoked in the *Oresteia*, there is a clear shift from female power (under which matricide is the most heinous crime) to male power (legitimately housed in the father, the only true parent).[32]

The myth of the naming of Athens is perhaps the clearest statement in classical Greek literature of a transition from female to male power. According to this myth, an olive tree and a spring appeared in the area that was to become Athens, and the residents asked Apollo what these marvels meant. Apollo replied that the olive tree came from Athena and the spring from Poseidon, and that the residents of the city could choose to name their city after one or the other of these gods. The citizens—both male and female—placed their votes. All the men voted for Poseidon, while all the women voted for Athena; because the women were in a majority of one, the decision was in favor of Athena. This so outraged Poseidon that he caused a great flood to occur. He demanded that the Athenians be punished for choosing Athena over him, and his punishment was this: that women should no longer be able to vote; that women's children should no longer be named after them, but after their fathers; and that women should not be called Athenians. Here indeed is a patriarchal revolution, as matriliny and women's suffrage are overthrown in favor of a society in which women have no political status or power.[33]

Myths and legends of Amazons are also sometimes read by feminist matriarchalists as accounts of patriarchal revolution. Amazons are documented very early in Greek literature (in Homer's epics), and they later become a staple of classical Greek discourse. The Greeks describe the Amazons as valiant warriors, but in legend and pictorial representations they always lose to men; either they are defeated directly in battle or they revert to domesticated femininity—roles of wife and mother—upon falling in love with their Greek enemies.[34] In feminist matriarchalist interpretations, Amazon legends record the efforts of armed defenders of matriarchy. The only reason Amazons are portrayed as losers or reluctant warriors is because the Greeks wrote these stories from their own misogynistic, post-patriarchal-revolution point of view.

If Amazons are held by feminist matriarchalists to represent the dying days of matriarchal civilization, its zenith is thought to be portrayed in ancient accounts of the golden age. The adjective "golden" was first applied to the past by Hesiod, who wrote of a golden race of men[35] who "lived like gods, carefree in their hearts, shielded from pain and misery."[36] Hesiod inspired later poets and philosophers, who by the first century CE were habitually referring to a "golden age," a time when life was easy and good.[37] Interpreting golden age myths quite literally, feminist matriarchalists find in them "folk memories of a more peaceful partnership-oriented epoch."[38]

Myth as History

Throughout feminist matriarchalist interpretations of myth lies the assumption that ancient myths are encoded versions of classical and preclassical history. This idea has been around for quite some time, and has led to some important archaeological discoveries. For example, Heinrich Schliemann's discovery of Troy was guided by Homer's texts, which had previously been believed to be fictional. Feminist matriarchalists continue this tradition of regarding myth as "a vast mirror that faithfully reflects the reality of the past."[39]

But discovering a prehistoric patriarchal revolution through ancient myth is no simple matter. Feminist matriarchalists are tripped up first by the fact that the myths they say reflect a patriarchal revolution

are not very close to the event in question. Classicist H. J. Rose suggests a date for the myth of the naming of Athens of no earlier than
the fourth century BCE. The *Oresteia* is an older story, dating at least to
Homer's time, but many of the more damning details in Aeschylus's
version—Athena's speech defending male supremacy, the tied vote,
Apollo serving as defense attorney for Orestes—are most likely original to Aeschylus, writing in the mid-fifth century BCE. In the Homeric version of the Orestes legend, in contrast, Clytemnestra gets
what she deserves, and Orestes need suffer no guilt over his matricide,
a theme that seems to reflect an entrenched patriarchy rather than a
new one.[40] It is the *later* myth rather than the earlier one that reads like
a record of patriarchal revolution.

Beyond these sorts of specifics, if a patriarchal revolution occurred in 3000 BCE, the memory of it would have to have been pre-
served for more than two thousand years to be written into Greek
myth. This would be like us having accurate accounts of events in
classical Greece passed down through oral tradition alone—an unlikely scenario. Gimbutas's editor, Joan Marler, claims that "mythology and folklore are conservative and slow to change," implying that
any history contained within myths could be carried along intact for
many generations. But myths may not be as old or static as we typically take them to be. In *The Myth of the Eternal Return*, Mircea Eliade
gives a striking example of how quickly history can become myth,
and in the process become sufficiently corrupted that it bears little relation to historical events. Folklorist Constantin Brailoiu discovered a
ballad in a small Romanian village relating the story of a young man
who, about to be married, was bewitched by a mountain fairy who
threw him off a cliff out of jealousy. His body was brought back to the
village, where his fiancée "poured out a funeral lament, full of mythological allusions." Brailoiu's informants told him that it was a "very
old story," an event that happened "long ago." However, Brailoiu
eventually discovered that the events in question had occurred less
than forty years earlier, and that the fiancée who was said to have
composed the funeral lament was still alive. Upon speaking with her,
Brailoiu learned that the young man had slipped and fallen from a
cliff and been brought back to the village alive, where he eventually
died, and that he was mourned in the customary way, with no unusual lament.[41]

This is an interesting case, since clearly there is an historical event embodied in the myth, a story of untimely (if ordinary) death lying underneath the story of the jealous mountain fairy. But without access to living informants or texts, it is not a trivial matter to decide which parts of the story represent history, and which are mythic themes and fabrications.

Feminist matriarchalists do not suggest that history happened exactly as myth says it did. None claim that a great male hero named Marduk actually dismembered the goddess Tiamat, or that prehistoric Athenians voted for Athena as their patron goddess, thus so enraging Poseidon that women were cursed from that point forward. In feminist matriarchalist interpretation, Tiamat and Marduk are metaphors for the shift from female power to male power; the vote of the Athenian assembly is a compact mythic telling of an event that took place over the course of hundreds or even thousands of years.

There is an enormous project of sorting and judging going on here. Plausible connections between myth and reality must be drawn; more fanciful elements (for example, Athena being born from the head of Zeus) must be dispensed with or read as metaphors; certain elements or certain myths must be credited with greater importance than others; and so on.[42] This can be a very messy business, characterized by legions of unspoken assumptions.

Feminist matriarchalists often give as their justification for parsing Greek myth as they do the fact that they are stripping away "patriarchal accretions."[43] These elements can be recognized because they do not conform to the pattern that feminist matriarchalists expect to find in ancient myth (however covered over by the purposeful political machinations of later redactors). This is a very convenient method of interpreting ancient myth: once the assumption is in place that prehistoric societies were matriarchal and goddess-worshipping, myth yields up that conclusion quite naturally. Critics who point to aspects of a myth that do not support that conclusion can be dismissed by the claim that those aspects are patriarchal accretions, and not the "original myth." If anything, troublesome aspects of a myth—for example, that it was a goddess, Athena, who championed patriarchy—lend even more credence to the matriarchal thesis, since they illustrate that a conspiracy took place within the text of the myth itself to eradicate even the memory of ancient matriarchies.

Feminist matriarchalists encourage one another to adopt this methodology of taking their conclusions as their premises. For example, Hallie Austen Iglehart encourages her readers to "'fill in the gaps' left by patriarchal researchers with your own knowledge, common sense, and intuition. . . . Soon you will begin to see matrifocal influence in art and civilizations that you had not noticed before."[44] What feminist matriarchalists do *not* do is to encourage one another to seek out evidence that might disprove their thesis. If the evidence contradicts the theory, it is the evidence that is wrong.

Myth as Charter
Granted that feminist matriarchalists are making some unwarranted leaps in interpreting myth as history, this still does not rule out the basic premise that myth could in fact be encoding a history of patriarchal revolution. Certainly some of the Greek myths to which feminist matriarchalists appeal offer a clear account of the imposition of male dominance on formerly free (or freer) women. And classical Greece is not the only place such myths are found. These myths of former female dominance are found around the globe. They are full of local details, but they contain some interesting similarities. The most common pattern is that certain powerful and/or magical ceremonial objects (hats, flutes, trumpets, masks) were originally owned or created by women, and possessing them gave women greater social power. Eventually, men confiscated these objects and withheld them from women and, as a result, women's social status is lower to this day.[45]

A good example of such a myth comes from the Selk'nam of Tierra del Fuego. The Selk'nam were a hunting and fishing people, mostly undisturbed by outsiders until white colonization of their land began in 1880. According to Selk'nam myth, women originally "ruled over men without mercy." The men did all the hunting, but also all the child-tending and domestic work, while the women met in private in the Hain, a large hut where they lived apart from the men, to deliberate on and resolve important social matters. Despite the men being physically larger and armed with hunting weapons, the women kept them subjugated by impersonating demons and spirits. In these disguises they visited the village during ceremonies, frightening and punishing men who threatened to get out of line. The women periodically ordered the men to deliver meat to them to satiate the demons' voracious appetites. The men did as they were told, and the women feasted on the meat and laughed "with malice at the men's incredible naïveté and stupidity." [46]

Things continued in this manner until one day Sun, a male culture hero, spied on two young women as they practiced the parts they would play in the ceremony. When Sun reported the women's secret back to the men, they responded by immediately attacking and killing the women. (Men who could not bear to kill their own daughters or wives asked other men to kill them for them.) Only the youngest girls and infants were spared. In order to prevent these girls from growing up to revive the rule of women, the men hatched a plan: they would live in the Hain apart from the women, and they would periodically impersonate demons and spirits to scare the women into submission—not a very original plan, to be sure, but a time-tested one. [47]

Feminist matriarchalists hold that these myths of former female dominance, like all "legends that won't die," contain a "race-memory." [48] They would not be so widespread, they argue, if there weren't some historical basis for them. The primary competing explanation for these cross-cultural myths of women's former dominance is that they are a "social charter" for male dominance.

The idea of myth as "charter" was first proposed by anthropologist Bronislaw Malinowski in the 1920s. Interested in the functions of myth, Malinowski claimed that for any group myth could be understood as a collection of narratives that dictate belief, define ritual, and act "as the chart of their social order and the pattern of their moral behaviour." Malinowski suggested that myth tends to promote the status quo, since its function "is to strengthen tradition and endow it with a greater value and prestige by tracing it back to a higher, better, more supernatural reality of initial events." Such mythic charters are said to operate especially in areas of sociological strain, such as significant differences in status or power. Gender disparities certainly fit in this category, and indeed Malinowski drew special attention to them: "Nothing is more familiar to the native than the different occupations of the male and female sex," Malinowski wrote. "There is nothing to be *explained* about it. But though familiar, such differences are at times irksome, unpleasant, or at least limiting, and there is the need to justify them, to vouch for their antiquity and reality, in short to buttress their validity." [49]

This theory seems ready-made to account for cross-cultural myths of women's former dominance. The aim of the myth is to justify the present state of affairs: in this case, male dominance. If women had power before—especially if they misused it, as they frequently did—then it is only fair that men should have it now, these myths seem to say. The myth-as-charter view suggests that myths of women's former dominance merely "mystify the inevitable inequities of any social order and . . . win the consent of those over whom power is exercised, thereby obviating the need for the direct coercive use of force and transforming simple power into 'legitimate' authority." In short, "ideology masquerades as aetiology." [50]

That these myths of women's former dominance are working to justify male dominance is often quite plain in the contexts in which they are deployed. When the Selk'nam congregate for the Hain festival which celebrates the male takeover, women are terrorized by men dressed as deities and demons. As anthropologist Anne McKaye Chapman reports, "women whose behaviour has not conformed to the model of subservient wife" are singled out by these demons: their huts are shaken, their hearths stirred up, their belongings dragged out of their huts or thrown at them; they may even be beaten and stabbed with a stick. And in at least some of the groups that hold a myth of women's former dominance, the men self-consciously use the myth to retain their power. For example, male informants from a tribe in Papua New Guinea have told anthropologists that without their myth and the sacred flutes associated with it, the women "would laugh at us and we men would lose all authority over them, they would no longer cook for us nor rear our pigs." Marie Reay, speaking of a group that credits women with inventing marriage during a time of female dominance, notes that the men "admit freely that they wish women to think that marriage was the women's own idea so that they may become reconciled to an institution in which all the advantage lies with the men." [51]

Classicists who have concerned themselves with ancient Greek myths of women's former dominance tend to interpret them in this same way, as justifications for male dominance which are "didactic rather than historical." Even in antiquity, there was some dispute about whether Amazons were fictional or historical.[52] Today most scholars are agreed that Amazons existed strictly in myth, and that legends about them served as morality tales teaching that women's rule is dangerous and unnatural. Amazon societies are constructed as a reversal of Greek practices, an "antitype to the patriarchal social order that the Greeks identified with civilization."[53] They display what the world would be like in the absence of patriarchal gender norms, and it is a frightening place.

It is not just the Amazons to whom the ancient Greeks attributed an unnatural level of power for women. The Egyptians, the Lycians, the Lemnians, and others are all credited with this "barbaric" arrangement. Indeed, the ancient Greeks show a preoccupation with the rule of women not unlike that found in tribal New Guinea or South America. A myth such as that of the naming of Athens clearly "justifies the lowly estate of women in society" and pins it squarely on women, who voted the wrong way and thus earned their lot in society.[54]

In general, feminist matriarchalists have no trouble believing that myths of women's former dominance, whether from ancient Greece or contemporary New Guinea, are used to keep women down. To this extent, they are in agreement with their critics. The key difference is that feminist matriarchalists believe that the myth is not only a charter, but also a history, a belief their critics do not share. "We don't fear something that doesn't exist, something that never happened, something that never could happen,"[55] reasons Phyllis Chesler. But we fear all sorts of things that don't exist (monsters, dragons, and the like) or that haven't happened (extraterrestrial invasions, all-out nuclear war). Some of our fears are reasonable, others are not, but the relevant factor in whether or not we find things frightening is not their prior, documented existence. It seems perfectly plausible that men could find the rule of women frightening even if women have never ruled; perhaps *especially* because women have never ruled and how they would behave is therefore unknown. Men have ample reason to fear that the desire for revenge would run high if the tables were ever turned and women took power. Myths of women's former dominance—which have in fact been invented exclusively by men, as far as we can tell—could well exist only to quell men's anxieties about their social position.[56]

Feminist matriarchalist interpretations of ancient myth are rather transparently driven by ideology. Mythical evidence can by its nature be given various incommensurable interpretations. In this case, it provides no real support for the proposed prehistoric patriarchal revolution, though it does offer a fertile field for imagination. In contrast, linguistic, archaeological, and genetic evidence offer some support for the theory of Indo-European invasions from the steppes in the fifth and fourth millennia BCE. It is not implausible that the people and concepts that spread out from the Russian steppes into neighboring lands were patriarchal, patrilineal, and warlike. But as previous chapters have shown, it is likewise not implausible that the peoples who came in contact with them were already as patriarchal, patrilineal, and warlike as their enemies. Neither is there any positive evidence that the Kurgans from the Russian steppes were an exceptionally brutal, supremely patriarchal people. Their stock of weaponry, as it has been uncovered archaeologically, does not dwarf that of Neolithic peoples to the south, nor do Kurgan skeletons give unusual evidence of violence toward women. Therefore an Indo-European military conquest—if one occurred, which is by no means certain—cannot be assumed to count as the birth of patriarchy.

CHAPTER 9

On the Usefulness of Origin Myths

The myth of matriarchal prehistory is an impressive—and to some, a beautiful and enticing—house of cards. The cards of which it is built are not totally flimsy. Some are plausible interpretations of historical and artifactual data. But others are patently absurd. They are either bad interpretations of the available data, or assertions based on no data at all. Taken together, the entire structure is unstable, and if there were not things stronger than archaeological or historical evidence holding it up—things like passionate hope and religious faith—it would be in imminent danger of collapse.

We cannot know nearly as much as we would like to about prehistory. Interpretation of "gendered" data especially is so overburdened by observers' wishes and assumptions that it is very difficult to bracket off present concerns and discover past reality. But what we do know (or can judge to be probable) about gender in prehistory is not particularly encouraging regarding the status of women. Ethnographic analogies to contemporary groups with lifeways similar to those of prehistoric times (hunting and gathering or horticulture, practiced in small groups) show little sex egalitarianism and no matriarchy. Indeed, these societies always discriminate in some way between women and men, usually to women's detriment. Women may have powerful roles, but their power does not undermine or seriously challenge an overall system of male dominance in either these groups or ours, and there is no reason to believe that it would have in prehistoric societies either. If there are in fact societies where women's position is high and secure, these exceptions cannot lead us to believe that it was *this* pattern (rather than the more prevalent pattern of discrimination against women) which held in prehistory.

There is also nothing in the archaeological record that is at odds with an image of prehistoric life as nasty, brutish, short, and male-dominated. This does not mean that it *was* this way, but only that it could have been, as easily as—more easily than, actually—it could have been blissful, peaceful, long, and matriarchal. Female and male grave goods of equivalent wealth do not prove that men were not dominant, nor does the absence of weapons of war among the material remains we have uncovered mean that there was no warfare. But beyond this simple absence of proof positive, we have some disconfirming evidence: suggestions that prehistoric peoples did not live in peace, and that the division of labor between women and men resembled that found in later societies, which have consistently given disproportionate value to the labors of men.

There is no question that some prehistoric groups in Europe and the Near East made vast numbers of artistic representations of women, and the suggestion that many (if not all) of these images were meant to represent goddesses is plausible. The major monotheistic religions of the world notwithstanding, most peoples worship goddesses. It would be distinctly odd if it were the case that prehistoric cultures were uniformly non-theistic, or worshipped only male deities. But it would also be odd if prehistoric goddess worship was exclusive. Judging from ethnographic data, gods were probably worshipped too, whether or not they were represented in anthropomorphic form. And whatever religions prehistoric peoples practiced, we can be fairly sure that goddess worship did not automatically yield cultures of peace and plenty led by the goddess's priestesses. This pattern has been found nowhere.

Prehistoric human societies may have been different from all those that came after them, but any such assertion runs into three perhaps insurmountable obstacles: first, there is no evidence that they were; second, there is no reason to expect that they would be (at least not when we are talking about the past thirty to forty thousand years of *Homo sapiens sapiens*, as feminist matriarchalists typically are); and third, if they were utterly different, and universally so, we need a compelling explanation of why things changed so drastically. Feminist matriarchalists' make their strongest case for patriarchal revolution in southeast Europe and the Near East, where it is at best one possible explanation among others. Elsewhere in the world, patriarchal revolution is an even less likely scenario. Feminist matriarchalists' arguments explaining how, why, or even when patriarchy became a worldwide phenomenon simply do not square with the available evidence.

In spite of all these difficulties, the house of cards that is feminist matriarchal myth continues to stand. Certainly I do not anticipate that the puff of wind I offer in this book will blow it down. The image of prehistoric social life as matricentric and goddess-worshipping is far too valuable to those who treasure it to be sacrificed out of a concern for historical veracity. Feminist matriarchal myth provides answers to questions that are troubling to anyone hoping to secure freedom, safety, and equality for women, questions like, "Why is it that where gender hierarchy has developed, women have always been the dominated gender?" or "How did men succeed in enforcing the subordination of women?" Questions that seek to uncover the historical (or prehistorical) roots of male dominance, particularly institutionalized male dominance, have long held a special fascination for feminist writers, who have asked again and again, "Were things always as they are today?" and "When did 'it' start?"[1] The care and imagination feminist matriarchalists have devoted to these "origins" questions is in itself an impressive achievement.

Perhaps the solution then is to embrace the myth of matriarchal prehistory as myth. If feminist matriarchalists abandon their ambitions to historical veracity, then accusations of sloppy or wishful thinking will not tarnish their myth (or the feminist movement more generally), and perhaps it could perform the functions for which it was intended. In other words, while there *is* a problem with the historical inaccuracy of matriarchal myth, there does not *have* to be one. For in theory, little can be said against the propriety of imagining a time—prehistoric, if necessary—when women were treated well rather than badly, with respect rather than condescension or outright hatred. Envisioning a feminist future is arguably a necessary task. And insofar as envisioning a feminist past helps accomplish this—as it clearly does for many people—it would seem to have obvious merit. In the face of this, quibbling over archaeological evidence seems, as

Theodore Roszak has put it, "a minor pedantic objection . . . [which] once it has been spoken as a sort of cautionary footnote . . . has nothing more to offer."[2]

Nevertheless, though it might seem that only the hardest of antifeminist hearts could resist the appeal of matriarchal myth once it is stripped of its pretensions to historical truth, there are many feminists, myself included, who must continue to protest against it. The very attempt to ask and answer origins questions about sexism—which is both matriarchal myth's motivation and method—is fraught with danger. To begin with, origin stories tend to reduce historically specific facts and values to timeless archetypes (this is particularly the case with "femininity," as we have seen). Therefore the solutions proposed by origins thinking are not tailored to specific cultural environments, but rather to a totalizing image of "patriarchy." Also, origins thinking is often characterized by nostalgia for a lost past, a feeling that "things ain't so good as they used to be." If this nostalgia enables those who experience it to imagine a different future and take steps to secure it, then it is functional. But nostalgia is rarely this functional; or rather, its function is usually escapist.[3]

In addition, origins thinking usually rests on a rather curious (though also quite common) notion of "the natural." According to this view, there is a way of living and thinking that is in harmony with our "natural" proclivities, and there was a time when we effortlessly lived like this. This way of being is precultural, instinctual. Life since then, by contrast, is false, constructed. To know who we really are, to decide what we must do to foster our happiness and that of the rest of the ecosystem, we need to be in dialogue with who we were: which is at the same time who we are truly supposed to be. It is this kind of thinking that imagines that by observing how foraging peoples live, we will know how we ourselves should live. If they breastfeed their children for four years, then so should we; if they eat a diet high in protein and fiber, then so should we; if they honor motherhood and worship an earth goddess, we can do no less if we want to be true to our "nature." But it should be obvious that when we reach foraging cultures, we have not reached "nature": we have merely uncovered other cultures, ones which mediate as thoroughly between themselves and any imagined human "nature" as ours does (though in quite different ways). As discussed earlier, it is simply not possible to find human nature "uncontaminated" by culture, no matter how far back one looks in human evolution.

This vision of the "natural" is produced in part by a common misunderstanding of the principles of Darwinian evolution. "Survival of the fittest" has trickled down into popular thinking as the conviction that if no one gets in the way of natural selection, evolutionary processes will produce the very best organisms and societies. That is, "nature" is thought not merely to *select*, but also to *optimize*. Thinking like Dr. Pangloss, it is now natural selection (rather than god or fate) that makes everything for the best, in this, the best of all possible worlds. Feminist matriarchalists surely do not see this drive toward goodness operating in the cultural sphere (where things like the patriarchal revolution happen), but they do tend to see "nature" as a force that operates to our eternal benefit, and this conspires to make them reach into the past—where nature supposedly dominates culture—to find a template for living. But natural selection does not choose what is best, it merely finds something that works, and continues to do it. So long as one generation is surviving and producing the next, natural selection will not keep endeavoring to find a better way. Biological evolution is full of accidents, some of which get turned to interesting good fortune and others to disaster.[4]

Apart from the search for our true nature, feminist matriarchalists justify their commitment to origin stories by claiming that since "our analysis of causes affects strategies for change," we cannot usefully proceed without knowing where sexism came from. This makes a lot of intuitive sense, especially for those of us who were told in every history class we ever took that those who don't learn from history are doomed to repeat it. There is only one wrench in the works: if sexism had an origin—that is, if it were not always present from the beginning of hominid evolution—then we know that it came into being during prehistory. And when it comes to detecting ideological developments in prehistory, we *can't* learn the relevant history: it is "in principle unobtainable."[5]

More importantly, to say that learning the origins of sexism will inform our political strategies reverses the order in which these steps actually take place: it is our present political interests that determine the origin stories we offer for sexism, not vice versa. The story feminist matriarchalists tell us, the one that says what's wrong with us and how we should proceed, is not history capable of teaching us how to avoid past mistakes. It is a myth. Feminist matriarchalists, like other myth-makers, begin with a vision of the world as they would like it to be, project it into the past, and then find a way (narratively speaking) to make present conditions emerge from ideal ones. Given the paucity of information with which anyone seeking the prehistoric origins of sexism is working, the only thing feminist matriarchalists can count on is the reappearance of the assumptions with which they began.

If we are not going to discover history at the end of the day, but simply create myth, then the *only* grounds upon which feminist origins thinking can be justified is that it serves feminist political purposes. I have already dwelled at length on the problems inherent in pinning sexism on universalizing notions of the differences between women and men. Insofar as strong theories of sex difference are an unavoidable component of matriarchal myth, we should be suspicious about the myth's feminist utility from the start. But it is problematic on another level too. As archaeologist Sarah Taylor remarks, "I for one do not find it very comforting to think that once, in a very distant and 'primitive' society, women held power, especially if we have been moving away from that condition ever since." [6]

Many do find this comforting. Matriarchal myth addresses one of the feminist movement's most difficult questions: How can women attain real power when it seems we have never had it before? How can we hope that sex egalitarianism is possible, that male dominance can be ended, when it has been a mark of who we are as a species from time immemorial? Feminist matriarchal myth answers that question in what I think has to be admitted is an emotionally compelling, inspiring way. But it raises new questions, equally difficult to answer: Why did matriarchy collapse—and not just in one place or time, but everywhere, all around the world? And how can we hope to get it back, under conditions so radically different from those which supposedly fostered it in the first place? If male dominance followed naturally on the discovery of biological paternity, is the only way to reclaim matriarchy to ensure that no one knows who the fathers of individual children are? Though this could be easily achieved through artificial insemination or promiscuous sex, no one who puts the patriarchal revolution down to the discovery of paternity seriously advocates this as a desirable public policy.[7] Others have pinned male dominance to the development of agriculture, but we cannot return the world to a sustainable foraging technology without euthanizing 99 percent of the world's population.

None of these questions are easy to answer. I once asked a class of students which problem they would rather live with, all claims to historical truth aside: that of explaining women's (pre)historical loss of power in such a way that it does not rule out women's power in the future, or that of explaining how male dominance—universal up until now—can be ended at some point in the future. Roughly half chose the first, the other half the second. As one woman who chose the first option remarked, "I need to have an Eden, a belief that things once were right." [8]

I am a partisan of the second option, and I would like to make a case for asking and answering it. The most alluring feature of matriarchal myth is the precedent it offers. But a precedent is not, as some feminist matriarchalists claim, required. Its absence need not "doom women from the start, from the point of origin." Indeed, there is a respected tradition among liberal social reformers to call for redressing the wrongs of the ages, without any concomitant attempt—or any felt necessity—to say that things were ever different. As Kate Millett observes, John Stuart Mill "saw no further back in time than a universal rule of force and took the subjection of women to be an eternal feature of human life," but he firmly believed that " 'progress' and moral suasion" could alter this reality, just as they had made inroads against tyranny and slavery. [9]

Whether patriarchy is our only history, or merely one history, we are not in either case bound "to clone the past." We can comfort ourselves with the thought that many of the conditions we suspect have worked to create male dominance are no longer with us, or need no longer produce the same response as they did in the past. If in fact it is a hunting and gathering division of labor that gives rise to male dominance, as anthropologist Richard Leakey argues, then presumably the farther we grow from those roots, the less we need to be affected by social roles that made sense only in the past. That we have not already shed the legacy of male dominance some ten thousand years after the West left foraging technologies behind does not mean that we cannot: social systems can continue to thrive long after the conditions that formed them have become irrelevant. Male dominance may be perpetuated through inertia and have no better reason to exist than tradition. The fact that "anatomy *once was* destiny," then, does not mean that it need be so any longer.[10]

If modern technologies give us one kind of freedom to innovate, the very fact of cross-cultural diversity gives us another. Sex roles and gender expectations are extremely diverse from one culture to another, to the point of being almost completely arbitrary. Motherhood, a cross-cultural universal, is acted out in a huge variety of ways and given a wide range of meanings. Heterosexual sex, present in all cultures for reproduction, is sometimes the norm, the only approved sexual activity, and at other times accepted only as a grudging necessity. Gender, another cross-cultural universal, varies from being tremendously significant to comparatively minor. There is, as anthropologist Christine Ward Gailey says, "no global content to gender roles."[11]

One could choose to interpret this as evidence that male dominance has many cunning tools in its toolbox, but one could as easily read the sheer amount of ethnographic variety in matters of gender and sex as proof that we have a lot more latitude in setting up gender relations than any amount of sorrowful recounting of the sins of Western patriarchy would lead us to believe. As anthropologist Martin King Whyte concludes from his cross-cultural study of the status of women, "our analysis suggests that there is no *inevitable* obstacle to change in the role of women; no *inherent* or *biological* barrier that must prevent women from attaining equality in any area of social life [my emphasis]."[12]

If there are no inherent barriers to women's equality, then the future of women does not rest on biological destiny or historical precedent, but rather on moral choice. What we must be and what we have been will of course have an effect on our gender relations, but ultimately these cannot and should not dictate what we *want* to be. If we are certain that we want to get rid of sexism, we do not need a mythical time of women's past greatness to get on with the effort toward ending it.

But suppose for a moment that there *are* inherent barriers to women's equality; that male dominance is so hard-wired into our genes that we can never completely overcome it. How does this change the picture? Less than one might think. We have ample reason to believe that human beings will always do bad things: they will lie, they will steal, they will injure one another. Some cultural contexts encourage this, others discourage it; cruelty and crime are rampant in some places and relatively rare in others. But at base, these seem to be cross-cultural universals. So what do we do in the face of these facts of human nature? Do we wake up in the morning and say, "there is no escaping it, people do bad things . . . I may as well go out today and rob a bank"? This is neither the motivation for the crime, nor is it an excuse. Similarly, even if we conclude that male dominance is universal and inevitable, this is not a charter for writing the oppression of women into law, or pardoning men who hurt women on the basis that they were only responding to their genetic inclinations. The fact that a goal—in this case, eradicating sexism—is in principle unreachable does not mean it is not worth pursuing with every ounce of moral fiber we can muster. In short, if our moral resolve is in place, there is nothing in the "facts" of biology or history that need detain us any longer.

Accounts of history and origins have a place. Ignorance of the history of a particular injustice may trip us up in our efforts to rectify it. For example, it is helpful to know that Africans were kidnapped and brought to America as slaves when we seek to address racism in America. But this history is not nearly as important as the clear conviction that racism is bad and must end. It is white Americans' ambivalence about the worthiness of this goal and the amount of energy that they feel should be devoted to it that is more likely to limit progress.

The same is true of sexism. Feminist matriarchal myth does not actually recount the history of sexism, as it purports to do. It may provide us with a vision of what it considers to be socially desirable and the hope that it can be attained. But we do not need matriarchal myth to tell us that sexism is bad or that change is possible. With the help of all feminists, matriarchalist and otherwise, we need to decide what we want and set about getting it. Next to this, the "knowledge" that we once had it will pale into insignificance.

NOTES

1. Meeting Matriarchy

1. Steinem, *Wonder Woman*, n.p.

2. This ethnographic study was published under the title *Living in the Lap of the Goddess: The Feminist Spirituality Movement in America.*

3. The intellectual history of the myth of matriarchal prehistory, from Bachofen to the present, will be treated in depth in my forthcoming book, *From Motherright to Gylany: The Myth of Matriarchal Prehistory, 1861–2000.*

4. Noble, *Shakti Woman,* 235; Mara Lynn Keller, "The Interface of Archaeology and Mythology," in Marler, ed., *Realm of the Ancestors,* 381.

2. Popularizing the Past

1. See, for example, Múten, *Return of the Great Goddess,* 167–68.

2. Min, ed., *Chalice and the Blade in Chinese Culture.* There was already substantial interest in and commitment to the myth of matriarchal prehistory in China prior to Eisler, since Chinese anthropologists and archaeologists were influenced by an earlier generation of socialists and communists championing this myth. See Eller, *From Motherright to Gylany.*

3. Cantarella, *Pandora's Daughters,* 13–14; Daly, *Beyond God the Father,* 94; Ruth, *Take Back the Light,* 131; Adler, *Drawing Down the Moon,* 187.

4. See Gross, *Feminism and Religion,* 153; Christ, "Eliade and the Feminist Paradigm Shift," 76.

5. See, for example, Sjöö and Mor, *Great Cosmic Mother,* 433–34; Noble, *Shakti Woman,* 215–16; Tiffany, "Power of Matriarchal Ideas," 138; Grønborg, "Matriarchy—Why Not?" 219.

6. Feminist matriarchalists frequently blame researchers' maleness for the fact that information about prehistoric matriarchies has been studiously ignored. When female researchers likewise ignore or refute the theory of matriarchal prehistory,

they are said to do so either because they are unwittingly in the grip of male-dominated professions or are actively trying to "curry favor with the backlash against feminism" (Charlene Spretnak, "Beyond the Backlash: An Appreciation for the Work of Marija Gimbutas," in Marler, ed., *Realm of the Ancestors*, 399).

7. Carson, *Feminist Spirituality*, 6.

8. Keller, "Archaeology and Mythology," in Marler, ed., *Realm of the Ancestors*, 393; Wilshire, *Virgin Mother Crone*, 3.

9. A few feminist matriarchalists are willing to shake off any need to have their myth be historically accurate, usually because they take the myth's significance to be psychological rather than historical. The myth is, for them, a translation of psychoanalytic object relations theory to the species level: We are born into a world of oneness with our mothers, akin to goddess-worshipping matriarchal societies; and just as the peace of the prehistoric matriarchies is disrupted by the patriarchal revolution, so the mother-oriented world of infancy ends inevitably and tragically as we grow up—especially when we grow to find that our mothers are not adequately respected in the world at large (see Downing, *The Goddess*, 6; Chernin, *Reinventing Eve*, 123–24; Naomi Goldenberg, cited in Young, "Goddesses, Feminists, and Scholars," 110–11).

10. It has long been believed that myths have functions, reasons for being told of which the myth's narrators may or may not be conscious. (The foremost twentieth-century exponent of the functionalist interpretation of myth was Bronislaw Malinowski. See Malinowski, *Sex, Culture, and Myth*, 247–48, 291–92, and *Myth in Primitive Psychology*, 91–92.) There are many today who reject this notion, arguing that myth need not necessarily serve any particular function, or no direct or simple one. These thinkers describe myth as "tropic," "metaphoric," or "expressive," or even as "a literary and largely modern construction" developed by Western romantics (see James F. Weiner, "The Abandoned String Skirt: The Origin of Sexual Complementarity Among the Foi," Annette Hamilton, "Knowledge and Misrecognition: Mythology and Gender in Aboriginal Australia," and Nicholas Thomas, "The Contradictions of Hierarchy: Myths, Women and Power in Eastern Polynesia," in Gewertz, ed., *Myths of Matriarchy Reconsidered*, 30, 58, 171; and Robert S. Ellwood, letter to author, December 1995). But whether or not all myths should be read through a functionalist lens, it is clear that the myth of matriarchal prehistory in particular *does* have a function, one clearly articulated by its proponents.

11. Múten, *Return of the Great Goddess*, 3; Spretnak, ed., *Politics of Women's Spirituality*, rev. ed., xv.

12. Ann and Imel, *Goddesses in World Mythology*, v.

13. Miriam Sidell, quoted in Stone, *Return of the Goddess*.

14. These categories of feminist thought—"liberal feminism," "radical feminism," "cultural feminism"—should not be understood as distinct camps within the feminist movement, but rather as a helpful index to the variety of mindsets and intellectual and political influences operative under the umbrella of feminism.

15. For a discussion of these threads within nineteenth- and twentieth-century thought, see Donovan, *Feminist Theory*.

16. See chapter 3, and Donovan, *Feminist Theory*, 31–54.

17. Most feminist matriarchalists count themselves as ecofeminists, though the obverse is not true. See Carson, *Goddesses and Wise Women*, 4; Getty, *Goddess*, 5; Orenstein, *Reflowering*, 15; Stephenson, *Women's Roots*, 327. Ecofeminists who have been critical of matriarchal myth include Janet Biehl *(Rethinking Eco-feminist Politics)* and Noël Sturgeon *(Ecofeminist Natures)*.

18. See Donovan, *Feminist Theory*, 141–56; Eller, *Living in the Lap*, 42–46.

19. As Starhawk explains, "What we term *religion* is the soil of culture, in which the belief systems, the stories, the thought-forms upon which all other institutions are based are consciously or unconsciously grown" *(Dreaming the Dark*, 72).

20. Christ, "Symbols of Goddess and God," 250; Redmond, "Rhythm and the Frame Drum," 20; Rowbotham, "When Adam Delved," 10. Bronislaw Malinowski sees this an enduring function of myth: "Myth, coming from the true past, is the precedent which holds a promise of a better future if only the evils of the present be overcome" *(Sex, Culture, and Myth*, 291–92).

21. Janine Canan, "Goddesses, Goddesses: From Archaeology to Poetry of the Feminine," in Marler, ed., *Realm of the Ancestors*, 555.

22. Heide Göttner-Abendroth, cited in Hauser-Schäublin, "Mutterrecht und Frauenbewegung," 140 (Göttner-Abendroth's four-volume work is titled *Das Matriarchat)*; Sjöö and Mor, *Great Cosmic Mother*, 46, 235, 424; Stein, *Dreaming the Past*, 32; Matthew Fox, cited in Ruether, *Gaia and God*, 146.

23. Getty, *Goddess*; Austen, *Heart of the Goddess*; Poth, *Goddess Speaks*. The Frauen-Museum in Wiesbaden, Germany has an ongoing exhibit of reproductions of prehistoric statuary thought to illustrate matriarchal themes (LaMonte, "'My Desire is Life,'" 31). Slide shows have been reported by Robb, "In Goddess They Trust," 32, 36; Eisler and Loye, *Partnership Way*; Noble, *Motherpeace*; and are a frequent listing in *Goddessing Regenerated's* "Cauldron of Events." One slide show is available on videotape (Hopkins, *Great Mother Earth* and *From Earth Mother to Love Goddess).*

24. Gloria F. Orenstein, "The Artistic Legacy of Marija Gimbutas," in Marler, ed., *Realm of the Ancestors*, 461–62. Feminist and spiritual feminist art with matriarchal themes is documented at length in Gadon, *Once and Future Goddess*, 225–337, and Orenstein, *Reflowering*.

25. For a discussion of Edelson's work, see Orenstein, *Reflowering*, 104. Wilshire's piece was one segment of a presentation given to a packed house at the Museum of Natural History in New York in March 1997 titled "The Great Goddess: Her Enduring Presence, Power, and Personality." A similar program took place at the Smithsonian Museum in Washington DC in June 1997 under the auspices of the Smithsonian Associates. This two-day seminar included a performance by the Anima Mundi Dance Company that portrayed "a mythopoetic journey to the ancient sacred feminine."

26. Kosse, interviewed in Stone, *Return of the Goddess* (Jenny Malmquist wrote the text for "The Return of the Great Mother"); Redmond, *When the Drummers Were Women*. Mary Timony, Helium's singer and songwriter, says that she "was reading a lot of Mary Daly" as she worked on *Pirate Prude* (and later, on *The Dirt of Luck)* and that she meant to convey an image of "the fall of Western civilization, patriarchy," and a future society that "would be more egalitarian, more female gods, women . . . more important in society" (Noël, interview with Mary Timony of Helium, http://www.bunnyhop.com/BH6/helium.html, 1996; Todd Polenberg, review of *Dirt of Luck* by Helium, http://pantheon.cis.yale.edu/tpole/nadine/11__6/helium.html, n.d.) I have listened to *The Dirt of Luck*, and must confess that I could discern nothing about matriarchy in the lyrics, though I wouldn't want to dispute the songwriter's and reviewers' assertion that it is there.

27. See especially Canan, "Goddesses, Goddesses," in Marler, ed., *Realm of the Ancestors*, 566–67; Lee/Libana, *You Said, What is This For?*; Apara Borrowes "Three Poems for Marija," in Marler, ed., *Realm of the Ancestors*, 549. Brindel clearly believes she is drawing on historical events. As she explains in an author's note, "Some time between 1800 and 1400 BC, the last matriarchies in the Western world were crushed. With them died a system of belief that regarded childbirth as the primary miracle, all women as intrinsically holy, and the Great Mother Goddess as supreme deity" *(Ariadne*, n.p.). Other fictional accounts drawing on the themes of matriarchal myth include Chernin, *Flame Bearers* and Robbins, *Skinny Legs and All*.

28. The subgenre of prehistoric romance novels is increasingly toying with the tropes of matriarchal myth—goddess worship, matrilineal chiefs and clans, horse-riding patriarchal invaders—bringing these ideas to a wider, frequently nonfeminist audience. The trend was kicked off by Jean Auel's *Clan of the Cave Bear* and its sequels and is also present in Prentiss, *Children of the Ice*; Wolf, *Horsemasters*; Thomas, *Reindeer Moon*; and Pesando, *Sisters of the Black Moon*.

29. Rufus and Lawson, *Goddess Sites*, back cover blurb; *Goddessing Regenerated* 7 (Summer/Fall 1997): 35. In an interview with Marguerite Rigoglioso, Luisah Teish notes that some African-American women have made goddess pilgrimages to Africa, though they do not appear to be as organized or popular as the white feminist industry of goddess pilgrimages to Europe.

30. Read, *Goddess Remembered*; Davis, *Goddess Unmasked*, 24–25; Ranck, *Cakes for the Queen of Heaven* (UUA); Eisler and Loye, *Partnership Way*.

31. See, for example, Pleiades, "Living Goddesses," advertisement in *Goddessing Regenerated* 6 (Spring 1997): 23. *Metis* is produced under the auspices of the California Institute of Integral Studies; *Goddessing Regenerated* is based in Malta, though published in the United States; the *Matriarchy Research and Reclaim Network Newsletter* is published in London. Earlier feminist spirituality journals and newsletters such as *Woman of Power, SageWoman* (still in print), and *Womanspirit* included frequent features on matriarchal prehistory, but had a wider mission of serving all aspects of the feminist spirituality movement. Examples of goddess calendars are Nancy Passmore, *The Lunar Calendar: Dedicated to the Goddess in Her Many Guises* (Boston: Luna Press,

1988); Betsy Bayley, Amy Chirman, Grace Darcy, and Elaine Gill, *Celebrating Women's Spirituality: An Engagement Calendar* (Freedom, CA: Crossing Press, 1989). Goddess reproductions are shown in catalogues including Grand Adventure (Stroudsburg, PA); Jane Iris Designs (Graton, CA); Slitherings Shamanic Art (Atlanta, GA); JBL Devotional Statues (Crozet, VA); Kate Cartwright, "Goddess Stamps and T-Shirts" (Graton, CA); Pleiades (Brimfield, MA); Star River Productions (New Brunswick, NJ). There is even a gift shop in Rockport, Massachusetts—"The Sea Goddess"—devoted entirely to goddess materials (see advertisement in *Goddessing Regenerated* 5 [Summer/Fall 1996]: 16).

32. Aburdene and Naisbitt, *Megatrends for Women*, chap. 9; NOW flyer, cited in Denfeld, *New Victorians*, 128–29; Lexington, Massachusetts NOW chapter, "Unearthing Pandora's Treasure," email advertisement, March 1999.

33. Gilligan and Brown, *Meeting at the Crossroads*; Pipher, *Reviving Ophelia*.

34. Mann, *The Difference*, 197.

35. Thurer, *Myths of Motherhood*, xxvi.

36. Sarah Bertucci, personal communication, March 1997; Candace E. West, personal communication, February 1997; Owen-Smith et al., "Feminist Teaching Across the Curriculum"; LaMonte, "Black Virgins," 15; Barbara Myerhoff and Karen Segal, "Goddess and the Matriarchy Controversy," course syllabus, University of Southern California, 1984. (Going on the assumption that "history" is really "his story," the history of men, the word "herstory" was coined to stand for "her story," women's history.) I attended part of the course "The Goddess and the Matriarchy Controversy," and though its title indicated an intention to look at prehistoric matriarchy skeptically, the course was very much geared toward the promotion of the myth.

37. Gross, *Feminism and Religion*, 159–60. Another guardedly sympathetic treatment of matriarchal myth can be found in Martha Ward's anthropology textbook, *A World Full of Women*.

38. Lerner, *Creation of Patriarchy*, 6–7, 31, 228–29.

39. Sreenivasan, *Moon Over Crete*, back cover blurb; Shannon, *Why It's Great to Be a Girl*, xiv–xv, 17–18, 122–23. The first treatment of matriarchal myth in children's literature was Charlene Spretnak's *Lost Goddesses of Early Greece*, published in 1981, which Spretnak wrote with the intention of giving her daughter a more female-friendly—and, she said, more accurate, earlier, prepatriarchal—version of Greek mythology (10).

40. Steven Goldberg, "Dr. Goldberg Replies to 'Patriarchy' Debate," http://www.vix.com/men/books/goldberg/patriarch.html, November 1992; Robert Sheaffer, "'The Goddess Remembered'—A Case of 'False Memory Syndrome,'" http://www.patriarchy.com/shaeffer/texts/goddess_rem.html, December 1993. Goldberg's *The Inevitability of Patriarchy* was republished in 1993 as *Why Men Rule*. Populist feminist critiques of matriarchal myth include Denfeld, *New Victorians*,

127−53, and Tavris, *Mismeasure of Women*, 71−79. More academic critiques can be found in Davis, *Goddess Unmasked*; Lefkowitz, "Twilight of the Goddess"; Pomeroy, *Goddesses, Whores, Wives, and Slaves*, x–xi; Walters, "Caught in the Web"; Biehl, *Rethinking Eco-feminist Politics;* Rowbotham, "When Adam Delved"; Kristol, "Just the Facts"; Bermond and Georgoudi, "Matriarcat n'a Jamais Existé!"; Stella Georgoudi, "Creating a Myth of Matriarchy," in Pantel, ed., *History of Women;* Lo Russo, "Idea d'una Societa Matriarcale"; Townsend, "Goddess"; Cantarella, *Pandora's Daughters;* Barbara Chesser, letter to the editor, *Women's Review of Books* 14/8 (May 1997): 4−5; Magli, ed., *Matriarcato*; Ruether, *Gaia and God;* Young, "Goddesses, Feminists, and Scholars"; Perkins, "Myth of the Matriarchy"; Janssen-Jurreit, *Sexism*. Critiques from archaeologists and classicists include Meskell, "Goddesses"; Conkey and Tringham, "Archaeology and the Goddess"; Brian Hayden, "Observing Prehistoric Women" in Claassen, ed., *Exploring Gender through Archaeology;* Brian Hayden, "Old Europe: Sacred Matriarchy or Complementary Opposition?" in Bonanno, ed., *Archaeology and Fertility Cult*; Anthony, "Nazi and Eco-feminist Prehistories"; Burkert, *Greek Religion*; Talalay, "Feminist Boomerang"; Samson, "Superwomen"; Barnett, review of *Language of the Goddess.*

41. Noble, *Shakti Woman*, 235; Marler, ed., *Realm of the Ancestors;* Vicki Noble, quoted in Starhawk and Donna Read, "Marija Gimbutas Film Project," http://www.webcom.com/gimbutas/belili, 1997.

42. Gore mentions in passing the notion of "a single earth goddess" worshipped throughout "prehistoric Europe and much of the world" replaced by later religions with "their distinctly masculine orientation." Gore also notes however that "the antiquity of the evidence and the elaborate and imaginative analysis used to interpret the artifacts leave much room for skepticism about our ability to know exactly what this belief system . . . taught" *(Earth in the Balance*, 260).

43. See especially Diop, *Cultural Unity of Black Africa*, and Amadiume, *Reinventing Africa.*

3. The Story They Tell

1. Efforts to trace the origins of social institutions through myth date back to classical Greece (Marcel Detienne, quoted in Blundell, *Origins of Civilisation*, 103; Vidal-Naquet, "Slavery," 188) and are, according to Lisa Marie Fedigan, a cross-cultural universal ("Changing Role of Women," 58).

2. Freud, *Totem and Taboo*, 144; Freud, *Moses and Monotheism*, 104.

3. Engels was far more enthusiastic about both Morgan and the concept of matriarchy than Marx had been, though in the *Origin* Engels claimed to be representing Marx's ideas. See Krader, ed., *Ethnological Notebooks* (the *Ethnological Notebooks* consist of Marx's notes on his anthropological readings).

4. Gage, *Woman, Church, and State*; Stanton, "Matriarchate"; Gamble, *Evolution of*

Woman; Hartley, *Age of Mother-Power;* Spencer, *Woman's Share in Social Culture;* Gilman, *Man-Made World.*

5. See Tolstoy, "Soviet Anthropological Thought"; Gellner, "Soviet and the Savage."

6. For matriarchal themes in classical scholarship, see Harrison, *Prolegomena* and *Epilegomena and Themis;* Thomson, *Ancient Greek Society;* Willetts, *Cretan Cults;* Hutchinson, *Prehistoric Crete;* Vermeule, *Greece in the Bronze Age;* Butterworth, *Traces of the Preolympian World.* Archaeologists working with themes of matriarchy or goddess worship included Crawford, *Eye Goddess;* Hawkes, *Dawn of the Gods;* Murray, "Female Fertility Figures"; Levy, *Gate of Horn.* For matriarchalists informed by psychoanalysis and Jungianism, see Fromm, "Theory of Mother Right"; Reich, *Compulsory Sex-Morality;* Neumann, *Great Mother;* M. Esther Harding, *Woman's Mysteries.*

7. This movement began with the "Kosmische Runde"—a group of poets and intellectuals centered around the poet Stefan George—who revived Bachofen's work around the turn of the century and over the next few decades (see, for example, Schuler, "Mutterdunkel"; Klages, *Kosmogonischen Eros;* Bäumler and Schröter, *Mythos von Orient und Okzident).* The myth of matriarchal prehistory occasionally emerged among the ideologues of the Third Reich (see Göttner-Abendroth, *Matriarchat,* vol. 1, 138–41).

8. Durant, *Story of Civilization,* vol. 1, 30–31, 33, 34.

9. Hawkes and Woolley, *Prehistory,* 117, 123, 264. For a discussion of Hawkes's position in regard to matriarchal ideas, see Hutton, "Neolithic Great Goddess."

10. The clearest exception from the past twenty-five years is Amaury de Riencourt's *Sex and Power in History* (1974), which tells a straightforward tale of men's triumph over the retarding forces of women's rule. Writers like Ken Wilber *(Up From Eden,* 1981) regard the patriarchy as an improvement over matriarchy, but introduce a feminist component into their story by insisting that patriarchy should soon be superseded by a society that is more congenial to women's rights. This is a pattern that occurred as well in nineteenth-century matriarchal myth; see Eller, *From Motherright to Gylany.*

11. Fisher, *Women's Creation,* 220 ff.; Davis, *First Sex,* 177–78.

12. Ortner, "Is Female to Male," 5, 8; Borun et al., *Women's Liberation,* 6.

13. This socialist feminist literature includes Karen Sacks, "Engels Revisited: Women, the Organization of Production, and Private Property," in Rosaldo and Lamphere, eds., *Woman, Culture, and Society,* and *Sisters and Wives;* Leacock, "Women's Status," "Women in Egalitarian Societies," *Myths of Male Dominance,* and "Origins of Gender Inequality"; Rohrlich-Leavitt, "Women in Transition"; Rohrlich, "State Formation"; Fluehr-Lobban, "Marxist Reappraisal" and "Marxism and the Matriarchate"; Al-Hibri, "Capitalism is an Advanced Stage of Patriarchy"; Gailey, "Evolutionary Perspectives," "State of the State," and *Kinship to Kingship.*

14. Estimates of the number of spiritual feminists or followers of the broader neopagan movement vary from 100,000 to 500,000 (Denfeld, *New Victorians*, 299, n. 1; Kelly, "Update"), but these estimates are extremely rough and doubtless inaccurate. Suffice it to say that feminist spirituality is a strong cultural force within the women's movement and a significant presence in New Age circles.

15. Ironically, this is especially true outside the feminist spirituality movement, where goddesses are *not* worshipped, but simply observed for what they are believed to reveal about women's prehistoric prominence. Within feminist spirituality, goddesses serve other functions as well: as role models to emulate, as divine companions offering succor, as supernatural forces making magic efficacious, and so on.

16. See, for example, Hutton, "Neolithic Great Goddess," 93; Ucko, *Anthropomorphic Figurines*, 409.

17. Stone, *When God Was a Woman*, 5, 22, 228.

18. Joan Marler, "The Circle is Unbroken: A Brief Biography," in Marler, ed., *Realm of the Ancestors*, 11–15; Steinfels, "Idyllic Theory," C1, C12.

19. Steinfels, "Idyllic Theory," C1, C12. In her later years, Gimbutas's reputation among linguists was considerably stronger than her reputation among archaeologists. Although linguists were no more interested in Gimbutas's goddess theories than were her archaeological peers, they, unlike archaeologists, continued to give serious attention to her work on the spread of Indo-European languages (see, for example, Lehmann, "Frozen Residues," 223).

20. Gimbutas, quoted in Steinfels, "Idyllic Theory," C12.

21. Ronald Hutton notes that Gimbutas's *Gods and Goddesses* portrays the goddesses of Old Europe primarily as mothers and symbol of fertility and sexuality, while *Language of the Goddess* and *Civilization of the Goddess* portray the goddess as "a mighty creatrix, presiding over all life and death" ("Neolithic Great Goddess," 97–98).

22. Noble, "Marija Gimbutas," 5; Spretnak, ed., *Politics of Women's Spirituality*, rev. ed., x; Pollack, *Body of the Goddess*, xi ; Judy Grahn, "Marija Gimbutas and Metaformic Theory," in Marler, ed., *Realm of the Ancestors*, 546.

23. Fritz Muntean, personal communication, November 1998.

24. Cavin, *Lesbian Origins*, 5–6; Noble, *Shakti Woman*, 215–16; French, *Beyond Power*, 27; Schmerl and Ritter, "Matriarchats-debatte," 86.

25. See, for example, Eisler, *Sacred Pleasure*, chap. 2.

26. JBL Devotional Statues, "The Acheulian Goddess," http://www.jblstatue.com/acheulian.html, 1998. See also Gimbutas, *World of the Goddess*; Noble, *Shakti Woman*, 38–39.

27. This is when Neolithic cultures are under consideration. When Paleolithic cultures are the topic of choice, the geography of the myth cuts a swath from southwestern France to Siberia, which is the approximate geographic spread of the so-called "Venus" figurines (see chapter 7).

28. Kristie Neslen *(The Origin)* and Starhawk *(Truth or Dare,* 33) have defended this focus on the "cradle of Western civilization" as appropriate to the study of the rise of Western patriarchy, "which is probably our worst enemy" (Neslen, *The Origin,* 3). European and European-American writers who have spent significant time investigating potential prehistoric matriarchies outside the "cradle of Western civilization" include DeMeo, "Origins and Diffusion of Patrism" (China and the Americas); Ellwood, "Sujin Religious Revolution" (Japan); Tsultrim Allione, quoted in Jamal, *Shape Shifters* (India); Noble, *Shakti Woman* (Mexico); Campbell, *Traveller in Space* (Tibet); Daniel F. McCall, "Mother Earth," in Preston, ed., *Mother Worship* (West Africa); Hubbs, *Mother Russia* (Russia); Cameron, *Daughters of Copper Woman* (Northwest America).

29. For Latina and Native American treatments of matriarchal themes, see Paula Gunn Allen, "Grandmother of the Sun," and Gloria Anzaldúa, "Entering into the Serpent," in Plaskow and Christ, eds., *Weaving the Visions,* 22–28, 77–86. African-American treatments can be found in Lorde, *Sister Outsider,* 67; Sabrina Sojourner, "From the House of Yemanja," in Spretnak, ed., *Politics of Women's Spirituality,* 57–63; Teish, *Jambalaya,* ix, 70–71; Luisah Teish, quoted in Stone, *Return of the Goddess,* and Asian-American ones in Rita Nakashima Brock, "On Mirrors, Mists, and Murmurs," in Plaskow and Christ, eds., *Weaving the Visions,* 241–42. For an example of Indian use of matriarchal themes, see Jayakar, *Earth Mother.*

30. The most detailed myths of matriarchal prehistory for the African continent are told by Africans, most notably Cheikh Anta Diop *(The Cultural Unity of Black Africa),* and Ifi Amadiume *(Afrikan Matriarchal Foundations* and *Reinventing Africa).* But there is also interest in prehistoric African matriarchies among white feminist matriarchalists, mostly related to their enthusiasm for the "black madonnas" of Europe, which, they argue, are related to African goddesses, especially Isis (see Bolen, *Crossing to Avalon,* 26–27; Rufus and Lawson, *Goddess Sites,* v–ix; Birnbaum, *Black Madonnas;* Rose, "Black Madonnas"). A critique of this practice can be found in Eller, "White Women and the Dark Mother." Chinese versions of matriarchal myth (which, unlike African ones, have not been incorporated into Western matriarchal myth) include Zhang, "Yuanjunmiao Cemetery" and Min, ed., *Chalice and the Blade in Chinese Culture.*

31. See Walker, *Skeptical Feminist,* 265–76; Eisler and Loye, *Partnership Way,* 217.

32. Wilshire, *Virgin Mother Crone,* 61.

33. Starr Goode, "Tea with Marija," in Marler, ed., *Realm of the Ancestors,* 40.

34. Bolen, *Crossing to Avalon,* 128–29; Mor and Sjöö, "Respell the World," 18.

35. Noble, *Shakti Woman,* 227–28. The claim that systems of writing were invented by matriarchal cultures must be made with some dexterity, since the earliest languages that have been deciphered all give evidence of nonmatriarchal social organizations (see chapter 8). Those who make this claim include Gimbutas, *Civilization of the Goddess,* 308–21; and Harald Haarmann, "Writing in the Ancient Mediterra-

nean: The Old European Legacy," Keller, "Archaeology and Mythology," James Harrod, "The Upper Paleolithic 'Double Goddess': 'Venus' Figurines as Sacred Female Transformation Processes in the Light of a Decipherment of European Upper Paleolithic Language," in Marler, ed., *Realm of the Ancestors*, 110 ff., 391, 492.

36. Wilshire, *Virgin Mother Crone*, 56; Merlin Stone, "9978: Repairing the Time Warp," in Heresies Collective, ed., *Great Goddess*, 125; Spretnak, "Female Psyche/ Soma."

37. This is an argument that has—predictably—been advanced most often by socialist feminists (see, for example, Leacock, "Women in Egalitarian Societies," 32−33; Reed, *Problems of Women's Liberation*, 21; Silverblatt, "Women in States," 430−31). It is less important to feminist matriarchalists whose roots are in feminist spirituality.

38. Stephenson, *Women's Roots*, 5; Alpert, "Mother Right," 91−92.

39. Sjöö , *New Age and Armageddon*, 66−67; Vicki Noble, quoted in Jamal, *Shape Shifters*, 113.

40. Grace Shinell calls lesbianism "the hidden sexual preference throughout history" and "the normal sexual union in prepatriarchal eras" ("Women's Collective Spirit," in Spretnak, ed., *Politics of Women's Spirituality*, 515−16; see also Cavin, *Lesbian Origins*, 40−41).

41. Stone, *When God Was a Woman*, 154.

42. Gimbutas, *Civilization of the Goddess*, x; Johnson, *Lady of the Beasts*, 3; Gimbutas, *Goddesses and Gods*, 152. There is some tension in the feminist spirituality movement, and American neopaganism generally, between those who revere numerous deities as manifestations of a single goddess, and those who believe that there truly are numerous deities who are incommensurable (see Eller, *Living in the Lap*, 132−35). However, in discussions of matriarchal prehistory, the goddess is virtually always singular. This cannot be interpreted as a verbal accident, for justifications of this singularity are easy to find (see, for example, Gimbutas, *Civilization of the Goddess*, 223; Spretnak, *Lost Goddesses*, 20; Göttner-Abendroth, *Matriarchal Mythology*, 13).

43. Brindel, *Ariadne*, 119.

44. Bolen, *Crossing to Avalon*, 128−29; Neslen, *The Origin*, 14; Starhawk, "Witchcraft and Women's Culture," 260; Redmond, *When the Drummers Were Women*, 1.

45. French, *Beyond Power*, 27.

46. Phyllis Chesler, "Foreword," in Budapest, *Holy Book of Women's Mysteries*, xx; Göttner-Abendroth, *Dancing Goddess*, 85.

47. See Reed, *Woman's Evolution*, 142; Cavin, *Lesbian Origins*, 40−41; Anna Perenna, "Towards a Matriarchal Manifesto," in Matriarchy Study Group, ed., *Politics of Matriarchy*, 10; Wilshire, *Virgin Mother Crone*, 23; Noble, *Shakti Woman*, 197.

48. Some matriarchalists argue that women knew perfectly well where babies came from but declined to share this knowledge with men, since they intuited that it

would weaken their social power if men knew that women could not produce children unaided (see, for example, Stein, *Women's Spirituality Book*, 5; Davis, *First Sex*, 133; Wabun Wind, "This God Is," in King, ed., *Divine Mosaic*, 106). Others say that both women and men were fully aware of the connection between sexual intercourse and conception, but simply did not attach the sort of meanings to that fact that came to hold sway in patriarchal times.

49. Janet Balaskas, "The Feminine Power of Birth," in Noble, ed., *Uncoiling the Snake*, 26; Múten, *Return of the Great Goddess*, 2; Francia, *Dragontime*, 13–14; Sjöö, *New Age and Armageddon*, 14–15; Iglehart, *Womanspirit*, 10–11; Wilshire, *Virgin Mother Crone*, 123. Women past menopause are said to have been especially respected in matriarchal societies since "their wise blood" was "stored in the body like the wisdom stored in their psyches" (Noble, *Shakti Woman*, 35; Cassidy, "Post-Modern Menstrual Lodge").

50. Eisler, *Sacred Pleasure*, 25.

51. This is almost always the figure given "on the fly," when an author or speaker is simply recapping the myth of matriarchal prehistory. Marija Gimbutas offers more precision, postulating "waves" of patriarchal invasions into Old Europe occurring in 4400–4300 BCE, 3400–3200 BCE, and 3000–2900 BCE (Marija Gimbutas, "Women and Culture in Goddess-Oriented Old Europe," in Plaskow and Christ, eds., *Weaving the Visions*, 70). In spite of this general consensus, some feminist matriarchalists date the patriarchal revolution considerably earlier, sometimes equating it with the Neolithic revolution, or much later, saying that patriarchal power was not truly consolidated until the Constantinian revolution, the medieval witchcraft persecutions, the Reformation, the rise of feudalism or capitalism, or even the industrial revolution. Different dates, usually much later ones, are given for patriarchal revolutions in England, Ireland, India, Mexico, Russia, and China.

52. See, for example, Mason, *Unnatural Order*, 69; Achterberg, *Woman as Healer*, 10; Getty, *Goddess*, 15; Wind, "This God Is," in King, ed., *Divine Mosaic*, 107. Amusingly, Elizabeth Judd argues that paternity was first recognized in the shamanistic cultures of north central Asia and Siberia owing to "the habitual consumption of certain hallucinogens" which "brings out a belief (in men) in a central male reproductive role" ("The Myths of the Golden Age and the Fall: From Matriarchy to Patriarchy," in Keller, ed., *Views of Women's Lives*, 63). Judd states that this is a "well known" effect of hallucinogens.

53. French, *War Against Women*, 19; Rich, *Of Woman Born*, 126; Walker, *Skeptical Feminist*, 51; Deming, "Remembering"; Wilshire, *Virgin Mother Crone*, 130; Francia, *Dragontime*, 13–14; Brindel, *Ariadne*, 236; Stein, *Women's Spirituality Book*, 119.

54. See Stephenson, *Women's Roots*, 29; Moltmann-Wendel, *Land Flowing with Milk and Honey*, 51–52; Deckard, *Women's Movement*, 194; d'Eaubonne, *Femmes avant le Patriarcat*. This theory was developed by early anthropologists, and refined by feminist and socialist anthropologists in the late twentieth century (for a summary of

this literature, see Silverblatt, "Women in States"). I regard this as another version of the myth of matriarchal prehistory and will be treating it as such in my forthcoming *From Motherright to Gylany*. I will not, however, be treating it here, except as it is picked up and used in more popular contemporary versions of the myth of matriarchal prehistory.

55. Kurgan is not the only term in use among feminist matriarchalists; reference is also made to "sky god-worshipping invaders," "pastoral nomads," "patriarchal invaders," and occasionally to "Aryans." I will use the term Kurgans, since it more precisely locates this particular group of putative patriarchal invaders without calling up the Nazi associations of the term "Aryans."

56. See, for example, Mackey, *Year the Horses Came*, 38; Neslen, *The Origin*, 45; Sjöö and Mor, *Great Cosmic Mother*, 258. There is a subtle contradiction here between the matriarchy imagined for Paleolithic times, which was characterized by nomadism, and the implication in discussions of the patriarchal revolution that nomadism produces male-dominant social relations.

57. It would make sense, if this were a strongly patriarchal society, that Kurgan women would stay home while their menfolk were off conquering new lands, and also that Kurgan men would marry or mate with women from the lands they conquered. But some suggest that Kurgan women were not prehistoric stay-at-home moms, but were rather the fabled Thermodon Amazons: blond, blue-eyed, horse-riding, fire-worshipping warriors from the Black Sea region (see Neslen, *The Origin*, 45; Sojourner, "House of Yemanja," in Spretnak, ed., *Politics of Women's Spirituality*, 62; Phyllis Chesler, "The Amazon Legacy," in Spretnak, ed., *Politics of Women's Spirituality*, 104–106). Notably, these women are not held responsible for the patriarchal revolution, as are their male counterparts.

58. Gimbutas, *Civilization of the Goddess*, 352; Gimbutas, "Women and Culture," in Plaskow and Christ, eds., *Weaving the Visions*, 69; Marler, ed., *Realm of the Ancestors*, 52.

59. Nano Valaoritis, "Cosmic Conflict of Male and Female in Greek Mythology," in Marler, ed., *Realm of the Ancestors*, 248. I think it significant that feminist matriarchalists, writing mainly from North America and Europe during the Cold War era, place the patriarchal homeland in Russia—already, by common Western consensus, the source of world evil.

60. The only maps I have seen of the patriarchal homeland are supplied by Gimbutas *(Civilization of the Goddess*, 358, 359, 368, 385, and elsewhere in the Gimbutas corpus), Mackey *(Year the Horses Came*, 6–7), and DeMeo ("Origins and Diffusion of Patrism," 268—though DeMeo places the "patrist heartland" considerably south and east of Gimbutas's proposed Kurgan homeland). The fact that Gimbutas has been so clear about the geographical boundaries of the patriarchal homelands does, to an extent, allow others to omit discussions of geography, but I suspect that the neglect of such discussions has more to do with a lack of interest in them on the part of feminist matriarchalists.

61. Mary Kelly, quoted in Stone, *Return of the Goddess;* Eisler, "Chalice and the Blade," 8. Eisler also uses the phrases "arid fringes of our globe," "peripheral areas of our globe," "fringe areas of our globe," and "edges of the earth" (see Eisler, *Sacred Pleasure*, 88; *Chalice and the Blade*, xvii, 43, 47−48; "Rediscovering Our Past, Reclaiming Our Future: Toward a New Paradigm for History," in Marler, ed., *Realm of the Ancestors*, 339).

62. See, for example, Gimbutas, quoted in Brown and Novick, "Unearthing the Goddess," 18; Eisler, *Sacred Pleasure*, 91; Pollack, *Body of the Goddess*, 121−22.

63. Stone, *When God Was a Woman*, 62; Gimbutas, *Civilization of the Goddess*, 352.

64. Davis, *First Sex*, 141. Others who name the Hebrews as patriarchal invaders include Ferguson, *Women and Religion*, 40−41; Baring and Cashford, *Myth of the Goddess*, 688; Eisler, *Chalice and the Blade*, 44. This anti-Semitism is critiqued both within and outside feminist matriarchalist circles. Carol Christ has been particularly outspoken against it (see, for example, *Rebirth of the Goddess*, 47), as has Katharina von Kellenbach *(Anti-Judaism*, 99−100).

65. Neslen, *The Origin*, 44. On natural disasters and resultant intertribal warfare as an explanation for patriarchal revolution, see Achterberg, *Woman as Healer*, 12, 28; Eisler, *Chalice and the Blade*, 43, 57; Lerner, *Creation of Patriarchy*, 46; Peggy Reeves Sanday, cited in Gross, *Feminism and Religion*, 167. For astrological explanations, see Noble, *Motherpeace*, 47; Jade, *To Know*, 168−69; Demetra George, "The Dark Moon Phase of the Goddess," in Noble, ed., *Uncoiling the Snake*, 19−20, 23. For discussion of genetic mutations, see Davis, *First Sex*, 34−35; Miles, *Women's History of the World*, 3; Jade River, "In the Beginning . . . We Were One," anonymous spiritual feminist publication, 1989; Shinell, "Woman's Primacy," in Heresies Collective, ed., *Great Goddess*, 46; Sjöö and Mor, *Great Cosmic Mother*, 2−3. I have heard the theory of extraterrestrial invasions offered—sometimes casually, sometimes seriously—at lectures and workshops and in interviews. Noting that patriarchal invaders "seem like anomalies that appeared out of nowhere," Vicki Noble remarks that it is "no wonder people are driven to posit extraterrestrial landings to explain the mystery" *(Shakti Woman*, 231).

66. Eisler, *Chalice and the Blade*, xxiii, 38; Eisler and Loye, *Partnership Way*, 85; Eisler, "The Goddess of Nature and Spirituality: An Ecomanifesto," in Campbell and Musès, eds., *In All Her Names*, 21. Those who see patriarchy as surviving largely through inertia include Borun et al., *Women's Liberation*, 39; DeMeo, "Origins and Diffusion of Patrism," 252, 254; Deckard, *Women's Movement*, 189.

67. Donna Henes, speaking at The American Museum of Natural History in New York as part of the program "The Great Goddess: Her Enduring Presence, Power, and Personality," moderated by Cristina Biaggi, 22 March 1997; Neslen, *The Origin*, 45. See also Noble, *Shakti Woman*, 231.

68. There is some internal dissension on this point. Many celebrate armed resistance on the part of the matriarchies as a manifestation of women's strength and bravery (see Rohrlich, "State Formation," 90; Jade, *To Know*, 168; d'Eaubonne, *Femmes*

avant le Patriarcat, chap. 4). But others beg to differ. As Donna Wilshire writes in a letter to the editor of *Goddessing Regenerated*, "it distresses me to see that Vicki Noble is writing about female warriors as if that were a wonderful occupation for women, then or now. Marija would be very sad. Old Europe was the time of peace, the time before the Bronze Age warriors—male and later female—destroyed the matristic Great Goddess cultures" ([Summer/Fall 1996]: 4).

69. Lerner, *Creation of Patriarchy*, 48, 81.

70. Hopkins, *Great Mother Earth*; Pollack, *Body of the Goddess*, 47. Some feminist matriarchalists see hope so long as goddesses are still in the picture, and do not regard patriarchy as having triumphed until the Roman Empire, under the banner of Christianity, forbade the worship of the ancient goddesses (see, for example, Redmond, *When the Drummers Were Women*, 137; Eisler, *Sacred Pleasure*, 30; Christ, *Rebirth of the Goddess*, 47).

71. See Cavin, *Lesbian Origins*, 84; Walker, *Skeptical Feminist*, 188–89; Christ, *Rebirth of the Goddess*, 94.

72. See Bolen, *Crossing to Avalon*, 24; Read, *Goddess Remembered*; Streep, *Sanctuaries*, 200; Abrahamsen, "Essays in Honor of Gimbutas," 73; Rose, "Black Madonnas," 18.

73. Neslen, *The Origin*, 47; Eisler, "Chalice and the Blade," 7; Austen, *Heart of the Goddess*, xviii. This belief that patriarchy is currently self-destructing is sometimes accompanied by the conviction that things will get worse before they get better. As Elizabeth Gould Davis explains in *The First Sex*, "The ages of masculism are now drawing to a close. Their dying days are lit up by a final flare of universal violence and despair such as the world has seldom before seen" (339).

74. Stephenson, *Women's Roots*, 327.

75. Canan, "Goddesses, Goddesses," in Marler, ed., *Realm of the Ancestors*, 568; Stein, *Dreaming the Past*, 118; Brooke Medicine Eagle, "Introduction," in Francia, *Dragontime*, xiii; Spretnak, "Female Psyche/Soma"; Walker, *Skeptical Feminist*, 128; Read, *Goddess Remembered*.

76. Christ, *Rebirth of the Goddess*, 164–65.

77. Mor and Sjöö, "Respell the World," 21; Shekhinah Mountainwater, *Moonspell* (self-published pamphlet, 1983), 2–3; Stein, *Dreaming the Past*, 149; Zsuzsanna Budapest, quoted in Adler, *Drawing Down the Moon*, 183.

78. Davis, *First Sex*, 18. Descriptions of utopian futures can be found in Eisler, *Chalice and the Blade*, 198–203; Walker, *Skeptical Feminist*, 265–77; Starhawk, *Truth or Dare*, 334–36.

4. The Eternal Feminine

1. Bolen, *Crossing to Avalon*, 52–53; Margaret Roy, "Politics of Women's Power," in Matriarchy Study Group, ed., *Politics of Matriarchy*, 47; Henes, *Mythology*; Noble, *Shakti Woman*, 6; Wilshire, *Virgin Mother Crone*, 123.

2. See, for example, "Oneness," a newsgroup posting by Joan, http://boris.qub.ac.-uk/archives/fox/fox-12–1995/0002.html, November 1995; Sjöö, *New Age and Armageddon*, 15; Iglehart, *Womanspirit*, 146–47.

3. Wilshire, *Virgin Mother Crone*, 272–73; Spretnak, "Female Psyche/Soma." Spretnak calls this "the matriarchal uncertainty principle."

4. Alpert, "Mother Right," 92; Mackey, *Horses at the Gate*, 136–54.

5. It has been my impression in researching the feminist spirituality movement (in which matriarchal myth is especially prevalent) that there are a disproportionate number of childless women, whether married or single, heterosexual or lesbian. Silverskye, a former goddess worshipper, complains in a newsgroup posting that "sometimes, Goddess spirituality seems like a reversion to the 'biology is destiny' argument, as if womanhood meant motherhood and birthing only. I chose not to have kids. I get a little tired of birthing imagery sometimes!" ("The Madeline Threads," http://boris/qub.ac.uk/archives/fox/fox-01–1996/0163.html, January 1996).

6. Meinrad Craighead, quoted in Gadon, *Once and Future Goddess*, 241.

7. Carson, *Goddesses and Wise Women*, 4. Focusing on menstruation also has the potential to offend, however, since not all women menstruate. Feminist matriarchalists apologize for this also. For example, in *Dragontime*, Luisa Francia insists that all women can participate in menstrual rituals, whether they are menstruating at that time or not, or even if they are past menopause or lack a uterus (81).

8. Göttner-Abendroth, *Dancing Goddess*, 225. It is also considerably easier to romanticize childbirth now that it is relatively safer. At least in the middle and upper classes of the industrialized world where feminist matriarchalist myth thrives, one can choose whether or not to experience childbirth and can be assured that one will almost certainly live through it. Though some feminist matriarchalists have rhetorically located the power of childbirth in its stance between life and death (see especially Noble, *Shakti Woman*, 68), the fact remains that people are less likely to view childbirth as an awesome miracle when there is a good chance that it will kill them or their loved ones (see King, *Women and Spirituality*, 80).

9. Murdock, *Heroine's Journey*, 173–74; Dexter, *Whence the Goddesses*,183; Walker, *Skeptical Feminist*, 16–17; Chesler, "Amazon Legacy," in Spretnak, ed., *Politics of Women's Spirituality*, 101.

10. Spretnak, ed., *Politics of Women's Spirituality*, 571; Davis, *First Sex*, 335–36; Gaube and von Pechmann, *Magie, Matriarchat, und Marienkult*, 211.

11. Stone, *Return of the Goddess;* Walker, *Skeptical Feminist*, 90; Shinell, "Women's Primacy," in Heresies Collective, ed., *Great Goddess*, 49; Barbara Starrett, "The Metaphors of Power," in Spretnak, ed., *Politics of Women's Spirituality*, 187–88.

12. Davis, *First Sex*, 34–35. See also Neslen, *The Origin*, 44; Shinell, "Woman's Primacy," in Heresies Collective, ed., *Great Goddess*, 46; Pollack, *Body of the Goddess*, 22.

13. Ranck, *Cakes for the Queen of Heaven* [Delphi], 39; Miles, *Women's History of the*

World, 3. See also Sherfey, *Female Sexuality,* 141. In her review article "Hormones, Sex, and Gender," Carol Worthman says that recent embryological research renders the "female default model" obsolete. It is now thought that sex determination does not follow a "switch model," where at a certain point in fetal development males are switched onto another track, but rather that it follows a "guided-path model," in which sex differences are part of fetal development before the differentation of their sex organs (604).

14. See, for example, Starhawk, *Dreaming the Dark,* 11; Zsuzsanna Budapest, quoted in Kimball, *Women's Culture,* 240–41; Noble, "Shakti Woman," 28; Paper, *Through the Earth Darkly,* 266.

15. Noble, *Motherpeace,* 201, and *Shakti Woman,* 235; Sjöö, *New Age and Armageddon,* 212.

16. Woolger and Woolger, *Goddess Within,* 10; Iglehart, *Womanspirit,* xiii; Poth, *Goddess Speaks,* 4; Murdock, *Heroine's Journey,* 156.

17. Starhawk, quoted in Edelson, "Story Box," 60.

18. Eisler, "Rediscovering Our Past," in Marler, ed., *Realm of the Ancestors,* 336; Eisler, *Sacred Pleasure,* 21, 403–405.

19. Wilshire, *Virgin Mother Crone,* 5, 277.

20. Judd, "Myths of the Golden Age," in Keller, ed., *Views of Women's Lives,* 54.

21. Eisler, *Chalice and the Blade,* xix–xx, and "Rediscovering Our Past," in Marler, ed., *Realm of the Ancestors,* 335–36; Eisler and Loye, *Partnership Way,* 179, 183–85. Another such table, "Categories of Opposition in Matriarchy and Patriarchy," can be found in Ruth, *Take Back the Light,* 132–33.

22. Alpert, "Mother Right," 91; Reis, *Through the Goddess,* 18; Shinell, "Woman's Primacy," in Heresies Collective, ed., *Great Goddess,* 46. An exception is Christine Downing, who believes that it might be desirable to free ourselves from "thinking always primarily along this fault line" of gender. However, she also cautions that "fantasies of nongenderedness are fantasies which deny otherness, separation, finitude, and particularity," and as such, are unrealistic *(Women's Mysteries,* 40, 76).

23. Chodorow, *Reproduction of Mothering.* See also Starrett, "Metaphors of Power," in Spretnak, ed., *Politics of Women's Spirituality,* 188.

24. See Gross, *Feminism and Religion,* 23; Christ, "Eliade and the Feminist Paradigm Shift," 75; Lerner, "Writing Women into History," 7.

25. Socialist matriarchalists, in contrast, do insist that gender as we know it is a patriarchal invention. See, for example, Coontz and Henderson, eds., *Women's Work,* 1; Leacock, "Origins of Gender Inequality," 267; Gailey, "Evolutionary Perspectives," 54; Dobbins, *From Kin to Class,* 7–8.

26. Appiah, *In My Father's House,* 175; Grosz, *Volatile Bodies,* 208. See also Cott, "Feminist Theory," 59; Sered, "Ideology, Autonomy, and Sisterhood," 500–503; Joan Scott, cited in Kristol, "Just the Facts," 41. Difference feminism is the most general term available for those feminists who emphasize sex differences and female

"specialness" in their political programs. However, there are other terms available that describe the type of feminism held in favor by feminist matriarchalists. Judith Clavir's term "metaphysical feminism" (Eisenstein, *Contemporary Feminist Thought*, 134) applies to feminist matriarchalists, as does Jean Bethke Elshtain's "sex polarity" ("New Feminist Scholarship," 15).

27. Jordanova, *Sexual Visions*, 21. See also Micaela di Leonardo, cited in Conkey and Tringham, "Archaeology and the Goddess," 234; Silvia Bovenschen, quoted in Walters, "Caught in the Web," 29. On women's exclusion from historical processes, see Talalay, "Feminist Boomerang," 173; Riley, *"Am I That Name?"* 103; Purkiss, *Witch in History*, 46; Blok, "Sexual Asymmetry," 11, 39–40. Though feminist matriarchalists are eager to buy their way back into history by putting matriarchy and patriarchy on a linear timeline, one can't fail to notice the relative stasis of prehistory, during which motherhood was the hub of society and the locus of religion, as compared to the dramatic events touched off by the patriarchal revolution.

28. Ortner, *Making Gender*, 179–80, and "Is Female to Male," 10; Simone de Beauvoir, quoted in King, "Healing the Wounds," 110. Others who have made this critique of feminist matriarchalist thought include Walters, "Caught in the Web," 25–26; Denfeld, *New Victorians*, 143; Nelson, *Gender in Archaeology*, 161; Pateman, *Sexual Contract*, 219; Biehl, *Rethinking Eco-feminist Politics*, 13, 16–17; Hewitt, *Critical Theory of Religion*, 201–2.

29. Bolen, *Crossing to Avalon*, 242. The term pseudomen comes from Kim Chernin's *Reinventing Eve* (xv).

30. Murdock, *Heroine's Journey*, 1–2, 7, 9, 14, 73.

31. Perera, *Descent to the Goddess*, 7–8.

32. Chernin, *Reinventing Eve*, xv.

33. Dworkin, *Right-Wing Women*, 206–207.

34. Kwame Anthony Appiah makes this point in distinguishing between "racialism," the belief that there is a "racial essence" which entails "moral and intellectual dispositions," and "racism," the belief that certain races are to be preferred to others because of these differential moral and intellectual dispositions. He suggests that the first is a question of fact (or in this case, of factual error), the second of value *(In My Father's House,* 13).

35. If, as Sherry Ortner suggests, "gender is itself centrally a prestige system," differential value for the genders may be unavoidable *(Making Gender,* 143).

36. For its role in the Nazi Holocaust, see Davis, "Goddess and the Academy," 62.

37. Kidd, *Dance of the Dissident Daughter,* 2–3. For a critique of this view, see Moore, *Feminism and Anthropology,* 190, 196; Sherry Ortner, "Gender and Sexuality in Hierarchical Societies," in Ortner and Whitehead, eds., *Sexual Meanings,* 397, 401.

38. Worthman, "Hormones, Sex, and Gender," 607.

39. Bleier, *Science and Gender,* 94.

40. Bleier, *Science and Gender*, 94, 104–5; Morelli, "Growing up Female," 212; Mann, *The Difference*, 23.

41. The human ability to negotiate the basic facts of biological life—through cultural innovation—is arguably the central defining feature of our species. It, more than anything else, is what explains the fact that we have covered the globe, adapting to climates ranging from deserts to jungles to arctic tundra. Thanks to Linda van Blerkom of the Anthropology Department at Drew University for an illuminating discussion of this point.

42. Goldberg, "Status of Women."

43. Gross, *Feminism and Religion*, 163.

44. Schor, "Feminist and Gender Studies," 277–78; Laqueur, *Making Sex*, viii, 11, 152–53. See also Pateman, *Sexual Contract*, 225.

45. Vicki Noble, quoted in Wynne, *Womanspirit Sourcebook*, 261. See also Virginia Beane Rutter, "Marija Gimbutas: Archaeologist of the Feminine Soul," in Marler, ed., *Realm of the Ancestors*, 600; Hopkins, *Great Mother Earth*. Elsewhere Noble seems to say that women do have a special access to the feminine, through the "blood mysteries" of the female body *(Shakti Woman,* 11).

46. Judith Butler, cited in Morris, "All Made Up," 572–73. The classic formulation of this position is Judith Butler's *Gender Trouble*.

47. Salvatore Cucchiari, "The Gender Revolution and the Transition from Bisexual Horde to Patrilocal Band: The Origins of Gender Hierarchy," in Ortner and Whitehead, eds., *Sexual Meanings*, 52; Appiah, *In My Father's House*, 13; Appiah, "Race," 276–77. As Appiah points out, the presumed existence of other racial traits does not downgrade the absolute primacy of skin color, for "if, without evidence about his or her impulses, we can say who is a Negro, than it cannot be part of what it is to be a Negro that he or she has them; rather it must be an a posteriori claim that people of a common race, defined by descent and biology, have impulses, for whatever reason, in common" (33).

48. Riley, *"Am I That Name?"* 1–2, 112.

49. Coward, *Patriarchal Precedents*, 286; Verena Stolcke, "Is Sex to Gender as Race is to Ethnicity?" in del Valle, ed., *Gendered Anthropology*, 18–19; Appiah, "Race," 276.

50. Delphy, *Close to Home*, 23.

51. Riley, *"Am I That Name?"* 2–3.

52. Downing, *Women's Mysteries*, 19–20.

53. Millicent Fawcett, quoted in Sheila Ryan Johansson, "'Herstory' as History: A New Field or Another Fad?" in Carroll, ed., *Liberating Women's History*, 403.

5. Finding Gender in Prehistory

1. On the face of it, it seems suspicious that literate cultures, which by their very nature are better documented, should all turn out to be male dominated, while pre-

literate, more poorly documented cultures are supposed to have been matriarchal. Feminist matriarchalists never suggest that the skill of writing can only develop under social conditions of male dominance—in fact some suggest it was already in use in matriarchal societies (see chapter 3)—so it seems a peculiar coincidence that matriarchies should turn out to be preliterate. In *The Alphabet Versus the Goddess*, Leonard Shlain suggests that there is a direct correlation between literacy and patriarchy, which would explain why matriarchal cultures are not documented textually. I suspect that this view will soon be adopted by feminist matriarchalists, since it provides an explanation of the coincidence of literacy and the patriarchal revolution that is not demeaning to women.

2. Noble, *Shakti Woman*, 173; Christ, "Eliade and the Feminist Paradigm Shift," 77–78.

3. Frazer, *Golden Bough*, viii–ix; McLennan, "Early History of Man," 541–42; Morgan, *Ancient Society*, vii. Sue Blundell notes that this habit of seeing other cultures as reflecting an earlier portion of one's own history was already present among the ancient Greeks and Romans *(Origins of Civilisation*, 198). The quintessential definition of "survivals" and their usage can be found in E. B. Tylor's *Primitive Culture* (16) and is summarized in Tambiah, *Magic, Science, Religion*, 44.

4. An early, and still one of the best critiques of "survivals" doctrine can be found in Boas, "Limitations of the Comparative Method," 277.

5. Marvin Harris makes the case for continuing to regard "contemporary primitive groups" as "surviving stone-age cultures" in *The Rise of Anthropological Theory* (154–55).

6. Conkey with Williams, "Original Narratives," 105; Gill, "Making Them Speak," 7; Keesing, "Exotic Readings of Cultural Texts." I thank my anthropologist brother-in-law, Robert Wolfe, for his explanation of the Kamchatka syndrome.

7. Some anthropologists sought to work around this conundrum by becoming more analytically precise about what constitutes women's social status and how it can be properly assessed. Arguing that women's status is made up of many things, they divided it, for example, into "their productive activities and control over production, their formal authority and decision-making power in sacred and secular domains . . . [and] their relative cultural valuation/devaluation" (Maureen Giovanni, in Leacock, "Women's Status," 262). One anthropologist, Martin King Whyte, developed fifty-two different scales—including such items as female infanticide, authority over children, menstrual taboos, control of property, sexual double standards, etc.—against which women's status relative to men's could be measured. But applying these scales to ninety-three culture groups, Whyte came to the daunting conclusion that "we can find no evidence for the existence of any general 'status of women' complex that varies consistently from culture to culture." In a phrase, he argued, "there is no such thing as *the* status of women" *(Status of Women*, 10, 116, 169). Other feminist efforts to dissect the various elements of the status of women can be found in Johansson, "'Herstory' as History," in Carroll, ed., *Liberating*

Women's History; Janssen-Jurreit, *Sexism,* 89; Schlegel, *Sexual Stratification,* 3; and Ortner, *Making Gender,* 140–41.

8. The best twentieth-century example of this is the various ethnographies of Australian aborigines, which report wildly different statuses for women even within the same population groups. For a review of this literature, see Merlan, "Gender in Aboriginal Social Life."

9. Ortner, *Making Gender,* 18, 141, 146. See also Moore, *Feminism and Anthropology,* 30. Ortner discusses the entire "status of women" debate within anthropology in her article "Gender Hegemonies," included in the *Making Gender* volume. She draws a fairly sharp distinction between differential prestige for men—which by itself, she argues, makes a society male dominant—and any power that women may actually wield behind the scenes (142).

10. Schlegel, *Sexual Stratification,* 264. Another example of this phenomenon is this description of the position of women among the Agta of the Philippine Islands offered by anthropologists Agnes Estioko-Griffin and P. Bion Griffin: "They . . . control the distribution of their acquired food, sharing first with their own nuclear family and extended family, then trading as they see fit. They may procure nonfood goods as they desire. Men may do the same; generally spouses discuss what work to do, what needs should be satisfied, and who will do what. . . . Women are as vocal and as critical in reaching decisions as are men" ("Woman the Hunter: The Agta," in Dahlberg, ed., *Woman the Gatherer,* 136). This is a fitting description of the majority of American families, even some that most feminists would regard as reprehensibly sexist.

11. Silverblatt, "Women in States," 429; Marianne Gullestad, "Home Decoration as Popular Culture," in del Valle, ed., *Gendered Anthropology,* 128. See also Yanagisako and Collier, "Unified Analysis," 35, 48; Morris, "All Made Up," 570.

12. Stuart Piggott, quoted in Finley, "Archaeology and History," 169–70.

13. Nurit S. Goldman-Finn, Sandra L. Dunavan, and J. Benjamin Fitzhugh, "Introduction," in Bacus et al., eds., *Gendered Past,* 3. See also Alison Wylie, "Foreword," in Bacus et al., eds., *Gendered Past,* ix. The seminal article which critiqued the implicit sexism of earlier archaeological interpretation was "Archaeology and the Study of Gender" by Margaret Conkey and Janet Spector, which was published in 1984.

14. See Cheryl Claassen, "Questioning Gender: An Introduction," in Claassen, ed., *Exploring Gender through Archaeology,* 3. The most frequently cited case of a third gender is that of the "two-spirit" or *berdache* found in one form or another in several Native American cultures. Others include the *hijra* of India, the *kathoey* of Thailand, the *mahu* of Hawaii, the *xanith* of Oman, and the *sarombavy* of the Malagasy Republic (see Herdt, ed., *Third Sex;* Morris, "All Made Up," 570; Weston, "Lesbian/Gay Studies," 350–53). These "third genders" are not all the same by any means, but they most commonly refer to men who to some degree take on the outward signs of what that culture defines as femininity, either in dress, occupation,

kinship status, or sexuality. A description of the range of genetic and morphological "intersex" anomalies can be found in Fausto-Sterling, *Myths of Gender*, 77–88.

15. Most of the much-celebrated cases of third genders are susceptible to critique. It is not clear whether what has been observed ethnographically is the exotic (to us) presence of a "third gender" or merely what we already—less prosaically—name transvestism or homosexuality. Certainly the Polynesian examples cited by Niko Besnier sound hauntingly like stereotypical American images of effeminate male homosexuals, right down to the taunting of male children with the name of these "third gendered" individuals as a form of discipline ("Polynesian Gender Liminality," in Herdt, ed., *Third Sex*, 310). All these "third genders" lack the typical linguistic accoutrement of gender: a set of pronouns and/or kinship terms unique to them. They are also more frequently biological males than females (Weston, "Lesbian/Gay Studies," 354). Furthermore, since "third gender" categories are so frequently derived from masculine and feminine gender characteristics, it could be said with a certain justice that "far from undermining the two-gender model, [they] underwrite it" (Cucchiari, "Gender Revolution," 34). In short, I don't think it is untoward to assume—recognizing that we may be wrong—that when we dig up a female skeleton we are looking at a woman.

16. Catherine Roberts, "A Critical Approach to Gender as a Category of Analysis in Archaeology," in du Cros and Smith, eds., *Women and Archaeology*, 18. Conkey and Tringham, "Archaeology and the Goddess," 204; Engelstad, "Images of Power," 504–505; Barbara Bender, "Writing Gender," in Moore and Scott, eds., *Invisible People and Processes*, 180. The claim is frequently made that one can practice a "gendered archaeology" without attributing particular material remains to one sex or the other (see, for example, Shelby Brown, "Feminist Research in Archaeology: What Does it Mean? Why Is it Taking So Long?" in Rabinowitz and Richlin, eds., *Feminist Theory and the Classics*, 252; Bailey, "Representation of Gender," 216–17), though just how this would be done is rarely made clear, at least to the nonspecialist such as myself.

17. See, for example, Naomi R. Goldenberg, "Marija Gimbutas and the King's Archaeologist," in Marler, ed., *Realm of the Ancestors*, 45.

18. Bernard Wailes, quoted in Steinfels, "Idyllic Theory," C12. Shelby Brown argues that "professional disagreement with Gimbutas's view of a powerful gynocentric past is largely expressed through silence," adding that "Gimbutas is an 'insider' with an impressive record of excavation and publication, and she does not threaten the archaeological status quo by criticizing her colleagues" ("Feminist Research in Archaeology," in Rabinowitz and Richlin, eds., *Feminist Theory and the Classics*, 256). Most early criticism of Gimbutas by archaeologists appeared in book reviews (see, for example, Fagan, "Sexist View") or was offered informally in interviews with journalists (see Leslie, "Goddess Theory"; Knaster, "Raider of the Lost Goddess"; Steinfels, "Idyllic Theory"). An early article-length critique of Gimbutas's theories was offered by Brian Hayden ("Old Europe," in Bonanno, ed., *Archaeology and Fertility Cult*). There has been considerably less silence since Gimbutas's death in

1994. Archaeologists are much more likely to criticize Gimbutas vigorously now that she is gone and all that is left are her nonarchaeologically trained disciples.

19. Amy Richlin, "The Ethnographer's Dilemma and the Dream of a Lost Golden Age," in Rabinowitz and Richlin, eds., *Feminist Theory and the Classics*, 285.

20. Christ, *Rebirth of the Goddess*, 31, 34–35; Hodder, *Reading the Past*, 106.

21. Bell, *Reconstructing Prehistory*, 22, 28, 51–52. Problems with falsifiability arise perhaps most strongly when feminist matriarchalists reconstruct prehistory by offering evidence from memories of past lives, channelled information from disembodied spirits, or questionable sources of information such as the "collective unconscious" or "cellular memory," as they sometimes do (see, for example, Rigoglioso, "Awakening to the Goddess," 65; Stein, *Dreaming the Past*; Lucia Chiavola Birnbaum, "Marija Gimbutas and the Change of Paradigm," in Marler, ed., *Realm of the Ancestors*, 350; George, "Dark Moon," 31; Mor and Sjöö, "Respell the World," 18–19; Gadon, *Once and Future Goddess*, 261; Starhawk, *Truth or Dare*, 32). For the purposes of this book, I am going to rule all evidence of this kind inadmissible, on the grounds that it is not falsifiable: not that it is not true, or potentially true, or that its sources are unconventional. For it could well be that the collective unconscious exists, and that we all go fishing in it from time to time (while we are asleep, perhaps), pulling out stunningly detailed and accurate information about our prehistoric past, far richer than the pathetic scraps we are able to dig out of archaeological sites. But if what the collective unconscious tells you turns out to be different from what it tells me, who will—who can—referee our debate? There is simply no agreed upon method for adjudicating competing truth claims amongst different dreams, past lives, or disembodied spirits. (Such methods exist in some cultures which rely on dreams or trances to attain knowledge, but this is not the case in Western culture.)

6. The Case Against Prehistoric Matriarchies I: Other Societies, Early Societies

1. W. E. Roth, quoted in Leach, "Virgin Birth," 86–87; Malinowski, *Father in Primitive Psychology*, 12.

2. Malinowski, *Father in Primitive Psychology*, 70–71; 87–88, 93; Powell, *Social Structure in the Trobriands*, 277–78. An even later ethnographer, Annette Weiner, claimed that the official denial of physiological paternity in the Trobriands was a social mechanism directed toward "preventing shame and open conflict" under the circumstance of widely practiced extramarital sex *(Women of Value*, 122). Malinowski's comments on how Trobrianders believed pigs to reproduce were published in 1916; in the 1927 publication of *The Father in Primitive Psychology*, Malinowski stated that his earlier remarks were in error and that his Trobriand informants insisted that pigs, like humans, did not require sexual intercourse to become pregnant (63–64, 66). A few anthropologists continue to believe that some cultures are or were ignorant of a connection between sexual intercourse and conception; see Cucchiari, "Gender

Revolution," in Ortner and Whitehead, eds., *Sexual Meanings*, 45; Spiro, "Virgin Birth."

3. Dixon, "Virgin Birth" correspondence, 653−54; Leach, "Virgin Birth," 90, 119−20 n. 1.

4. Montagu, *Coming into Being*, 226, 332.

5. Delaney, "Meaning of Paternity," 497; René Grémaux, "Woman Becomes Man in the Balkans," in Herdt, ed., *Third Sex*, 268. Delaney notes that human reproduction was explained to her in 1950s America with these same metaphors of male/seed and female/earth. For descriptions of Aristotle's views of conception, see Laqueur, *Making Sex*, 41, 255 n. 36; Cantarella, *Pandora's Daughters*, 60.

6. Leach, "Virgin Birth," 93−94; Anderson and Zinsser, *History of Their Own*, 6; Mellaart, *Neolithic of the Near East*, 107, fig. 57. Riane Eisler calls the plaque from Çatalhöyük "a lesson in sex education, demonstrating that our Neolithic ancestors understood the connection between sexual intercourse and birth" *(Sacred Pleasure*, 63).

7. In my research on this issue, I was unable to find any ethnographies of groups that do not give fathers—whether biological or adoptive—strong and frequently decisive roles in relationship to their children. Many groups leave much of the basic caretaking work to women but still regard men as significantly and legitimately concerned with their children's welfare and able to make decisions on their behalf.

8. This transition is explained by some as being related to the rise of property, and men's desire to transmit it to their own progeny, but most feminist matriarchalists leave this transition virtually untheorized.

9. Ortner, "Gender and Sexuality," in Ortner and Whitehead, eds., *Sexual Meanings*. On the improved status of menopausal or otherwise sterile women, see Godelier, "Male Domination," 12−13; Murphy and Murphy, *Women of the Forest*, 105.

10. Schlegel, *Sexual Stratification*, 7. As Timothy Taylor notes, "child-rearing is hardly ever recognized as a job in market economic terms" *(Prehistory of Sex*, 205).

11. See, for example, Luisa Francia, "Dance of Life," anonymous spiritual feminist publication, 1; Chernin, *Reinventing Eve*, 174, 177−78; Walker, *Skeptical Feminist*, 51, 115, 186; Stein, *Women's Spirituality Book*, 6−7; Davis, *First Sex*, 148, 152−53; Deming, "Remembering."

12. Hiatt, "Pseudo-Procreation Rites," 77−80; Meigs, *Food, Sex, and Pollution*, 131−32; Cucchiari, "Gender Revolution," in Ortner and Whitehead, eds., *Sexual Meanings*, 33. In Wogeo, New Guinea, men periodically cut their penises and bleed into the ocean, explaining that they do so to rid their bodies of contamination, just as women rid their bodies of contamination by menstruating. In fact, the same word, *baras*, is used to refer to both menstruating women and men who have recently bled their penises (Hobgin, *Island of Menstruating Men*, 88). The same cleansing function is achieved among Sambia men by inducing bleeding from their noses (Herdt, *Guardians of the Flutes*, 64−65). Subincision as practiced among some Australian abo-

rigines seems to be a different matter. It is performed once, as an initiation rite, and permanently alters the penis. Some feminist matriarchalists who have discussed this ritual regard subincision as an effort to "make the penis more closely resemble the female vulva" (Davis, *First Sex*, 152–53; Judy Grahn, "From Sacred Blood to the Curse and Beyond," in Spretnak, ed., *Politics of Women's Spirituality*, 273), and anthropologist Ashley Montagu concurs, claiming that the subincised penis "is called by the same name as that of the female vulva" *(Natural Superiority of Women*, 20). But Philip Singer and Daniel Desole report that there is "no mention at all, either in a derogatory or favorable way, of the penis as vulva, or, in fact, of the penis resembling a vulva in either form or function." In fact, Singer and Desole make a rather persuasive case for regarding subincision as an effort to make human penises resemble those of kangaroos. They note that Australian aboriginal cultures stress erotic pleasure, and that in such a context, "the prolonged copulation of the kangaroo, up to two hours," would not go unnoticed. They also point out that subincision greatly enlarges the width of the penis, causing it to look more like a kangaroo's. In any event, subincision does not entail a great deal of bleeding, and thus is unlikely to be an explicit imitation of menstruation ("Australian Subincision Ceremony Reconsidered," 356–58).

13. Hiatt, "Pseudo-Procreation Rites," 77; Meigs, *Food, Sex, and Pollution*, 37, 131–32.

14. See Estioko-Griffin and Griffin, "Woman the Hunter," in Dahlberg, ed., *Woman the Gatherer*, 138–39; Gell, *Metamorphosis of the Cassowaries*, 94–95; Divale and Harris, "Male Supremacist Complex," 525; Poewe, "Universal Male Dominance," 116.

15. Mark N. Cohen and Sharon Bennett, "Skeletal Evidence for Sex Roles and Gender Hierarchies in Prehistory," in Miller, ed., *Sex and Gender Hierarchies*, 287; Naomi Hamilton, "Figurines, Clay Balls, Small Finds, and Burials" in Hodder, ed., *On the Surface*, 255; Theya Molleson and Peter Andrews, "The Human Remains," in *Çatalhöyük Newsletter*, ed. Ian Hodder, 4 (December 1997), http://catal.arch.-cam.ac.uk/catal/Newsletter4; Hays, "When is a Symbol Archaeologically Meaningful?" 84. These estimates are in close accord with ethnographic parallels. Anthropologists estimate life expectancy at birth for tribal peoples as being anywhere from seventeen to thirty-three, figures also typical in most parts of the world through the nineteenth century, and in many parts of the world yet today (see Cavalli-Sforza and Cavalli-Sforza, *Great Human Diasporas*, 8). This is in sharp contrast with the picture painted by feminist matriarchalists. Mary Mackey's novels of prehistoric matriarchy are filled with queens, priestesses, and elders in their fifties and sixties, some over ninety years old, not to mention the more commonplace mothers and grandmothers whose age must average between thirty and fifty, even if they had their children at a very young age (Mackey, *Year the Horses Came*, 64, 74, and *Horses at the Gate*, 258). Though some individuals in any population live to an advanced age, regardless of the average age at death (see Andrew T. Chamberlain, "Missing Stages of Life—Toward the Perception of Children in Archaeology," in Moore and Scott, eds., *Invisible People and Processes*, 249), it is still difficult to reconcile "the good life" which fem-

inist matriarchalists attribute to Paleolithic and Neolithic peoples with the fact that few women would live to see four decades.

16. DeMeo, "Origins and Diffusion of Patrism," 261; Feder and Park, *Human Antiquity*, 75. See also Gimbutas, "Women and Culture," in Plaskow and Christ, eds., *Weaving the Visions*, 64.

17. Mellaart, *Çatal Hüyük*, 60, 79, 208–209; Mellaart, *Neolithic of the Near East*, 101–102.

18. See Gadon, *Once and Future Goddess*, 27–28; Lerner, *Creation of Patriarchy*, 32–35; Eisler, *Chalice and the Blade*, 25.

19. Hamilton, "Figurines," in Hodder, ed., *On the Surface*, 257.

20. Hamilton, "Figurines," in Hodder, ed., *On the Surface*, 252, 262; Theya Molleson and Peter Andrews, "The Human Remains," in *Çatalhöyük Newsletter*, ed. Ian Hodder, 4 (December 1997), http://catal.arch.cam.ac.uk/catal/Newsletter4; Ian Hodder and Anita Louise, "Discussions with the Goddess Community," http://-catal.arch.cam.ac.uk/catal/goddess.html, n.d.

21. Mellaart, *Çatal Hüyük*, 205–206; Hamilton, "Figurines," in Hodder, ed., *On the Surface*, 254, 256.

22. Sherratt, "Mobile Resources," 14; Mellaart, *Çatal Hüyük*, 212.

23. Whyte, *Status of Women*, 171. Of the 1,179 societies in the HRAF files compiled by Murdock, 75 percent are patrilocal while only 10 percent are matrilocal (Divale and Harris, "Male Supremacist Complex," 521). I am using the term "patrilocal" to include residence with the husband's family and "matrilocal" to include residence with the wife's family rather than the more precise terms "virilocal" and "uxorilocal."

24. Rose, "Prehistoric Greece," 214–15; Murphy and Murphy, *Women of the Forest*, 76–77; Malinowski, *Father in Primitive Psychology*, 16–17; Hogbin, *Island of Menstruating Men*, 17–19, 99; Hultkrantz, *Native Religions*, 89–90; Thomas L. Jackson, "Pounding Acorn: Women's Production as Social and Economic Focus," in Gero and Conkey, eds., *Engendering Archaeology*, 318–19; Panoff, "Patrifiliation," 178–79; Janssen-Jurreit, *Sexism*, 66; Fluehr-Lobban, "Marxist Reappraisal," 348; Divale, *Matrilocal Residence*, 35, 194. Marvin Harris claims that there is "universal recognition of some degree of kinship with both maternal and paternal relatives, regardless of the nature of the unilineal rule *(Rise of Anthropological Theory*, 187).

25. Ortner, "Gender and Sexuality," in Ortner and Whitehead, eds., *Sexual Meanings*, ed. 400; Colin M. Turnbull, "Mbuti Womanhood," in Dahlberg, ed., *Woman the Gatherer*, 205–206.

26. Frayser, *Sexual Experience*, 355; Merlan, "Gender in Aboriginal Social Life," 28, 49; Raymond, review of *The Subordinate Sex*, 457.

27. Mann, *The Difference*, 211. The line of direction here is important, for sometimes goddesses are said to legitimize power for women, but just as often it is said

that goddesses were invented as a reflection of human women's power (see, for example, Johnson, *Lady of the Beasts*, 348–49; Miles, *Women's History of the World*, 17; Gimbutas, *Civilization of the Goddess*, 342; Judd, "Myths of the Golden Age," in Keller, ed., *Views of Women's Lives*, 58). The assumption that goddesses are projections of human women can lead to some rather ridiculous interpretations of goddess myths. For example, Ruby Rohrlich concludes that in early Sumer, women were "involved as warriors and generals" since in Sumerian myth Inanna slayed "the dragon Kur" ("State Formation," 90). One might as easily state that women in the first two millennia CE seem to have reproduced parthenogenetically, as reflected in the myth of the Virgin Mary giving birth to Jesus.

28. See chapter 3, note 42.

29. Lefkowitz, "New Cults of the Goddess," 266; Nicole Loraux, "What is a Goddess?" in Pantel, ed., *History of Women*, 35. Native Americans and aboriginal Australians have often been said to worship a supreme mother goddess above all other deities, but in both cases, it has been quite conclusively shown that "Mother Earth" was a creation of European ethnographers rather than native peoples (see Gill, *Mother Earth*; Gill, "Making Them Speak"; Swain, "Mother Earth Conspiracy," *Interpreting Aboriginal Religion*; Hamilton, "Knowledge and Misrecognition," in Gewertz, ed., *Myths of Matriarchy Reconsidered*, 62). John Stratton Hawley notes that Hindu goddesses "tend to be seen as close relatives of one another . . . in a way that is somehow less true of the male side of the Hindu pantheon" ("The Goddess in India," in Hawley and Wulff, eds., *Devī*, 6). This would hint at a sort of goddess monotheism (the presence of so many male gods alongside "the Goddess" notwithstanding). But one could also interpret the perceived unity of the goddesses as a revealing example of a general attitude that regards women as being more undifferentiated—more defined by their group status as females—and less individuated than men. Furthermore, in her article "The Western Kali," Rachel Fell McDermott suggests that this tendency to view the Hindu goddesses as representatives of "an overarching female power" did not develop until the sixth century CE, before which time a more traditional form of polytheism probably prevailed (in Hawley and Wulff, eds., *Devī*, 297).

30. Ras Shamra text, quoted in Heine, *Matriarchs*, 47; Frymer-Kensky, *Wake of the Goddesses*, 29; Motz, *Faces of the Goddess*, 12–13; Ralph W. Nicholas, "The Village Mother in Bengal," in Preston, ed., *Mother Worship*, 205–206.

31. Stern, *Prehistoric Europe*, 286. Goddesses sometimes function as warnings to men of the dangers women pose. For example, scholars of Hinduism have drawn a distinction between "small" goddesses, who are "beneficent and auspicious"—and, not incidentally, "controlled by males"—and "big" goddesses, who, since they are celibate, are independent of males and who are dangerous, death-dealing figures. As John Stratton Hawley concludes, "it is hard to consider Hindu visions of how the sexes may interact at the divine level without developing a powerful sense of men's fear of women. Such fear is often expressed as the desire to control" ("Goddess in India," in Hawley and Wulff, eds., *Devī*, 14). On the other hand, Hawley also notes

that not all Hindu goddesses fit this schema and may be both independent of males and benevolently maternal (15–18).

32. Cynthia Ann Humes, "Glorifying the Great Goddess or Great Woman?" in King, ed., *Women and Goddess Traditions*, 51–52; Hawley, "Goddess in India," in Hawley and Wulff, eds., *Devī*, 23 (Hawley is citing Humes's work). Humes found exceptions to this rule, women who saw the goddess as empowering for women, but they had all "been educated in westernized Christian schools or had actually lived in the West" and "already occupied a privileged position in society."

33. See Frymer-Kensky, *Wake of the Goddesses*, vii. James Preston remarks on the absence of Mariolatry in Protestantism, where women's rights have been most stressed within Christianity *(Mother Worship*, 338).

34. Eisler, *Chalice and the Blade*, xvi; Riane Eisler, cited in Mason, *Unnatural Order*, 157; Kidd, *Dissident Daughter*, 168. See also Perenna, "Matriarchal Manifesto," in Matriarchy Study Group, ed., *Politics of Matriarchy*, 17; Ranck, *Cakes for the Queen of Heaven*, 28–29, 31 [UUA]; Daly, *Beyond God the Father*, 13, 19.

35. Woolger and Woolger, *Goddess Within*, 18–19; Lerner, *Creation of Patriarchy*, 160. Feminist matriarchalists are not directly contradicting themselves when they revel in the goddess worship of classical Greek culture, for they regard classical goddess worship as "the afterglow of Old European times" (Haarmann, "Writing in the Ancient Mediterranean," in Marler, ed., *Realm of the Ancestors*, 108–109). What they celebrate in classical religion is not the goddess worship of a patriarchal culture, but the persistence of matriarchal religion into patriarchal times. Thus it is possible to condemn Athenian patriarchy but still notice its "'softer,' more creative, more 'feminine' underside" (Eisler, "Rediscovering Our Past," in Marler, ed., *Realm of the Ancestors*, 341). Also, not all classicists agree with the dismal picture I have painted here for women in ancient Greece. Marilyn Skinner, for example, suggests the possibility that "women's domestic sphere may have constituted a separate and autonomous culture . . . that did not necessarily acquiesce in the attitudes of the dominant male culture" ("Greek Women and the Metronymic," 41). See also Monique Saliou, "The Process of Women's Subordination in Primitive and Archaic Greece," in Coontz and Henderson, eds., *Women's Work*, 171; Lefkowitz, *Women in Greek Myth*, 133–34.

36. Dexter, *Whence the Goddesses*, 85. An especially difficult test case for feminist matriarchalists is Mariolatry. Their theory would seem to predict that worship of Mary would at least mitigate the ill effects of patriarchal Christianity, and some matriarchalists argue that it has done just that. For example, Thomas Berry sees Western culture becoming more patriarchal in the sixteenth century, at the same time that Mary "was rejected as a 'pagan' intrusion into the Christian world" *(Dream of the Earth*, 150). However, the Catholic priests who authored the *Malleus Mallificarum*, and thus kicked off several centuries of witch-hunting that preferentially targeted women, were "ardent worshippers of Mary" (Heine, *Matriarchs*, 143).

37. Heine, *Matriarchs*, 105; Ena Campbell, "The Virgin of Guadalupe and the Female-Self-Image," in Preston, ed., *Mother Worship*, 10, 18, 21. Tullio Tentori makes a similar report for Marian worship in Naples, Italy ("An Italian Religious Feast," in Preston, ed., *Mother Worship*, 112).

38. Whyte, *Status of Women*, 7, 103. Peggy Reeves Sanday comes to different conclusions in her ethnographic survey, claiming that male gods correlate with male power, while goddess worship or mixed-sex pantheons correlate with greater status for women *(Female Power)*.

39. Leibowitz, "Sexual Division of Labor," 125, 139; Divale and Harris, "Male Supremacist Complex," 524. On horticultural divisions of labor, see Murphy and Murphy, *Women of the Forest*, 137–38; Reichel-Dolmatoff, *Amazonian Cosmos*, 3, 11; Tooker, "Women in Iroquois Society," 121; Lancaster, *Goba*, 186–87.

40. Milisauskas, *European Prehistory*, 172–73. It is possible of course that these items did not belong to the deceased, but were bestowed on them as part of funerary customs (see Hodder, *Reading the Past*, 53; Hayden, "Observing Prehistoric Women," in Claassen, ed., *Exploring Gender through Archaeology*, 37). Thus they may not reflect a sexual division of labor at all.

41. Faris, "Form to Content," 106; Burton and White, "Sexual Division of Labor," 569. For additional comments on the sexual division of labor, see Spector, "Male/Female Task Differentiation," 124; Liebowitz, "Sexual Division of Labor," 125.

42. Danziger, "Man and Language in Prehistory"; Aaby, "Engels and Women," 35; Leibowitz, "Sexual Division of Labor," 127.

43. Whyte, *Status of Women*, 153, 155; Marshall Sahlins, quoted in Flanagan, "'Egalitarian' Societies," 246; Begler, "Sex, Status, and Authority," 573; Flanagan, "'Egalitarian' Societies," 258. Earlier anthropologists regarded sex as a "natural" axis of inequality, and thus not worth noting as an exception to the egalitarianism of "egalitarian" societies (see Taylor, "'Brothers' in Arms?" 37).

44. Bonvillain, *Women and Men*, 21, 29; Begler, "Sex, Status, and Authority," 585; Marjorie Shostak, quoted in Marvin Harris, "The Evolution of Human Gender Hierarchies: A Trial Formulation," in Miller, ed., *Sex and Gender Hierarchies*, 59; Turnbull, "Mbuti Womanhood," in Dahlberg, ed., *Woman the Gatherer*, 207, 210; Janssen-Jurreit, *Sexism*, 89. For general statements on male dominance in foraging societies, see Ronald Cohen, quoted in Leacock, "Women's Status," 258; Rosaldo, "Use and Abuse," 411–12. Some feminist anthropologists and feminist matriarchalists, most notably Eleanor Leacock, have argued that none of these examples can be trusted to reflect what prehistory was like because the groups under observation had all already come under the unhealthy influence of the West. (A summary of Leacock's arguments on colonial influence can be found in Moore, *Feminism and Anthropology*, 31–32.) Before ethnographers had a chance to see them in their undefiled state, they had been missionized and colonized, or even been the victims of full-out imperialist conquest. This argument fails on several grounds. First, some ethnographers have shown that Western contact has improved women's status in

some cultures (see, for example, Ann McElroy, quoted in Leacock, "Women's Status," 264; Cara Richards, quoted in Sempowski, "Differential Mortuary Treatments," 35–36). Second, it is quite clear that male domination and/or violence against women predated Western contact in some cultures (see, for example, Matthew Spriggs, "Quantifying Women's Oppression in Prehistory: The Aneityum [Vanuatu] Case," in du Cros and Smith, eds., *Women and Archaeology*, 143–44; Herdt, *Guardians of the Flutes*). And finally, the argument fails not only on empirical grounds, but on theoretical ones, since it is unclear how we might discriminate between "products of the colonial experience" and those that "bespeak a persisting tradition" (Marilyn Strathern, quoted in Leacock, "Women's Status," 267). These can sometimes be sorted out: we may know that it was European imperialists who brought agriculture, horses, Christianity, or a cash economy to a native culture. But things are much more murky in the case of gender relations, which presumably existed in one form or another long before any Western contact. Without a preexisting theory to decide exactly what effect Western contact would necessarily have on gender relations—or direct evidence of precontact life—it is arbitrary to assign certain patterns (i.e., male dominance) to colonial influence and others (i.e., relative sexual equality) to aboriginal life (see Ortner, *Making Gender*, 142–43).

45. On foraging societies, see Lee and DeVore, cited in Aaby, "Engels and Women," 27; Chapman, *Drama and Power*, 63. On horticultural societies, see Aaby, "Engels and Women," 27; Ehrenberg, *Women in Prehistory*, 99, 155. For general statements regarding the correlation between women's work and women's status, see Peggy Reeves Sanday, cited in Parker and Parker, "Myth of Male Superiority," 293; Maureen Giovanni, quoted in Leacock, "Women's Status," 262.

46. See Delphy, *Close to Home*, 61.

47. Reichel-Dolmatoff, *Amazonian Cosmos*, 3, 11; Murphy and Murphy, *Women of the Forest*, 62, 64; Murphy, "Social Structure and Sex Antagonism," 92; Weiner, *Women of Value*, 137; Parker and Parker, "Myth of Male Superiority," 292; Divale and Harris, "Male Supremacist Complex," 524.

48. Tooker, "Women in Iroquois Society," 115–17; Murphy and Murphy, *Women of the Forest*, 5–6, 60–62, 78, 87, 106, 108, 127–28, 131–32; Murphy, "Social Structure and Sex Antagonism," 93. Rape and forced sex are so common among the Mundurucú that Mundurucú males joke "we tame our women with the banana" (Murphy, "Social Structure and Sex Antagonism," 95). Martin King Whyte undertook a cross-cultural investigation of relationships between women's control over the products of their labor and women's status in other spheres, and found them "generally very weak" *(Status of Women*, 145).

49. Until very recently, it was quite common for cultural anthropologists and archaeologists, like feminist matriarchalists, to defend or at least proclaim the theory that women invented agriculture (see, for example, Durant, *Story of Civilization*, 8, 34; Haaland and Haaland, "Levels of Meaning," 299). Given that there is no evidence for this theory and no way to verify it, one has to assume that these scholars were mouthing the theory mainly to throw women a bone, especially after all of the

major evolutionary advances of the human race had been handed over to "man the hunter." The irony is that once women were accorded this leading role in agriculture, the Neolithic revolution began to be viewed as the proverbial fall from paradise rather than as the great switching point between a primitive, apelike existence and "civilization." This is a particularly sharp irony since one of the best things about foraging societies, according to many commentators, was the relative equality it offered to women. Thus women are now blamed for creating the conditions of their own oppression.

50. See Crabtree, "Gender Hierarchies."

51. Bridges, "Changes in Activities"; Cassidy, cited in Cohen and Bennett, "Skeletal Evidence," in Miller, ed., *Sex and Gender Hierarchies*, 277–78; Goodman et al., cited in Cohen and Bennett, "Skeletal Evidence," in Miller, ed., *Sex and Gender Hierarchies*, 277–78.

52. Ammerman and Cavalli-Sforza, *Neolithic Transition*, 9–10, 63, 71, 133–34; Cavalli-Sforza and Cavalli-Sforza, *Great Human Diasporas*, 16, 138, 149; Washburn and Lancaster, "Evolution of Hunting," 303.

53. See Ortner, "Gender and Sexuality," in Ortner and Whitehead, eds., *Sexual Meanings*, 397.

54. In her textbook, *Women and Men: Cultural Constructs of Gender*, Nancy Bonvillain suggests that gender equality is "most likely" to be found in foraging societies, while gender inequality is "most marked" in complex state societies (3). Whatever the validity of these statements as generalizations, they are certainly not universal rules of the sort that could justify speculations about *the* status of women in prehistory.

55. Divale and Harris, "Male Supremacist Complex," 527; Steven J. Mithen, "The Mesolithic Age," in Cunliffe, ed., *Oxford Illustrated Prehistory*, 121; Hayden, "Archaeological Evaluation." Archaeologist Peter Warren suggests that the cut marks found on some children's skeletons from Minoan Crete resemble those found on slaughtered animals, and indeed these skeletons were found with the skeletons of slaughtered animals (Biehl, *Rethinking Eco-feminist Politics*, 38–39; Hewitt, *Critical Theory of Religion*, 191; for other comments on possible human sacrifice, see Anthony, "Nazi and Eco-feminist Prehistories," 94; Meskell, "Goddesses," 79). Marija Gimbutas has herself noted the possible "ritual offering of small children" or "dedicatory sacrifice" at certain Neolithic sites, though she elsewhere suggests that cut marks on skeletons can be attributed to burial practices rather than human sacrifice (cited in Biehl, *Rethinking Eco-feminist Politics*, 32; Gimbutas, *Civilization of the Goddess*, 292).

56. Gimbutas, *Civilization of the Goddess*, 352, "World View of the Culture of the Goddess," 46, and *Age of the Great Goddess;* Anthony, "Nazi and Eco-feminist Prehistories," 93–94, and quoted in Denfeld, *New Victorians*, 140.

57. Gimbutas, *Civilization of the Goddess*, 55, 160, 324, 352; Anthony, "Nazi and Eco-feminist Prehistories, 93–94; Milisauskas, *European Prehistory*, 177; Hayden, "Archaeological Evaluation." Elaborate fortifications are also noted for the Middle

Eastern site of Jericho as early as the eighth millennium BCE (Mellaart, *Çatal Hüyük*, 20; Motz, *Faces of the Goddess*, 36).

58. Harris, *Cultural Anthropology*, 246; Arthur Demarest, quoted in Wilford, "What Doomed the Maya?" C1, C10.

59. Such burials have actually been found in ancient Sumer (in the early dynastic period, 2600–2350 BCE), but so have burials in which a man was interred with murdered females. As these are royal tombs, the operative distinction would seem to be class rather than sex (Susan Pollock, "Women in a Men's World: Images of Sumerian Women," in Gero and Conkey, eds., *Engendering Archaeology*, 378). Feminist matriarchalists sometimes argue that these so-called *suttee* burials, when the principal corpse is male, are an early indicator of patriarchal revolution (see, for example, Dexter, *Whence the Goddesses*, 35; Gimbutas, "First Wave," 285, 304–305). Mary Mackey describes this form of burial for a patriarchal chief from the Sea of Grass (*Year the Horses Came*, 376). However, this type of burial is relatively rare; it is certainly not as though it suddenly became the general custom among, say, the late Neolithic peoples of the Russian steppes.

7. The Case Against Prehistoric Matriarchies II: Prehistoric Art and Architecture

1. Leroi-Gourhan, cited in Pollack, *Body of the Goddess*, 70; Jung, *Man and His Symbols*, 3.

2. Davis, "Goddess and the Academy," 52; Patricia Reis, quoted in Wynne, *Womanspirit Sourcebook*, 179.

3. See Roosevelt, "Interpreting Female Images," 2; Lauren Talalay, quoted in Osborne, "Women Warriors," 53.

4. Carol Christ has argued that the use of diminutives—"figurines" and "statuettes"—in reference to these artifacts "serves to trivialize them." However, they are almost all small, as Christ herself notes ("Eliade and the Feminist Paradigm Shift," 84). I intend no disrespect with the use of these terms.

5. Gro Mandt, "The Women of Vingen: Aspects of Gender Ideology in Rock Art," in Marler, ed., *Realm of the Ancestors*, 166. It is unquestionably Carl Jung, whose view of symbols has been absorbed by many feminist matriarchalists, who most influenced this method of deriving information from symbols. Gimbutas's first book on goddess symbology, *The Gods and Goddesses of Old Europe* [1974], explicitly drew upon the work of Erich Neumann, one of Jung's disciples. Though Gimbutas later ceased to acknowledge Neumann—or only acknowledged him to criticize him (see, for example, *Age of the Great Goddess*)—her debt to him and to other Jungians is clear (see Meskell, "Goddesses," 77). A detailed discussion of the scope and nature of Jung's influence upon feminist matriarchal myth will be included in my forthcoming book, *From Motherright to Gylany*.

6. For particularly egregious examples of tracking symbols across large spans of non-contiguous geography and time, see Baring and Cashford, *Myth of the Goddess*, 42; Streep, *Sanctuaries*, 41; Harrod, "Upper Paleolithic 'Double Goddess,'" in Marler, ed., *Realm of the Ancestors*, 493–94. Gimbutas seems to recognize, if only implicitly, the problem of generalizing across a huge swath of time and space. In *The Civilization of the Goddess*, she painstakingly describes the burial customs, pottery, technology, and so on of various sites in Old Europe and elsewhere, giving detailed evidence of local and chronological variations. It is not until she turns to the topic of prehistoric religion that evidence from a wide array of cultures suddenly becomes grist for a single goddess mill.

7. Conkey and Tringham, "Archaeology and the Goddess," 216–17. See also Anthony, "Nazi and Eco-feminist Prehistories," 95; Hutton, "Discovery of the Modern Goddess," 94. The lack of anthropomorphic art from prehistoric Britain and northwest Europe that might support the thesis of goddess religion has long been a thorn in the side of matriarchalists, so much so that someone apparently decided to remedy the situation with a forgery placed in a Neolithic flint mine in Norfolk in 1939. This "Grimes Graves Goddess" was immediately greeted as proof that Britons, like their prehistoric contemporaries, worshipped a great mother goddess. For details, see Hutton (94–95).

8. Bolen, *Crossing to Avalon*, ix; Streep, *Sanctuaries*, 95; Gadon, *Once and Future Goddess*, 12; Poth, *Goddess Speaks*, 99.

9. Wilshire, *Virgin Mother Crone*, 132.

10. This list is a compilation of ones found in Baring and Cashford, *Myth of the Goddess*, 39–40; Gadon, *Once and Future Goddess*, 73; Streep, *Sanctuaries*, 4, 20, 22, 31, 58, 97, 106, 113; Eisler, *Chalice and the Blade*, 18; Meskell, "Goddesses," 80; Rybakov, "Cosmogony and Mythology," 38; Wilshire, *Virgin Mother Crone*, 132; Hubbs, *Mother Russia*, 6; Poth, *Goddess Speaks*, 1; Gaube and von Pechmann, *Magie, Matriarchat, und Marienkult*, 211; Mandt, "Women of Vingen," in Marler, ed., *Realm of the Ancestors*, 166; Frances Stahl Bernstein, "The Goddess of the Garden in Pompeii," in Marler, ed., *Realm of the Ancestors*, 208.

11. Gimbutas, *Goddesses and Gods*, 114; Pollack, *Body of the Goddess*, 61.

12. Pollack, *Body of the Goddess*, 71.

13. Baring and Cashford take this illustration from Gimbutas's *Goddesses and Gods of Old Europe*. Gimbutas does not explicitly name these as images of the moon, but rather as "fourfold signs" that may represent the phases of the moon (91).

14. Paul Mellars, "The Upper Palaeolithic Revolution," in Cunliffe, ed., *Oxford Illustrated Prehistory*, 74; Bahn and Vertut, *Journey through the Ice Age*, 75–76. Bahn devotes an entire chapter to problems involved in accurately dating Paleolithic art (chap. 5). Initial efforts to date cave art by radiocarbon methods, like efforts to date it stylistically, have yielded these large ranges of dates for different sites and different individual paintings.

15. Mellars, "Upper Palaeolithic Revolution," in Cunliffe, ed., *Oxford Illustrated Prehistory*, 70–75; Bacus et al., eds., *Gendered Past*, 110; Kurtén, "Cave Art," 111. Rice and Paterson's study ("Anthropomorphs in Cave Art") reveals that slightly over half of the human representations are sexable, with roughly 75 percent of these being male, and 25 percent female.

16. L. Didon, quoted in Stoliar, "Upper Paleolithic Female Signs," 42–43; Bahn, "No Sex, Please," 99–100, 102. See also Mack, "Archaeology of the Female Body," 87; Marshack, *Roots of Civilization*, fig. 187.

17. Leroi-Gourhan, "Evolution of Paleolithic Art," 65–66; Stern, *Prehistoric Europe*, 134–35.

18. Redmond, *When the Drummers Were Women*, 29; Gimbutas, "Vulvas, Breasts, and Buttocks," 23.

19. Sally R. Binford, "Myths and Matriarchies," in Spretnak, ed., *Politics of Women's Spirituality*, 546–47.

20. Marija Gimbutas, interestingly, is an exception to this rule. She freely claims that though prehistoric art is full of disembodied vulvas and naked women graphically displaying their genitals, it is not "about" sex. Sounding quite puritanical, Gimbutas happily gives up the sex-is-good rule of feminist matriarchal myth in deference to saving prehistoric art for a chaste religious form of goddess worship. See, for example, "Vulvas, Breasts, and Buttocks," 39; Gimbutas, "The 'Monstrous Venus' of Prehistory: Divine Creatrix," in Campbell and Musès, eds., *In All Her Names*, 30; *Goddesses and Gods*, 166.

21. Eisler, *Sacred Pleasure*, 15, 18; Kingsolver, "Making Peace," 30.

22. Nelson, *Gender in Archaeology*, 156; Bahn, "No Sex, Please," 101–102.

23. Pollack, *Body of the Goddess*, 79, fig. cap. 5; Gimbutas, *Language of the Goddess*, 68, fig. cap. 107; Johnson, *Lady of the Beasts*, 11. Alexander Marshack notes that the canine teeth of deer, recovered from Paleolithic burials, have the same "buttocks image" shape that Buffie Johnson finds in the Paleolithic German carving *(Roots of Civilization*, 317). Rather than assuming that the teeth were chosen for their resemblance to "the buttocks image," we might conclude that the human-made pendant was crafted to resemble the teeth of deer.

24. Ucko, *Anthropomorphic Figurines*, 315–16, 335–36.

25. This is the logic employed by archaeologist A. L. a Campo (cited in Knapp and Meskell, "Bodies of Evidence," 97), who reads all Cypriot figurines of the cruciform type as being female, whether or not they are equipped with breasts, facial elaboration, or intricate necklaces. The breasts of some are used to attribute breasts to the others.

26. Baring and Cashford, *Myth of the Goddess*, 74–75; Gimbutas, quoted in Young, "Goddesses, Feminists, and Scholars," 124. Occasionally feminist matriarchalists suggest that these phallic figurines were intended to portray harmony between the

sexes rather than the containment of the male within the female (see, for example, Pollack, *Body of the Goddess*, 24).

27. Gadon, *Once and Future Goddess*, 7; Johnson, *Lady of the Beasts*, plate 7; Streep, *Sanctuaries*, 29; Redmond, *When the Drummers Were Women*, 30; Taylor, *Prehistory of Sex*, 128. The term *"batons de commandement"* was coined by the Abbé Breuil, who saw in them a resemblance to military batons.

28. Gimbutas, *Age of the Great Goddess;* Kehoe, "No Possible, Probable Shadow of Doubt," 129; Knapp and Meskell, "Bodies of Evidence," 194. There are some unambiguous phalluses that have been recovered from Neolithic sites (Talalay, "Feminist Boomerang," 167), though of course it is unknown whether they were used as sexual aids.

29. See Johnson, *Lady of the Beasts*, 3; Mackey, *Year the Horses Came*, 20; Thurer, *Myths of Motherhood*, 8; Streep, *Sanctuaries*, 63; Keller, "Archaeology and Mythology," in Marler, ed., *Realm of the Ancestors*, 382. In *Civilization of the Goddess*, Gimbutas describes a ceramic workshop and speculates that the stacks of bowls found there "may have been waiting to be used for certain rituals" (107) rather than, say, waiting to be used for dinner.

30. Moore, *Iconography of Religions*, 47; Kurtén, "Cave Art," 104; Maurice Bloch, "Questions Not to Ask of Malagasy Carvings," in Hodder et al., eds., *Interpreting Archaeology*, 212–14.

31. Rice, "Prehistoric Venuses," 412, n. 2; Mellars, "Upper Palaeolithic Revolution," in Cunliffe, ed., *Oxford Illustrated Prehistory*, 69–70; Bahn, "No Sex, Please," 99. Feminist matriarchalists are generally opposed to the term "Venus," since they see it as diminishing the importance of these figurines. They often substitute titles such as "Lady" or "Goddess." I use the term Venus for convenience.

32. Abramova, "Palaeolithic Art," 65, 67, 70, 88; Gvozdover, "Typology of Female Figurines," 44–45; Dobres, "Re-Considering Venus Figurines," 245, 252, 256; Ucko, *Anthropomorphic Figurines*, 409; Rice, "Prehistoric Venuses," 402; Nelson, "Diversity of 'Venus' Figurines," 15–17; Pamela Russell, "The Palaeolithic Mother-Goddess: Fact or Fiction?" in du Cros and Smith, eds., *Women and Archaeology*, 95.

33. See Gadon, *Once and Future Goddess*, 8; Göttner-Abendroth, *Matriarchal Mythology*, 3; Christ, *Rebirth of the Goddess*, 10; Ranck, *Cakes for the Queen of Heaven* [Delphi], 25.

34. Rice, "Prehistoric Venuses," 402, 409. Estimates of the percentage of Paleolithic Venuses who are pregnant range from 17 to 68 percent (McCoid and McDermott, "Decolonizing Gender," 323–24; Rice, "Prehistoric Venuses," 408). This range in itself indicates the difficulty of assessing the Venuses' reproductive status.

35. Gimbutas, *Civilization of the Goddess*, 174; Starhawk, "Marija Gimbutas's Work and the Question of the Sacred," in Marler, ed., *Realm of the Ancestors*, 519.

36. Pestalozza, "Mediterranean Matriarchate," 52; James, *Cult of the Mother-*

Goddess, 13; Tavris, *Mismeasure of Women*, 73; G. Chard, quoted in Nelson, "Diversity of 'Venus' Figurines," 15–16; Wendt, *In Search of Adam*, 359; Kurtén, "Cave Art," 112–13.

37. Spretnak, ed., *Politics of Women's Spirituality*, 577.

38. Abramova, "Paleolithic Art," 66; Faris, "Form to Content," 104–5; Gvozdover, "Typology of Female Figurines," 71. Marcia-Anne Dobres points out that faces are modeled in much greater detail on the Siberian Venuses ("Re-Considering Venus Figurines," 253). An alternative explanation for facelessness is offered by McCoid and McDermott, who speculate that the figurines are self-representations of women as they see themselves while pregnant: they look down on their swollen breasts and belly (which from that vantage point look "unnaturally large" even if of average size), see only tapering legs, and of course cannot see their own faces ("Decolonizing Gender"). Viewed in this light, the Venuses could be understood to have a didactic function, teaching women about the changes their bodies would undergo in the course of their reproductive lives. Though innovative, this interpretation has not been particularly well received (see, for example, Ucko, "Mother, Are You There?" 302–303).

39. Alasdair Whittle, "The First Farmers," in Cunliffe, ed., *Oxford Illustrated Prehistory*, 144; Talalay, "Feminist Boomerang," 169; Ucko, *Anthropomorphic Figurines*, 335–36; Dimitra Kokkinidou and Marianna Nikolaidou, "Body Imagery in the Aegean Neolithic: Ideological Implications of Anthropomorphic Figurines," in Moore and Scott, eds., *Invisible People and Processes*, 89–90. Similarly extensive figurine assemblages have been found in Neolithic China, India, and in the New World (see Jiao Tianlong, "Gender Relations in Prehistoric Chinese Society: Archaeological Discoveries," in Min, ed., *Chalice and the Blade in Chinese Culture*, 117; Jayakar, *Earth Mother*, 167; Roosevelt, "Interpreting Female Images," 1; Marcus, "Importance of Context," 285; Guillén, "Chalcatzingo Figurines," 99–100).

40. Kokkinidou and Nikolaidou, "Body Imagery," in Moore and Scott, eds., *Invisible People and Processes*, 89–90; Hamilton, "Figurines," in Hodder, ed., *On the Surface*, 225.

41. Rodriguez, *Our Lady of Guadalupe*, 29.

42. Emmanuel Anati, "The Question of 'Fertility Cults,'" in Bonanno, ed., *Archaeology and Fertility Cult;* Frymer-Kensky, *Wake of the Goddesses*, 92; Spaeth, *Roman Goddess Ceres*, 112–13. The idea that there is a connection between goddess worship and concern for agricultural fertility has a long history among scholars of religion, for example Mircea Eliade *(History of Religious Ideas*, vol. 1, 400).

43. Reichel-Dolmatoff, "Anthropomorphic Figurines from Colombia," 231–32, 239; Guillén, "Chalcatzingo Figurines," 99–100; Mathews, "Seneca Figurines"; Brumfiel, "Figurines and the Aztec State," 147; Ucko, *Anthropomorphic Figurines*, 422, 425; Haaland and Haaland, "Who Speaks the Goddess's Language?" 117–18; Roosevelt, "Interpreting Female Images," 10; Orphanides, "Anthropomorphic Figurines," 166.

44. Fleming, "Mother-Goddess," 251; Ucko, *Anthropomorphic Figurines*, 418.

45. Sherratt, review of *Language of the Goddess*, 346. Both Islam and Judaism have artistic and iconographic traditions (limited by a generalized suspicion of any representation), but neither permit any representation whatsoever of God Himself (see Unterman, "Judaism," 44−45; Neusner, "Studying Ancient Judaism," 30−31; Lamya'al-Faruqi, *Islam and Art*, 14−18; Annemarie Schimmel, "Islamic Iconography," in Eliade, ed., *Encyclopedia of Religion*, 64−65). Christianity shares this restraint to a degree, though it is not nearly so iconoclastic. Still, representation of the Father God of Christianity is comparatively rare (compared to representation of Jesus or Mary, for example) and is often limited to more abstract symbols (see Apostolos-Cappadona, *Dictionary of Christian Art*, 146).

46. Vermeule, *Greece in the Bronze Age*, 282; Dominique Collon, "Mesopotamian Iconography," in Eliade, ed., *Encyclopedia of Religion*, 27, 30−31. Walter Burkert sees this pattern in classical Greek religion as well *(Greek Religion*, 42).

47. Frymer-Kensky, *Wake of the Goddesses*, 160−61.

48. Savina J. Teubal's interpretation of these figurines is not far from this: she sees the pillar figurines as signifying "that the powerful tradition of female figurines associated with reproduction persisted among the women of Israel, even though the nurturing attributes were slowly being transferred to Yahweh, who opens the womb and rewards women with children" ("The Rise and Fall of Female Reproductive Control as Seen through Images of Women," in King, ed., *Women and Goddess Traditions*, 297).

49. Rohrlich, "State Formation," 80; Lydia Ruyle, letter to editor, *Goddessing Regenerated* 6 (Winter/ Spring 1997): 4; Hodder, "'Always Momentary,'" 693−94; Hodder, "Past as Passion," 131. The current excavations are slated to run for twenty-five years and are being carried out by an international team composed mainly of archaeologists from the United States, the United Kingdom, and Turkey. Thus far, the work has mainly involved sifting old evidence, sampling the site, and making decisions about how to approach the excavation as a whole. Findings from this preliminary phase are compiled in Hodder, ed., *On the Surface*.

50. Mellaart, *Çatal Hüyük*, 23, 30, 32, 49−51, 54−57, 82−84, 101, 167−68.

51. Christ, *Rebirth of the Goddess*, 13; Hamilton, "Figurines," in Hodder, ed., *On the Surface*, 215−20, 222−25; Mellaart, *Çatal Hüyük*, 106−7, 178−80. Many have been struck by the resemblance between the "goddess with leopards" and "the image of Cybele or Magna Mater" which appears some three thousand years later. Some have suggested that the two must be related. The much later cult of Cybele was primarily a men's cult, and there is no evidence that the two are connected. There is an enormous gap of space and time between them, and no one has proposed a definite link between the two (see Burkert, *Structure and History*, 119−20; Phillipe Borgeaud, private communication, November 1996).

52. Mellaart, *Çatal Hüyük*, 124; Hodder, "Contextual Archaeology," 44−45; Ian

Hodder and Anita Louise, "Discussions with the Goddess Community," http://-catal.arch.cam.ac.uk/catal/goddess.html, n.d.

53. Eliade, *History of Religious Ideas*, vol. 1, 46–47; Pollack, *Body of the Goddess*, 25–26; Streep, *Sanctuaries*, 145.

54. Gimbutas, *Language of the Goddess*, 244, 246, 266; Dorothy Cameron, "The Minoan Horns of Consecration," in Marler, ed., *Realm of the Ancestors*, 510; Noble, *Shakti Woman*, 187; Redmond, *When the Drummers Were Women*, 50.

55. Taylor, *Prehistory of Sex*, 156–57; William Barnett, cited in Denfeld, *New Victorians*, 139.

56. Getty, *Goddess*, 11–12; Hodder, "Contextual Archaeology," 45; Taylor, *Prehistory of Sex*, 158.

57. Read, *Goddess Remembered*; Rigoglioso, "Awakening to the Goddess," 144; Stern, *Prehistoric Europe*, 272; Colin Renfrew, "The Prehistoric Maltese Achievement and its Interpretation," in Bonanno, ed., *Archaeology and Fertility Cult*, 118. Both Gertrude Rachel Levy (*Gate of Horn*, 137) and Sibylle von Cles-Reden (*Realm of the Great Goddess*, 90) noted that the sex of the Maltese statuary was ambiguous.

58. Levy, *Gate of Horn*, 137; Trump et al., "New Light on Death," 100; Meskell, "Goddesses," 77, fig. cap. 2.

59. J. D. Evans, quoted in Streep, *Sanctuaries*, 89; Gimbutas, *Age of the Great Goddess*; Gimbutas, *Civilization of the Goddess*, 174. Feminist matriarchalists were not the first to advance this theory. As early as 1969, Philip Van Doren Stern was claiming that it had been "seriously suggested that the ground plans of these buildings follow the outlines of the grossly fat Mother Goddess figures that dominated the islands' art" (*Prehistoric Europe*, 272).

60. Cristina Biaggi, "Temple-Tombs and Sculptures in the Shape of the Body of the Great Goddess," in Marler, ed., *Realm of the Ancestors*, 499.

61. Sjöö, "Poem in Tribute to Gimbutas," 30.

62. Biaggi, *Habitations of the Great Goddess*, plate 7.

63. Getty, *Goddess*, 21; Trump, *Prehistory of the Mediterranean*, 178–79.

64. Mimi Lobell, quoted in Rachel Pollack, "Body of the Goddess," in Noble, ed., *Uncoiling the Snake*, 105–106.

65. Anderson and Zinsser, *History of Their Own*, 447, n. 17; Baring and Cashford, *Myth of the Goddess*, 121; Thomson, *Ancient Greek Society*, 178.

66. Thomas, "Matriarchy in Early Greece," 191–92, n. 13.

67. Ucko, *Anthropomorphic Figurines*, 434; Finley, "Archaeology and History," 170; Marinatos, *Minoan Religion*, 162, 166–67, 174; Younger, *Iconography of Late Minoan and Mycenaean Sealstones*, x–xi.

68. Baring and Cashford, *Myth of the Goddess*, 111–12. See also Poth, *Goddess Speaks*, 99.

69. Hutchinson, *Prehistoric Crete*, 208; Marinatos, *Minoan Religion*, 276−77, n. 5. Part of the reason the "snake goddesses" have been given such an exaggerated importance probably has to do with the eager reception they received when they were first discovered (one served as the frontispiece for the first volume of Sir Arthur Evans's *Palace of Minos*, published in 1921), and the fact that at least one, and probably several forgeries were successfully sold on the international antiquities market to museums (see Butcher and Gill, "The Director," 383, 401).

8. Was There a Patriarchal Revolution?

1. See, for example, Makkay, "Linear Pottery," 176−77; Renfrew, *Archaeology and Language*, 3; Cavalli-Sforza et al., "Reconstruction of Human Evolution," 6005.

2. David W. Anthony and Bernard Wailes, quoted in Renfrew, review of *Archaeology of Language*, 444; Sherratt, "Mobile Resources," 14.

3. See Renfrew, *Archaeology and Language*, 1; Mallory, *Indo-Europeans*, 24−26. Though it is assumed that there were other, non-Indo-European languages in Europe prehistorically, only Etruscan, Basque, and representatives of the Finno-Ugaric languages (Hungarian, Finnish, and Estonian) have survived into historical times, making it difficult to know what, if anything, preceded Indo-European linguistic dominance (Beekes, *Comparative Indo-European Linguistics*, 8; Renfrew, *Archaeology and Language*, 145).

4. The protolexicon is a very abbreviated list of words from what must have been a far larger vocabulary. For example, the protolexicon includes a word for "snow" but none for "rain," but it seems unlikely that these peoples lived in a region where it snowed but never rained (Renfrew, *Archaeology and Language*, 14; A. B. Keith, cited in Renfrew, *Archaeology and Language*, 81). A complete list of what is now thought to be in the Indo-European protolexicon can be found in Beekes, *Comparative Indo-European Linguistics*, arranged both topically (34−40) and alphabetically by English translation (350−54). Another such lexicon, linked to Gimbutas's work, is published as an appendix in Gimbutas's *Kurgan Culture* (Martin E. Huld, "The Vocabulary of Indo-European Culture," 373−93).

5. Beekes, *Comparative Indo-European Linguistics*, 34−35; D'iakonov, "Original Home," 61−62; Mallory, *Indo-Europeans*, 114−17, 120; Childe, *Aryans*, 82.

6. Szemerényi, "Kinship Terminology," 33, 73, 92, 198−99, 205−206; Beekes, *Comparative Indo-European Linguistics*, 38; Benveniste, *Indo-European Language*, 165, 167, 193, 195. Benveniste argues that special terms for "mother's uncle" in Indo-European languages suggest that the kinship system of the proto-Indo-Europeans may have included matrilineal features (180, 191−92, 221−22). His thesis has not won general favor, and Szemerényi in particular argues strenuously against it.

7. Mallory, *Indo-Europeans*, 131−32; Benveniste, *Indo-European Language*, 277. Mallory explains the lower castes in India as being made up of "the suppressed indigenous populations" (suppressed, he assumes, by Aryan invaders).

8. Beekes, *Comparative Indo-European Linguistics*, 37, 39, 41–42; Benveniste, *Indo-European Language*, 137; Childe, *Aryans*, 80–81.

9. V. Gordon Childe reviewed all the extant possibilities for a proto-Indo-European homeland in 1926 and settled—with equivocation—on southern Russia, as Gimbutas was to do decades later *(Aryans*, 200). This proposed homeland is now favored by Mallory, among others *(Indo-Europeans*, 177). W. P. Lehmann considers a southern Russian homeland to be "the standard view of the early history of the Indo-European community" ("Frozen Residues," 223).

10. D'iakonov, "Original Home," 51–52; Mallory, *Indo-Europeans*; Gimbutas, *Kurgan Culture*, 334–44; Gimbutas, "Homeland of the Indo-Europeans." Gimbutas makes a lucid and persuasive case against an Anatolian homeland for proto-Indo-European. Recent advocates of an Anatolian homeland include Renfrew *(Archaeology and Language)* and Gamkrelidze and Ivanov ("Ancient Near East and the Indo-European Question").

11. Cunliffe, ed., *Oxford Illustrated Prehistory*, 3; Beekes, *Comparative Indo-European Linguistics*, 52; Edgar C. Polomé, "The Impact of Marija Gimbutas on Indo-European Studies," in Marler, ed., *Realm of the Ancestors*, 103–104.

12. Mallory, *Indo-Europeans*, 23, 126–27; Andrew Sherratt, quoted in Renfrew, review of *Archaeology and Language*, 459; Beekes, *Comparative Indo-European Linguistics*, 49. It is possible that words associated with the secondary products revolution and metallurgy were developed after the initial dispersal, and then traded among the now differentiated Indo-European languages, so this cannot be regarded as an iron-clad argument for a dispersal after 4000 BCE.

13. See Beekes, *Comparative Indo-European Linguistics*, 45; Wolfgang Meid, "The Indo-Europeanization of Old European Concepts," in Marler, ed., *Realm of the Ancestors*, 123. In spite of this caution, the history of Indo-European linguistics is full of easy equivalences drawn between languages and people. This contributed, among other things, to propaganda for the Nazi Holocaust. Nazi ideologues assigned the Indo-European homeland to Germany and described the original Indo-Europeans as tall, blond, strong Aryans, a superior race to all those it overcame linguistically, and, so the theory went, militarily. In general, there have been only spotty and often clumsy attempts to line up the linguistic record with the archaeological record. Some feminist matriarchalists credit Gimbutas with being the first to marry archaeological and linguistic evidence (see, for example, Rigoglioso, "Awakening to the Goddess," 68; Marler, ed., *Realm of the Ancestors*, 50), but others before her, such as Gordon Childe, did essentially the same thing.

14. Beekes, *Comparative Indo-European Linguistics*, 50–51; Mallory, *Indo-Europeans*, 27–30; Gimbutas, *Civilization of the Goddess*, 219; Eisler, *Chalice and the Blade*, 17.

15. Andrew Sherratt, "The Transformation of Early Agrarian Europe," in Cunliffe, ed., *Oxford Illustrated Prehistory*, 191–93; Gimbutas, *Kurgan Culture*, 319, 327; L. Luca Cavalli-Sforza, "Genetic Evidence Supporting Marija Gimbutas's Work on the Origins of Indo-European People," in Marler, ed., *Realm of the Ancestors*, 98; Mal-

lory, *Indo-Europeans*, 259; Polomé, "Impact of Gimbutas," in Marler, ed., *Realm of the Ancestors*, 103–104; Anthony and Wailes, in Renfrew, review of *Archaeology and Langauge*, 444; Beekes, *Comparative Indo-European Linguistics*, 37, 50–52.

16. Robert Coleman, in Renfrew, review of *Archaeology and Language*, 452; Leach, "Aryan Invasions," 231; Mallory, *Indo-Europeans*, 259. Robert Coleman gives the example of the Roman Empire, which had a dramatic military impact on the eastern Mediterranean, but virtually no linguistic impact; Edmund Leach gives another example, that of the British Isles between the fifth and seventh centuries CE, when the linguistic dominance of Latin moved from west to east, while the military dominance of the Anglo-Saxons moved from east to west (Coleman, in Renfrew, review of *Archaeology and Language*, 452; Leach, "Aryan Invasions," 231). J. P. Mallory, on the other hand, notes that languages have spread under conditions of friendly trade *(Indo-Europeans*, 259).

17. Colin Renfrew, quoted in Young, "Goddesses, Feminists, and Scholars," 152; Renfrew, *Archaeology and Language*, 94–95.

18. An exception is Ian Hodder, who regards "the Corded Ware/Bell Beaker phenomena" as "a story about the foreign, imposed, violent nature of power," a story effectively told through artifacts ("Material Culture in Time," in Hodder et al., eds., *Interpreting Archaeology*, 165).

19. Anthony, "Nazi and Eco-feminist Prehistories," 95; David W. Anthony, quoted in Steinfels, "Idyllic Theory," C12; Mallory, *Indo-Europeans*, 185.

20. Ammerman and Cavalli-Sforza, *Neolithic Transition*, 139; Cavalli-Sforza, "Genetic Evidence," in Marler, ed., *Realm of the Ancestors*, 95.

21. Ammerman and Cavalli-Sforza, *Neolithic Transition*, 87, 105, 108, Cavalli-Sforza, "Genetic Evidence," in Marler, ed., *Realm of the Ancestors*, 96–97. In *The Neolithic Transition*, Cavalli-Sforza and Ammerman say the second principal component represents "movement from central Asia or parts of the Soviet Union toward Europe" rather than the north-to-south movement postulated in Cavalli-Sforza's earlier work, and they say this movement is potentially associated with "groups of pastoral nomads in the third millennium B.C. continuing through historical times" (107–108). But it is only the third principal component that Cavalli-Sforza has explicitly, if speculatively, linked to Indo-European migrations.

22. See, for example, Spretnak, ed., *Politics of Women's Spirituality*, rev. ed., x; Rigoglioso, "Awakening to the Goddess," 68; Abrahamsen, "Essays in Honor of Gimbutas," 70.

23. Ammerman and Cavalli-Sforza, *Neolithic Transition*, 108; Cavalli-Sforza, "Genetic Evidence," 97, 99; Jenny Blain, quoted in Kramer-Rolls, ed., "Reader's Forum."

24. Snell, *Ancient Near East*, 20, 34–35; Frymer-Kensky, *Wake of the Goddesses*, 48, 79, 92; Lerner, *Creation of Patriarchy*, 89, 102; Olsen, *Chronology*, 2. Some feminist matriarchalists still claim that Sumer—at least early Sumer—was matriarchal, espe-

cially on the basis of its goddess worship and women's roles as priestesses (see Getty, *Goddess*, 18; Redmond, *When the Drummers Were Women*, 59). However, Sumer is always regarded in feminist matriarchal thought as a transitional civilization, since by the time of its destruction in the second millennium BCE, it was clearly warlike and patriarchal (see, for example, Eisler, *Sacred Pleasure*, 68).

25. Marinatos, *Minoan Religion*, 165–66; Chadwick, *Linear B*, 37, 43, 45, 47; Ventris and Chadwick, *Mycenaean Greek*, 124, 134, 155–56, 162; Pomeroy, *Goddesses, Whores, Wives, and Slaves*, 2d ed., x–xi; Cantarella, *Pandora's Daughters*, 16.

26. Cantarella, *Pandora's Daughters*, 27, 32. See also Sarah B. Pomeroy, "A Classical Scholar's Perspective on Matriarchy," in Carroll, ed., *Liberating Women's History*, 219. Homer is thought to have been illiterate. The poems he gathered together and/or composed were transmitted orally until the sixth century BCE (Pomeroy, *Goddesses, Whores, Wives, and Slaves*, 17).

27. Anderson and Zinsser, *History of Their Own*, 27; Zeitlin, "Signifying Difference," 54–56, 57, 60–61, 84; Loraux, *Children of Athena*, 74. The myth of Pandora can be found in Hesiod, *Works and Days*, 90–105.

28. Zeitlin, "Signifying Difference," 59; Keuls, *Reign of the Phallus*, 1. See also Lerner, *Creation of Patriarchy*, 202; Cantarella, *Pandora's Daughters*, 40, 46, 85, 115; Pomeroy, *Goddesses, Whores, Wives, and Slaves*, 2d ed., xii–xiii; Blok, "Sexual Asymmetry," 9. Just as ethnographers of aboriginal Australia have offered widely divergent opinions on the status of women among the aborigines, so too have classicists disagreed on the status of women in classical antiquity. The history of this debate is recounted in Katz, "Ideology and 'The Status of Women'" and Blok, "Sexual Asymmetry."

29. Starhawk, *Truth or Dare*, 63; Noble, *Shakti Woman*, 3; Getty, *Goddess*, 20; Redmond, *When the Drummers Were Women*, 145; Antiga, "Goddess in Me," in King, ed., *Divine Mosaic*, 181. Translations of and commentary on the *Enuma Elish*, the Babylonian epic of creation featuring the story of Tiamat and Marduk, can be found in Kramer and Maier, *Myths of Enki*, and McCall, *Mesopotamian Myths*.

30. Pollack, *Body of the Goddess*, 6, 130; Valaoritis, "Cosmic Conflict," in Marler, ed., *Realm of the Ancestors*, 250. The myth of Athena's birth can be found in Hesiod, *Theogony*, 886–95.

31. Pomeroy, *Goddesses, Whores, Wives, and Slaves*, 1; Norman O. Brown, Introduction, Hesiod, *Theogony*, 15–18, 41.

32. Sheila Murnaghan, personal communication, January 1997; Alan Sommerstein, Introduction, Aeschylus, *Eumenides*, 1; Aeschylus, *Oresteian Trilogy*, 169–70, 172.

33. Augustine, *City of God*, 616. The flood was apparently standard operating procedure for Poseidon, who retaliated with a deluge when he faced other losses as well (Pembroke, "Women in Charge," 25).

34. Abby Wettan Kleinbaum, "Amazon Legends and Misogynists: The Women and Civilization Question," in Keller, ed., *Views of Women's Lives*, 84. As the Greek ora-

tor Lysias said of the Amazons in 389 BCE, "when matched with our Athenian ancestors they appeared in all the natural timidity of their sex, and showed themselves less women in their external appearance than in their weakness and cowardice" (quoted in Lefkowitz, *Women in Greek Myth*, 23). Interestingly, there is growing archaeological evidence for female warriors on the southern Russian steppes, one of the areas broadly defined in Greek myth as an Amazon homeland. A number of graves containing weapons of war with female skeletons—some displaying bowed legs, presumably from horse-riding, along with injuries from arrowheads—suggest that some women in this area were in fact warriors. However, these women were clearly part of a culture that included men, and most of their female peers were buried not with weapons, but with jewelry and domestic tools (see Davis-Kimball, "Warrior Women," 47; Timothy Taylor, "Thracians, Scythians, and Dacians, 800 BC−AD 300," in Cunliffe, ed., *Oxford Illustrated Prehistory*, 394−96; a summary of Davis-Kimball's findings and scholarly reactions to them can be found in Osborne, "Women Warriors").

35. Hesiod excludes women until the "silver race" appears. These men have "prudent mothers" *(Works and Days*, 131).

36. Hesiod, *Works and Days*, 113−14.

37. Blundell, *Origins of Civilisation*, 136. Histories of golden age myths and their narrators can be found in Blundell, and also in Levin, *Myth of the Golden Age*.

38. Eisler, *Sacred Pleasure*, 74.

39. Georgoudi, "Myth of Matriarchy," in Pantel, ed., *History of Women*, 455−56. See, for example, Gadon, *Once and Future Goddess*, 2; Iglehart, *Womanspirit*, 80−81.

40. Rose, "Alleged Evidence for Mother-Right," 289; Rose, "Prehistoric Greece," 235; Sommerstein, Introduction, Aeschylus, *Eumenides*, 1.

41. Marler, ed., *From the Realm of the Ancestors*, 212; Eliade, *Myth of the Eternal Return*, 44−45.

42. As Walter Burkert explains, "All interpretations [of myth as history] must use Procrustean methods to make the tale isomorphic with the purported reality, must cut off excesses attributed to uncontrolled 'fantasy' " *(Structure and History*, 4).

43. The term "patriarchal accretions" is Ranck's *(Cakes for the Queen of Heaven* [Delphi], 8−9).

44. Iglehart, *Womanspirit*, 99.

45. For descriptions of cross-cultural myths of women's former dominance, see Tuzin, *Voice of the Tambaran*, 34; Héritier, "Sang du Guerrir"; Murphy, "Social Structure and Sex Antagonism," 92−93; Murphy and Murphy, *Women of the Forest;* Borun et al., *Women's Liberation*, 21; Godelier, "Male Domination," 16; L. B. Glick, quoted in Gewertz, ed., *Myths of Matriarchy Reconsidered*, 113; Hobgin, *Island of Menstruating Men*, 100−101; Juillerat, "'An Odor of Man,' " 69−70; Hamilton, "Knowledge and Misrecognition," in Gewertz, ed., *Myths of Matriarchy Reconsidered*, 59−60; Meigs, *Food, Sex, and Pollution*, 37, 45; Gillison, "Cannibalism Among Women,"

44–45; Reichel-Dolmatoff, *Amazonian Cosmos*, 169–70. New Guinea and South America are the "hot spots" for myths of this type, but similar myths of women's former dominance can be found elsewhere. See Turnbull, "Mbuti Womanhood," in Dahlberg, ed., *Woman the Gatherer*, 218; Anna-Stina Nykänen, "Women in Finland: An Overview," http://www.helsinki.fi/kris_ntk/doc/etane95.html, 1995; Kenyatta, *Facing Mount Kenya*, 5–10.

46. Chapman, *Drama and Power*, 66–71.

47. Ibid.

48. Chesler, "Amazon Legacy," n.p.

49. Malinowski, *Sex, Culture, and Myth*, 249–50, and *Myth in Primitive Psychology*, 32–33, 58–59, 91–92.

50. Michael W. Young, "The Matriarchal Illusion in Kalauna Mythology," in Gewertz, ed., *Myths of Matriarchy Reconsidered*, 5; Parker and Parker, "Myth of Male Superiority," 292, 300; Juillerat, "'An Odor of Man,'" 90; Hauser-Schäublin, "Mutterrecht und Frauenbewegung," 147; Borun et al., *Women's Liberation*, 20–21; Lincoln, *Discourse and the Construction of Society*, 4–5. Joan Bamberger made the earliest, and still the best case that myths of women's former dominance work to legitimate male dominance ("The Myth of Matriarchy: Why Men Rule in Primitive Society," in Rosaldo and Lamphere, eds., *Woman, Culture, and Society*).

51. Chapman, *Drama and Power*, 113, 154; Terence Hays, "'Myths of Matriarchy' and the Sacred Flute Complex of the Papua New Guinea Highlands," in Gewertz, ed., *Myths of Matriarchy Reconsidered*, 106; Marie Reay, "Man-Made Myth and Women's Consciousness," in Gewertz, ed., *Myths of Matriarchy Reconsidered*, 130. It is interesting to note that for the women in this group, the myth of former female dominance apparently works as wish-fulfillment, in much the way that it does for contemporary feminist matriarchalists in the West (139).

52. Lefkowitz, *Women in Greek Myth*, 22. Sarah Pomeroy notes that Plutarch, writing about Amazons in Bronze Age Greece "apologizes for resorting to the use of legends as history" ("Classical Scholar's Perspective on Matriarchy," in Carroll, ed., *Liberating Women's History*, 221). William Blake Tyrell suggests that the Greeks "regarded myths as history because they told of universal truths, not the details we deem to be historical facts" *(Amazons*, 25; see also Veyne, *Did the Greeks Believe in Their Myths?).* In other words, it was not a chronological history that the Greeks wished to establish in their myths; rather it was a worldview they sought to capture. This was true not only for myths per se, but even for ancient Greek histories. The sort of truth standards that we seek to apply today were simply not relevant for most classical writers.

53. Arthur, review of *Amazons*, 592. See also Cantarella, *Pandora's Daughters*, 19; Vidal-Naquet, "Slavery," 190; Skinner, "Greek Women and the Metronymic," 39. Battles with Amazons were often set alongside battles with giants and centaurs in both Greek art and literature, so it is not immediately clear why Amazons should be viewed as any less mythical than centaurs. Furthermore, the purported homeland of

the Amazons shifted throughout Greek history as Greeks actually traveled to the places they believed Amazons to live and failed to find them there (see Lefkowitz, *Women in Greek Myth*, 20, 22; Pomeroy, "Classical Scholar's Perspective on Matriarchy," in Carroll, ed., *Liberating Women's History*, 221).

54. Cantarella, *Pandora's Daughters*, 16–17; Pembroke, "Women in Charge," 29–30; Vidal-Naquet, "Slavery," 190; Loraux, *Children of Athena*, 60; Loraux, "What is a Goddess?" in Pantel, ed., *History of Women*, 40; Tyrrell, *Amazons*, 30.

55. Chesler, "Amazon Legacy," n.p.

56. This seems to be the driving force behind much of the late nineteenth and early twentieth century preoccupation with prehistoric matriarchies, when scholarly men announced that prehistory was matriarchal, but that we could all rest easy since "progress" and "evolution" had elevated us to the high state of male dominance. (This topic will be covered at length in my forthcoming book, *From Motherright to Gylany.*)

9. On the Usefulness of Origin Myths

1. Miles, *Women's History of the World*, xiii; Gailey, "State of the State," 78–79; Rosaldo, "Use and Abuse," 391.

2. Theodore Roszak, quoted in Walters, "Caught in the Web," 28.

3. See, for example, Ruether, *Sexism and God-Talk*, 84–85.

4. See Stephen Jay Gould and Elisabeth Vrba, cited in Gable, *Timewalkers*, 5.

5. Rowbotham, "When Adam Delved," 10; Eichler, "Sex Inequality," 341, 345.

6. Taylor, "'Brothers' in Arms?" 37.

7. An exception is Cavin, *Lesbian Origins*, 170.

8. Given how closely feminist matriarchal myth mirrors the basic plot line of Jewish and Christian creation and eschatological myths, it is possible that part of the attraction of feminist matriarchal myth is its familiarity to a Western audience.

9. Cavin, *Lesbian Origins*, 22; Millett, *Sexual Politics*, 110.

10. Judith Ochshorn, "Goddesses and the Lives of Women," in King, ed., *Women and Goddess Traditions*, 380; Richard Leakey, cited in Dobbins, *From Kin to Class*, 19; Gerda Lerner, cited in Richlin, "Ethnographer's Dilemma," in Rabinowitz and Richlin, eds., *Feminist Theory and the Classics*, 284.

11. Kathleen Bolen, "Prehistoric Construction of Mothering," in Claassen, ed., *Exploring Gender through Archaeology*, 49; Cucchiari, "Gender Revolution," in Ortner and Whitehead, eds., *Sexual Meanings*, 33; Godelier, "Male Domination," 11; Gailey, "Evolutionary Perspectives," 37.

12. Whyte, *Status of Women*, 180.

REFERENCES

Aaby, Peter. "Engels and Women." *Critique of Anthropology* 3/9–10 (1977): 25–53.

Abrahamsen, Valerie. "Essays in Honor of Marija Gimbutas: A Response." *Journal of Feminist Studies in Religion* 13/2 (Fall 1997): 69–74.

Abramova, Z. A. "Palaeolithic Art in the USSR," trans. Catherine Page. *Arctic Anthropology* 4/2 (1967) [1962]: 1–179.

Aburdene, Patricia, and John Naisbitt. *Megatrends for Women*. New York: Villard Books, 1992.

Achterberg, Jeanne. *Woman as Healer*. Boston: Shambhala, 1990.

Adler, Margot. *Drawing Down the Moon: Witches, Druids, Goddess-Worshippers, and Other Pagans in America Today*. Boston: Beacon Press, 1979.

Aeschylus. *The Eumenides*. Edited by Alan Sommerstein. Cambridge: Cambridge University Press, 1989.

———. *The Oresteian Trilogy*. Translated by Philip Vellacott. Hammondsworth, England: Penguin, 1956.

Al-Hibri, Azizah. "Capitalism Is an Advanced Stage of Patriarchy: But Marxism Is Not Feminism." In *Women and Revolution: A Discussion of the Unhappy Marriage of Marxism and Feminism*, ed. L. Sargent, 165–93. Boston: South End Press, 1981.

Alpert, Jane. "Mother Right: A New Feminist Theory." *Ms.* 2/2 (August 1973): 52–55, 88–94.

Amadiume, Ifi. *Afrikan Matriarchal Foundations: The Igbo Case*. London: Karnak House, 1987.

———. *Reinventing Africa: Matriarchy, Religion, and Culture*. London: Zed Books, 1997.

Ammerman, Albert J., and L. L. Cavalli-Sforza. *The Neolithic Transition and the Genetics of Populations in Europe*. Princeton: Princeton University Press, 1984.

Anderson, Bonnie S., and Judith P. Zinsser. *A History of Their Own: Women in Europe from Prehistory to the Present*. Vol. 1. New York: Harper and Row, 1988.

Ann, Martha, and Dorothy Myers Imel. *Goddesses in World Mythology*. Santa Barbara, CA: ABC-Clio, 1993.

Anthony, David W. "Nazi and Eco-feminist Prehistories: Ideology and Empiricism in Indo-European Archaeology." In *Nationalism, Politics, and the Practice of Archaeology*, ed. Philip L. Kohl and Clare Fawcett, 1–32. Cambridge: Cambridge University Press, 1996.

Apostolos-Cappadona, Diane. *Dictionary of Christian Art*. New York: Continuum, 1994.

Appiah, Kwame Anthony. *In My Father's House: Africa in the Philosophy of Culture*. New York: Oxford University Press, 1992.

————. "Race." In *Critical Terms for Literary Study*, ed. Frank Lentricchia and Thomas McLaughlin, 274–87. 2d ed. Chicago: University of Chicago Press, 1995.

Arthur, Marilyn B. Review of *Amazons*, by William Blake Tyrrell. *Signs* 12 (Spring 1987): 589–93.

Auel, Jean M. *The Clan of the Cave Bear*. New York: Crown, 1980.

Augustine. *The City of God*. Translated by Marcus Dods. New York: Random House, 1950.

Austen, Hallie Iglehart. *The Heart of the Goddess: Art, Myth and Meditations of the World's Sacred Feminine*. Berkeley, CA: Wingbow Press, 1990.

Bachofen, Johann Jakob. *Myth, Religion, and Mother Right: Selected Writings of J. J. Bachofen* [1861]. Translated by Ralph Manheim. Princeton: Princeton University Press, 1967.

Bacus, Elisabeth A., et al., eds. *A Gendered Past: A Critical Bibliography of Gender in Archaeology*. Technical Report No. 25. Ann Arbor, MI: University of Michigan Museum of Anthropology, 1993.

Bahn, Paul G. "No Sex, Please, We're Aurignacians." *Rock Art Research* 3/2 (1986): 99–120.

Bahn, Paul G., and Jean Vertut. *Journey through the Ice Age*. Berkeley: University of California Press, 1997.

Bailey, Douglass W. "The Representation of Gender: Homology or Propaganda." *Journal of European Archaeology* 22 (1994): 189–202.

Baring, Anne, and Jules Cashford. *The Myth of the Goddess: Evolution of an Image*. London: Penguin/Arkana, 1991.

Barnett, William. Review of *The Language of the Goddess*, by Marija Gimbutas. *American Journal of Archaeology* 96/1 (1992): 170–71.

Bäumler, Alfred, and M. Schröter. *Der Mythos von Orient und Okzident: Eine Metaphysik der alten Welt aus den Werken von J. J. Bachofen* [1926]. München: C. H. Beck'sche Verlagsbuchhandlung, 1956.

Beekes, Robert S. P. *Comparative Indo-European Linguistics: An Introduction*. Amsterdam: John Benjamins Publishing Company, 1995.

Begler, Elsie B. "Sex, Status, and Authority in Egalitarian Society." *American Anthropologist* 80 (1978): 571–88.

Bell, James A. *Reconstructing Prehistory: Scientific Method in Archaeology*. Philadelphia: Temple University Press, 1994.

Benveniste, Emile. *Indo-European Language and Society* [1969]. Translated by Elizabeth Palmer. London: Faber and Faber, 1973.

Bermond, Daniel, and Stella Georgoudi. "Le Matriarcat n'a Jamais Existé!" *Histoire* 160 (November 1992): 40–43.

Berry, Thomas. *The Dream of the Earth*. San Francisco: Sierra Club Books, 1988.

Biaggi, Cristina. *Habitations of the Great Goddess*. Manchester, CT: Knowledge, Ideas, and Trends, Inc., 1994.

Biehl, Janet. *Rethinking Eco-feminist Politics*. Boston: South End Press, 1991.

Birnbaum, Lucia Chiavola. *Black Madonnas: Feminism, Religion, and Politics in Italy*. Boston: Northeastern University Press, 1993.

Bleier, Ruth. *Science and Gender: A Critique of Biology and Its Theories On Women*. New York: Pergamon Press, 1984.

Blok, Josine. "Sexual Asymmetry: A Historiographical Essay." In *Sexual Asymmetry: Studies in Ancient Society*, ed. Peter Mason, 1–57. Amsterdam: J. C. Gieben, 1987.

Blundell, Sue. *The Origins of Civilisation in Greek and Roman Thought*. London: Croom Helm, 1986.

Boas, Franz. "The Limitations of the Comparative Method of Anthropology" [1896]. In *Race, Language, and Culture*. New York: Macmillan, 1940.

Bolen, Jean Shinoda. *Crossing to Avalon: A Woman's Midlife Pilgrimage*. San Francisco: HarperSanFrancisco, 1994.

Bonanno, Anthony, ed. *Archaeology and Fertility Cult in the Ancient Mediterranean*. Amsterdam: B. R. Grüner Publishing Co., 1986.

Bonvillain, Nancy. *Women and Men: Cultural Constructs of Gender*. 2d ed. Upper Saddle River, NJ: Prentice Hall, 1998.

Borun, Minda, Molly McLaughlin, Gina Oboler, Norma Perchonock, and Lorraine Sexton (The Philadelphia Collective). *Women's Liberation: An Anthropological View*. Pittsburgh: Know, Inc., 1971.

Bridges, Patricia S. "Changes in Activities with the Shift to Agriculture in the Southeastern United States." *Current Anthropology* 30 (1989): 385–94.

Briffault, Robert. *The Mothers: A Study of the Origins of Sentiments and Institutions*. 3 vols. New York: Macmillan, 1927.

Brindel, June Rachuy. *Ariadne*. New York: St. Martin's Press, 1980.

Brown, David Jay, and Rebecca McClen Novick. "Unearthing the Goddess: An Interview with Marija Gimbutas." *Magical Blend* (date unknown).

Brumfiel, Elizabeth M. "Figurines and the Aztec State: Testing the Effectiveness of Ideological Domination." In *Gender and Archaeology*, ed. Rita P. Wright. Philadelphia: University of Pennsylvania Press, 1996.

Budapest, Zsuzsanna. *Holy Book of Women's Mysteries*. Rev. ed. Berkeley, CA: Wingbow Press, 1986.

Burkert, Walter. *Greek Religion*. Cambridge, MA: Harvard University Press, 1985.

———. *Structure and History in Greek Mythology and Ritual*. Berkeley: University of California Press, 1979.

Burton, Michael L., and Douglas R. White. "Sexual Division of Labor." *American Anthropologist* 86 (1984): 568–83.

Butcher, Kevin, and David W. J. Gill. "The Director, the Dealer, the Goddess, and Her Champions: The Acquisition of the Fitzwilliam Goddess." *American Journal of Archaeology* 97 (1993): 383–401.

Butler, Judith. *Gender Trouble: Feminism and the Subversion of Identity*. New York: Routledge, 1990.

Butterworth, E. A. S. *Some Traces of the Preolympian World in Greek Literature and Myth*. Berlin: de Gruyter, 1966.

Cameron, Anne. *Daughters of Copper Woman.* Vancouver, BC: Press Gang Publishers, 1981.

Campbell, Joseph, and Charles Musès, eds. *In All Her Names: Four Explanations of the Feminine in Divinity.* San Francisco: HarperSanFrancisco, 1991.

Campbell, June. *Traveller in Space: In Search of Female Identity in Tibetan Buddhism.* London: Athlone Press, 1996.

Cantarella, Eva. *Pandora's Daughters: The Role and Status of Women in Greek and Roman Antiquity.* Baltimore: Johns Hopkins University Press, 1987.

Carroll, Berenice A., ed. *Liberating Women's History.* Urbana: University of Illinois Press, 1976.

Carson, Anne. *Feminist Spirituality and the Feminine Divine: An Annotated Bibliography.* Trumansburg, NY: Crossing Press, 1986.

———. *Goddesses and Wise Women: The Literature of Feminist Spirituality 1980–1992, An Annotated Bibliography.* Freedom, CA: Crossing Press, 1992.

Cassidy, Kira. "In a Post-Modern Menstrual Lodge, Not Every Womon Bleeds." *Womonspeak* 2 (Fall/Winter 1997): n.p.

Cavalli-Sforza, Luigi Luca, and Francesco Cavalli-Sforza. *The Great Human Diasporas: The History of Diversity and Evolution.* Translated by Sarah Thorne. Reading, MA: Addison-Wesley, 1995.

Cavalli-Sforza, Luigi Luca, Alberto Piazza, Paolo Menozzi, and Joanna Mountain. "Reconstruction of Human Evolution: Bringing Together Genetic, Archaeological, and Linguistic Data." *Proceedings of the National Academy of Sciences* 85 (1988): 6002–6.

Cavin, Susan. *Lesbian Origins.* San Francisco: Ism Press, 1985.

Chadwick, John. *Linear B and Related Scripts.* London: British Museum Publications, 1987.

Chapman, Anne MacKaye. *Drama and Power in a Hunting Society: the Selk'nam of Tierra del Fuego.* Cambridge: Cambridge University Press, 1982.

Chernin, Kim. *The Flame Bearers.* New York: Random House, 1986.

———. *Reinventing Eve: Modern Woman in Search of Herself.* San Francisco: Harper and Row, 1987.

Chesler, Phyllis. "The Amazon Legacy." In *Wonder Woman.* New York: Holt, Rinehart, and Winston and Warner Books, 1972.

Childe, V. Gordon. *The Aryans: A Study of Indo-European Origins* [1926]. New York: Barnes and Noble Books, 1993.

Chodorow, Nancy. *The Reproduction of Mothering: Psychoanalysis and the Sociology of Gender.* Berkeley: University of California Press, 1989.

Christ, Carol P. "Mircea Eliade and the Feminist Paradigm Shift." *Journal of Feminist Studies in Religion* 7 (Fall 1991): 75–98.

———. *Rebirth of the Goddess: Finding Meaning in Feminist Spirituality.* Boston: Addison-Wesley, 1997.

———. "Symbols of Goddess and God in Feminist Theology." In *The Book of the Goddess,* ed. Carl Olson. New York: Crossroad, 1983.

Claassen, Cheryl, ed. *Exploring Gender through Archaeology: Selected Papers from the 1991 Boone Conference.* Madison, WI: Prehistory Press, 1992.

Conkey, Margaret W., and Janet D. Spector. "Archaeology and the Study of Gender." *Advances in Archaeological Method and Theory* 7 (1984): 1–38.

Conkey, Margaret W., and Ruth E. Tringham. "Archaeology and the Goddess: Exploring the Contours of Feminist Archaeology." In *Feminisms in the Academy: Rethinking the Disciplines*, ed. A. Stewart and D. Stanton, 199–247. Ann Arbor, MI: University of Michigan Press, 1995.

Conkey, Margaret W., with Sarah H. Williams. "Original Narratives: The Political Economy of Gender in Archaeology." In *Gender at the Crossroads of Knowledge: Feminist Anthropology in the Postmodern Era*, ed. Michaela di Leonardo, 102–39. Berkeley: University of California Press, 1991.

Coontz, Stephanie, and Peta Henderson, eds. *Women's Work, Men's Property: The Origins of Gender and Class*. London: Verson, 1986.

Cott, Nancy F. "Feminist Theory and Feminist Movements: The Past Before Us." In *What Is Feminism? A Reexamination*, ed. Juliet Mitchell and Ann Oakley, 49–62. New York: Pantheon, 1986.

Coward, Rosalind. *Patriarchal Precedents*. Boston: Routledge and Kegan Paul, 1983.

Crabtree, Pam. "Gender Hierarchies and the Sexual Division of Labor in the Natufian Culture of the Southern Levant." In *The Archaeology of Gender: Proceedings of the 22nd Annual Conference of the Archaeological Asssociation of the University of Calgary*, ed. Dale Walde and Noreen D. Willows. Calgary: University of Calgary Archaeological Association, 1991.

Crawford, Osbert Guy Stanhope. *The Eye Goddess*. London: Phoenix House, 1957.

Cunliffe, Barry, ed. *The Oxford Illustrated Prehistory of Europe*. Oxford: Oxford University Press, 1994.

D'Eaubonne, Francoise. *Les Femmes avant le Patriarcat*. Paris: Payot, 1977.

D'iakonov, I. M. "On the Original Home of the Speakers of Indo-European." *Soviet Anthropology and Archeology* 23/2 (1984): 3–87.

Dahlberg, Frances, ed. *Woman the Gatherer*. New Haven: Yale University Press, 1981.

Daly, Mary. *Beyond God the Father: Toward a Philosophy of Women's Liberation*. Boston: Beacon Press, 1973.

Davis, Elizabeth Gould. *The First Sex*. New York: Putnam, 1971.

Davis, Philip G. "The Goddess and the Academy." *Academic Questions* (Canada) 6/4 (Fall 1993): 49–66.

———. *Goddess Unmasked: The Rise of Neopagan Feminist Spirituality*. Dallas: Spence Publishing Co., 1998.

Davis-Kimball, Jeannine. "Warrior Women of the Eurasian Steppes." *Archaeology* (Jan/Feb) 1997: 44–48.

de Riencourt, Amaury. *Sex and Power in History*. New York: David McKay Co., 1974.

del Valle, Teresa, ed. *Gendered Anthropology*. London and New York: Routledge, 1993.

Delaney, Carol. "The Meaning of Paternity and the Virgin Birth Debate." *Man (n.s.)* 21/3 (1986): 494–513.

Delphy, Christine. *Close to Home: A Materialist Analysis of Women's Oppression*. Translated by D. Leonard. Amherst: University of Massachusetts Press, 1984.

DeMeo, James. "The Origins and Diffusion of Patrism in Saharasia, c. 4000 BCE: Evidence for a Worldwide, Climate-Linked Geographical Pattern in Human Behavior." *World Futures* 30/4 (1991): 247–71.

Deming, Barbara. "Remembering Who We Are." Lecture at Florida State University in Tallahassee, 4 March 1977 (http://www.rpi.edu/~mccadbd/rememberingwho.html).

Denfeld, Rene. *The New Victorians: A Young Woman's Challenge to the Old Feminist Order*. New York: Warner Books, 1995.

Dexter, Miriam Robbins. *Whence the Goddesses: A Source Book*. New York: Teachers College Press, 1990.

Diop, Cheikh Anta. *The Cultural Unity of Black Africa: The Domains of Patriarchy and of Matriarchy in Classical Antiquity*. London: Karnak House, 1989.

Divale, William. *Matrilocal Residence in Pre-Literate Society* [1974]. Ann Arbor, MI: UMI Research Press, 1984.

Divale, William, and Marvin Harris. "Population, Warfare, and the Male Supremacist Complex." *American Anthropologist* 78 (1976): 521–38.

Dixon, R. M. W. "Virgin Birth" correspondence. *Man (n.s.)* 3 (1968): 653–54.

Dobbins, Peggy Powell. *From Kin to Class: Speculations on the Origins and Development of the Family, Class Society, and Female Subordination*. Berkeley: Signmaker Press, 1981.

Dobres, Marcia-Anne. "Re-Considering Venus Figurines: A Feminist-Inspired Re-Analysis." In *Ancient Images, Ancient Thought: The Archaeology of Ideology*. Proceedings of the 1990 Chacmool Conference, ed. A. Sean Goldsmith, Sandra Garvie, David Selin, and Jeanette Smith, 245–62. Calgary, Alberta: University of Calgary, 1992.

Donovan, Josephine. *Feminist Theory: The Intellectual Traditions of American Feminism*. Rev. ed. New York: Continuum, 1992.

Downing, Christine. *The Goddess: Mythological Images of the Feminine*. New York: Crossroad, 1981.

———. *Women's Mysteries: Toward a Poetics of Gender*. New York: Crossroad, 1992.

du Cros, Hilary, and Laurajean Smith, eds. *Women and Archaeology: A Feminist Critique*. Occasional Papers in Prehistory, No. 23. Canberra: Australian National University, 1993.

Durant, Will. *The Story of Civilization*. Vol. 1. New York: Simon and Schuster, 1935.

Dworkin, Andrea. *Right-Wing Women*. New York: Perigree Books, 1983.

Edelson, Mary Beth. "Story Box: The Spirituality Question." *Heresies* 24 (1989): 57–62.

Ehrenberg, Margaret. *Women in Prehistory*. Vol. 4, Oklahoma Series in Classical Culture. Norman, OK: University of Oklahoma Press, 1989.

Eichler, Magrit. "The Origin of Sex Inequality: A Comparison and Critique of Different Theories and Their Implications for Social Policy." *Women's Studies International Quarterly* 2 (1979): 329–46.

Eisenstein, Hester. *Contemporary Feminist Thought*. Boston: G. K. Hall, 1984.

Eisler, Riane. *The Chalice and the Blade: Our History, Our Future*. San Francisco: Harper and Row, 1987.

————. "The Chalice and the Blade: Toward a Partnership with the Earth." Paper presented at the American Academy of Religion annual meeting, Anaheim, California, 1989.

————. *Sacred Pleasure: Sex, Myth, and the Politics of the Body — New Paths to Power and Love.* San Francisco: HarperSanFrancisco, 1995.

Eisler, Riane, and David Loye. *The Partnership Way: New Tools for Living and Learning, Healing Our Families, Our Communities, and Our World.* San Francisco: Harper and Row, 1990.

Eliade, Mircea, ed. *The Encyclopedia of Religion.* New York: Macmillan, 1987.

————. *A History of Religious Ideas.* Vol. 1, *From the Stone Age to the Eleusinian Mysteries.* Translated by Willard R. Trask. Chicago: University of Chicago Press, 1978.

————. *The Myth of the Eternal Return* [1949]. Translated by Willard R. Trask. Princeton: Princeton University Press, 1971.

Eller, Cynthia. *From Motherright to Gylany: The Myth of Matriarchal Prehistory, 1861–2000.* Forthcoming.

————. *Living in the Lap of the Goddess: The Feminist Spirituality Movement in America.* Boston: Beacon, 1995.

————. "White Women and the Dark Mother." Paper presented at the American Academy of Religion annual meeting, Orlando, Florida, 1998.

Ellwood, Robert S. "The Sujin Religious Revolution." *Japanese Journal of Religious Studies* 17/2–3 (1990): 199–217.

Elshtain, Jean Bethke. "The New Feminist Scholarship." *Salmagundi* 70/71 (1986): 3–26.

Engels, Frederick. *The Origin of the Family, Private Property and the State* [1884]. New York: International Publishers, 1972.

Engelstad, Ericka. "Images of Power and Contradiction: Feminist Theory and Post-Processual Archaeology." *Antiquity* 65/248 (1991): 502–14.

Fagan, Brian. "A Sexist View of Prehistory." *Archaeology* 45/2 (1992): 14–15, 18, 66.

Faris, J. "From Form to Content in the Structural Study of Aesthetic Systems." In *Structure and Cognition in Art*, ed. D. Washburn. Cambridge: Cambridge University Press, 1983.

Fausto-Sterling, Anne. *Myths of Gender: Biological Theories About Women and Men.* 2d ed. New York: Basic Books, 1992.

Feder, Kenneth L., and Michael Alan Park. *Human Antiquity: An Introduction to Physical Anthropology and Archaeology.* Mountain View, CA: Mayfield Publishing Co., 1989.

Fedigan, Linda Marie. "The Changing Role of Women in Models of Human Evolution." *Annual Review of Anthropology* 15 (1986): 25–66.

Ferguson, Marianne. *Women and Religion: From the Goddesses to the Present.* New York: Macmillan, 1994.

Finley, M. I. "Archaeology and History." *Daedalus* 100 (1971): 168–86.

Fisher, Elizabeth. *Woman's Creation.* New York: McGraw Hill, 1980.

Flanagan, James G. "Hierarchy in Simple 'Egalitarian' Societies." *Annual Review of Anthropology* 18 (1989): 245–66.

Fleming, Andrew. "The Myth of the Mother-Goddess." *World Archaeology* 1 (1969): 247–61.

Fluehr-Lobban, Carolyn. "Marxism and the Matriarchate: 100 Years after *The Origin of the Family, Private Property, and the State.*" *Critique of Anthropology* 7/1 (1987): 5–14.

———. "A Marxist Reappraisal of the Matriarchate." *Current Anthropology* 20 (1979): 341–59, 608–11.

Francia, Luisa. *Dragontime: Magic and Mystery of Menstruation.* Woodstock, NY: Ash Tree Publishing, 1991.

Fraser, Robert. *The Making of* The Golden Bough: *The Origins and Growth of an Argument.* London: Macmillan, 1990.

Frayser, Suzanne G. *Varieties of Sexual Experience: An Anthropological Perspective on Human Sexuality.* New Haven: HRAF Press, 1985.

Frazer, Sir James George. *The Golden Bough: A Study in Magic and Religion* [1894]. Abridged and rev. ed. New York: Macmillan, 1922.

French, Marilyn. *Beyond Power: On Women, Men, and Morals.* New York: Summit Books, 1985.

———. *The War Against Women.* New York: Summit Books, 1992.

Freud, Sigmund. *Moses and Monotheism* [1939]. New York: Vintage, 1955.

———. *Totem and Taboo: Some Points of Agreement between the Mental Lives of Savages and Neurotics* [1913]. Translated by James Strachey. New York: Norton, 1950.

Fromm, Erich. "The Theory of Mother Right and its Relevance for Social Psychology" [1934]. Chap. 7 in *The Crisis of Psychoanalysis.* New York: Holt, Rinehart, and Winston, 1970.

Frymer-Kensky, Tikva. *In the Wake of the Goddesses: Women, Culture, and the Biblical Transformation of Pagan Myth.* New York: Fawcett Columbine, 1993.

Gadon, Elinor W. *The Once and Future Goddess: A Symbol for Our Time.* San Francisco: Harper and Row, 1989.

Gage, Matilda Joslyn. *Woman, Church, and State: A Historical Account of the Status of Woman through the Christian Ages: With Reminiscences of the Matriarchate* [1900]. New York: Arno Press, 1972.

Gailey, Christine Ward. "Evolutionary Perspectives on Gender Hierarchy." In *Analyzing Gender,* ed. Beth B. Hess and Myra Marx Ferree, 32–67. Newbury Park, CA: Sage Publications, 1987.

———. *Kinship to Kingship: Gender Hierarchy and State Formation in the Tongan Islands.* Austin: University of Texas Press, 1987.

———. "The State of the State in Anthropology." *Dialectical Anthropology* 9 (1985): 65–89.

Gamble, Eliza Burt. *The Evolution of Woman: An Inquiry into the Dogma of Her Inferiority to Man.* New York: G. P. Putnam's, 1894.

Gamkrelidze, T., and V. Ivanov. "The Ancient Near East and the Indo-European Question [and] the Migration of Tribes Speaking Indo-European Dialects." *Journal of Indo-European Studies* 13 (1985): 3–91.

Gaube, Karin, and Alexander von Pechmann. *Magie, Matriarchat, und Marienkult:*

Frauen und Religion Versuch einer Bestandesaufnahme. Reinbek bei Hamburg: Rowohlt, 1986.

Gell, Alfred. *Metamorphosis of the Cassowaries: Umeda Society, Language, and Ritual.* London: Athlone Press, 1975.

Gellner, Ernest. "The Soviet and the Savage." *Current Anthropology* 16 (1973): 595–617.

George, Demetra. "Mysteries of the Dark Moon." *Woman of Power,* no. 8 (Winter 1988).

Gero, Joan M., and Margaret W. Conkey, eds. *Engendering Archaeology: Women and Prehistory.* Cambridge, MA: Blackwell, 1991.

Getty, Adele. *Goddess: Mother of Living Nature.* London: Thames and Hudson, 1990.

Gewertz, Deborah, ed. *Myths of Matriarchy Reconsidered.* Oceania Monograph 33. Sydney: University of Sydney Press, 1988.

Gill, Sam D. "Making Them Speak: Colonialism and the Study of Mythology." Paper presented at the American Academy of Religion annual meeting, New Orleans, Louisiana, November 1996.

———. *Mother Earth: An American Story.* Chicago: University of Chicago Press, 1987.

Gilligan, Carol, and Lyn Mikel Brown. *Meeting at the Crossroads: Women's Psychology and Girl's Development.* Cambridge: Harvard University Press, 1992.

Gillison, Gillian. "Cannibalism Among Women in the Eastern Highlands of Papua New Guinea." In *The Ethnography of Cannibalism,* ed. Paula Brown and Donald Tuzin, 33–50. Washington DC: Society for Psychological Anthropology, 1983.

Gilman, Charlotte Perkins. *The Man-Made World or Our Androcentric Culture.* London: Fischer Unwin, 1911.

Gimbutas, Marija. *The Age of the Great Goddess: Ancient Roots of the Emerging Feminine Consciousness.* Interview with Kell Kearns. Two audiocassettes. Boulder, CO: Sounds True Recordings, 1992.

———. *The Civilization of the Goddess: The World of Old Europe.* Edited by Joan Marler. San Francisco: HarperSanFrancisco, 1991.

———. "The First Wave of Eurasian Steppe Pastoralists into Copper Age Europe." *Journal of Indo-European Studies* 5 (1977): 277–338.

———. *The Gods and Goddesses of Old Europe: 6500–3500 BC.* Berkeley and Los Angeles: University of California Press, 1974.

———. *The Goddesses and Gods of Old Europe: 6500–3500 BC.* [Rev. ed. of *Gods and Goddesses of Old Europe.*] Berkeley and Los Angeles: University of California Press, 1982.

———. "Primary and Secondary Homeland of the Indo-Europeans." *Journal of Indo-European Studies* 13/1–2 (1985): 185–202.

———. *The Kurgan Culture and the Indo-Europeanization of Europe: Selected Articles from 1952 to 1993.* Edited by Miriam Robbins Dexter and Karlene Jones-Bley. Washington, DC: Journal of Indo-European Studies Monograph No. 18, 1997.

———. *The Language of the Goddess.* San Francisco: HarperSanFrancisco, 1989.

———. "Vulvas, Breasts, and Buttocks of the Goddess Creatress: Commentary on the Origins of Art." In *The Shape of the Past: Studies in Honor of Franklin D. Murphy*, ed. G. Buccellati and C. Speroni. Los Angeles: Institute of Archaeology and Office of the Chancellor, University of California, 1981.

———. *World of the Goddess*. Videocassette. New York: Mystic Fire Video, 1990.

———. "The World View of the Culture of the Goddess." *Snake Power* 1/1 (1989): 46.

Godelier, Maurice. "The Origins of Male Domination." *New Left Review* 127 (1981): 3–17.

Goldberg, Steven. *Why Men Rule: A Theory of Male Dominance*. Chicago: Open Court, 1993.

Gore, Al. *Earth in the Balance: Ecology and the Human Spirit*. Boston: Houghton Mifflin, 1992.

Göttner-Abendroth, Heide. *The Dancing Goddess: Principles of a Matriarchal Aesthetic* [1982]. Boston: Beacon Press, 1991.

———. *Matriarchal Mythology in Former Times and Today*. Freedom, CA: Crossing Press, 1987.

———. *Das Matriarchat I. Geschichte Seiner Erforschung*. Stuttgart: Verlag Kohlhammer, 1988.

Graves, Robert. *The White Goddess: A Historical Grammar of Poetic Myth* [1948]. Amended and enl. ed. New York: Farrar, Straus, and Giroux, 1966.

Gross, Rita. *Feminism and Religion: An Introduction*. Boston: Beacon Press, 1996.

Grosz, Elizabeth. *Volatile Bodies: Toward a Corporeal Feminism*. Bloomington, IN: Indiana University Press, 1994.

Grønborg, Ronni. "Matriarchy — Why Not?" *Folk* 21/22 (1979/80): 219–28.

Guillén, Ann Cyphers. "Thematic and Contextual Analyses of Chalcatzingo Figurines." *Mexicon* 10 (1988): 98–102.

Gvozdover, M. D. "The Typology of Female Figurines of the Kostenki Paleolithic Culture." *Soviet Anthropology and Archeology* 27/4 (1989): 32–94.

Haaland, Gunnar, and Randi Haaland. "Levels of Meaning in Symbolic Objects." In "Can We Interpret Figurines?" *Cambridge Archaeological Journal* 6/2 (1996): 295–300.

———. "Who Speaks the Goddess's Language? Imagination and Method in Archaeological Research." *Norwegian Archaeological Review* 28/2 (1995): 105–21.

Harding, M. Esther. *Woman's Mysteries: A Psychological Interpretation of the Feminine Principle as Portrayed in Myth, Story, and Dreams* [1955]. London: Rider Books, 1991.

Harris, Marvin. *Cultural Anthropology*. 3d ed. New York: Harper Collins, 1991.

———. *The Rise of Anthropological Theory*. New York: Thomas Crowell, 1968.

Harrison, Jane Ellen. *Epilegomena to the Study of Greek Religion* [1921] *and Themis* [1912]. New Hyde Park, NY: University Books, 1962.

———. *Prolegomena to the Study of Greek Religion* [1903]. New York: Meridian Books, 1955.

Hartland, E. S. "Matrilineal Kinship and the Question of its Priority." *Memoirs of the American Anthropological Association* 4 (1917): 1–87.

————. *Primitive Paternity.* 2 vols. London: Folk-Lore Society, 1909–10.

Hartley (Gallichan), Catherine Gasquoine. *The Age of Mother-Power: The Position of Woman in Primitive Society.* New York: Dodd Mead, 1914.

Hauser-Schäublin, Brigitta. "Mutterrecht und Frauenbewegung." In *Johann Jakob Bachofen (1815–1887).* Begleitpublikation zur Ausstellung im Historischen Museum Basel, 137–50. Basel: Historischen Museum Basel, 1987.

Hawkes, Jacquetta. *Dawn of the Gods.* London: Chatto & Windus, 1958.

Hawkes, Jacquetta, and Sir Leonard Woolley. *Prehistory and the Beginnings of Civilization.* Vol. 1 of *History of Mankind: Cultural and Scientific Development.* London: Allen and Unwin, 1963.

Hawley, John Stratton, and Donna Marie Wulff, eds. *Devī: Goddesses of India.* Berkeley: University of California Press, 1996.

Hayden, Brian. "An Archaeological Evaluation of the Gimbutas Paradigm." *Pomegranate,* no. 6 (November 1998): 35–46.

Hays, Kelley Ann. "When Is a Symbol Archaeologically Meaningful? Meaning, Function, and Prehistoric Visual Arts." In *Archaeological Theory: Who Sets the Agenda?* ed. Norman Yoffee and Andrew Sherratt, 81–92. Cambridge: Cambridge University Press, 1993.

Heine, Susanne. *Matriarchs, Goddesses, and Images of God: A Critique of a Feminist Theology.* Minneapolis: Augsburg, 1989.

Henes, Donna. *Mythology, the Matriarchy, and Me.* Audio compact disc. New York: Io Productions, 1998.

Herdt, Gilbert. *Guardians of the Flutes: Idioms of Masculinity.* New York: McGraw-Hill, 1981.

————, ed. *Third Sex, Third Gender: Beyond Sexual Dimorphism in Culture and History.* New York: Zone Books, 1993.

Heresies Collective, ed. *The Great Goddess.* Rev. ed. Special issue of *Heresies.* New York: Heresies Collective, 1982.

Héritier, F. "Le Sang du Guerrir et le Sang des Femmes: Notes Anthropologiques sur le Rapport des Sexes." *Africaines: Sexes et Signes. Cahiers du GRIF* 29 (1984): 5–11.

Hesiod. *Theogony.* Translated by Norman Brown. New York: Bobbs-Merrill, 1953.

————. *Works and Days.* In *Theogony, Works and Days, Shield.* Translated by Apostolos N. Athanassakis. Baltimore: Johns Hopkins Press, 1983.

Hewitt, Marsha Aileen. *Critical Theory of Religion: A Feminist Analysis.* Minneapolis: Fortress Press, 1995.

Hiatt, L. R., "Secret Pseudo-Procreation Rites among the Australian Aborigines." In *Anthropology in Oceania: Essays Presented to Ian Hogbin,* ed. L. R. Hiatt and C. Jayawardena, 77–88. Sydney: Angus and Robertson, 1971.

Hodder, Ian. "'Always Momentary, Fluid and Flexible': Towards a Reflexive Excavation Methodology." *Antiquity* 71/273 (September 1997): 691–700.

————. "Contextual Archaeology: An Interpretation of Çatal Hüyük and a Discussion of the Origins of Agriculture." *Institute of Archaeology Bulletin* 24 (1987): 43–56.

————, ed. *On the Surface: Çatalhöyük 1993–95.* Çatalhöyük Project Vol. 1/British

Institute of Archaeology at Ankara Monograph 22. Cambridge: McDonald
Institute of Archaeology, The Çatalhöyük Research Trust, 1996.

———. "The Past as Passion and Play: Çatalhöyük as a Site of Conflict in the Con-
struction of Multiple Pasts." In *Archaeology Under Fire: Politics, Nationalism, and
Heritage in the Eastern Mediterranean and Middle East*, ed. Lynn Meskell. London:
Routledge, 1998.

———. *Reading the Past: Current Approaches to Interpretation in Archaeology*. 2d ed.
Cambridge: Cambridge University Press, 1991.

Hodder, Ian, Michael Shanks, Alexandra Alexandri, Victor Buchli, John Carman,
Jonathan Last, and Gavin Lucas, eds. *Interpreting Archaeology: Finding Meaning in
the Past*. New York: Routledge, 1995.

Hogbin, Herbert Ian. *The Island of Menstruating Men: Religion in Wogeo, New Guinea*.
Scranton: Chandler, 1970.

Hopkins, Mary R. *The Great Mother Earth*. Part I of *Woman and Her Symbols*. Videocassette. 49 minutes. Distributed by Quaker Video, Maplewood, New Jersey,
1990.

———. *From Earth Mother to Love Goddess*. Part II of *Woman and Her Symbols*. Videocassette. 47 minutes. Distributed by Quaker Video, Maplewood, New Jersey,
1990.

Hubbs, Joanna. *Mother Russia: The Feminine Myth in Russian Culture*. Bloomington:
Indiana University Press, 1988.

Hultkrantz, Åke. *Native Religions of North America*. San Francisco: HarperSanFrancisco, 1987.

Hutchinson, R. W. *Prehistoric Crete*. London: Penguin, 1962.

Hutton, Ronald. "The Discovery of the Modern Goddess." In *Nature Religion
Today*, ed. Joanne Pearson et al., 89–100. Edinburgh: Edinburgh University
Press, 1998.

———. "The Neolithic Great Goddess: A Study in Modern Tradition." *Antiquity*
71 (1997): 91–99.

Iglehart, Hallie. *Womanspirit: A Guide to Women's Wisdom*. San Francisco: Harper
and Row, 1983.

Jade. *To Know: A Guide to Women's Magic and Spirituality*. Oak Park, IL: Delphi Press,
1991.

Jamal, Michele. *Shape Shifters: Shaman Women in Contemporary Society*. New York
and London: Arkana, 1988.

James, Edwin O. *The Cult of the Mother-Goddess*. New York: Praeger, 1959.

Janssen-Jurreit, Marielouise. *Sexism: The Male Monopoly on History and Thought*.
New York: Farrar Straus Giroux, 1982.

Jayakar, Pupul. *The Earth Mother*. San Francisco: HarperCollins, 1990.

Johnson, Buffie. *Lady of the Beasts: Ancient Images of the Great Goddess and her Sacred
Animals*. San Francisco: Harper and Row, 1988.

Jordanova, Ludmilla. *Sexual Visions: Images of Gender in Science and Medicine Between
the Eighteenth and Twentieth Centuries*. Madison: University of Wisconsin Press,
1989.

Juillerat, Bernard. "'An Odor of Man': Melanesian Evolutionism, Anthropological Mythology, and Matriarchy." Translated by R. Scott Walker. *Diogenes*, no. 144 (Winter 1988): 65–91.

Jung, Carl Gustav, ed. *Man and His Symbols*. Garden City, NY: Doubleday, 1964.

Katz, Marilyn A. "Ideology and 'The Status of Women' in Ancient Greece." In *Women and Antiquity: New Assessments*, ed. Richard Hawley and Barbara Levick, 21–43. New York: Routledge, 1995.

Keesing, Roger M. "Exotic Readings of Cultural Texts." *Cultural Anthropology* 30 (1989): 459–79.

Kehoe, Alice B. "No Possible, Probable Shadow of Doubt." *Antiquity* 65 (1991): 129–31.

Keller, Frances Richardson, ed. *Views of Women's Lives in Western Tradition: Frontiers of the Past and the Future*. New York: Edwin Mellen, 1990.

Kelly, Aidan. "An Update on Neopagan Witchcraft in America." In *Perspectives on the New Age*, ed. James Lewis. Albany: State University of New York Press, 1993.

Kenyatta, Jomo. *Facing Mount Kenya: The Tribal Life of the Gikuyu*. New York: Random House, 1965.

Keuls, Eva C. *The Reign of the Phallus: Sexual Politics in Ancient Athens*. Berkeley: University of California Press, 1985.

Kidd, Sue Monk. *The Dance of the Dissident Daughter: A Woman's Journey from Christian Tradition to the Sacred Feminine*. San Francisco: HarperSanFrancisco, 1996.

Kimball, Gayle, ed. *Women's Culture: The Women's Renaissance of the Seventies*. Metuchen, NJ: Scarecrow Press, 1981.

King, Karen, ed. *Women and Goddess Traditions*. Minneapolis: Fortress Press, 1997.

King, Theresa, ed. *The Divine Mosaic: Women's Images of the Sacred Other*. St. Paul, MN: Yes International Publishers, 1994.

King, Ursula. *Women and Spirituality: Voices of Protest and Promise*. New York: New Amsterdam, 1989.

King, Ynestra. "Healing the Wounds: Feminism, Ecology, and the Nature/Culture Dualism." In *Reweaving the World: The Emergence of Ecofeminism*, ed. Irene Diamond and Gloria Feman Orenstein. San Francisco: Sierra Club Books, 1990.

Kingsolver, Barbara. "Making Peace." In *High Tide in Tucson: Essays from Now or Never*. New York: Harper Collins, 1995.

Klages, Ludwig. *Vom Kosmogonischen Eros* [1922]. Stuttgart: Hans E. Günther Verlag, 1951.

Knapp, A. Bernard, and Lynn Meskell. "Bodies of Evidence on Prehistoric Cyprus." *Cambridge Archaeological Journal* 7/2 (October 1997): 183–204.

Knaster, Mirka. "Raider of the Lost Goddess." *East West* 19/12 (December 1990): 36–43, 68–69.

Kosse, Roberta. *Return of the Great Mother: An Oratorio for Women's Chorus and Chamber Orchestra*. Libretto by Jenny Malmquist. New York: Ars Pro Femina, no. 1, 1978.

Krader, Lawrence, ed. *The Ethnological Notebooks: Studies of Morgan, Phear, Maine, Lubbock*, by Karl Marx. 2d ed. Assen: Van Gorcum, 1974.

Kramer, Samuel Noah, and John Maier. *Myths of Enki, The Crafty God.* New York: Oxford University Press, 1989.

Kramer-Rolls, Dana, ed. "Reader's Forum." *Pomegranate*, no. 6 (November 1998): 2–5, 47–56.

Kristol, Elizabeth. "Just the Facts, Ma'am." *The American Spectator* 22 (July 1989): 39–41.

Kurtén, Björn. "Cave Art" [1981]. Chap. 14 in *How to Deep-Freeze a Mammoth.* Translated by Erik J. Friis. New York: Columbia University Press, 1986.

LaMonte, Willow. "The Black Virgins of Lydia Ruyle." *Goddessing Regenerated* 7 (Summer/Fall 1997): 15.

———. "'My Desire is Life': Goddess Traditions and Eco-Feminism." *Goddessing Regenerated* 7 (Summer/Fall 1997): 31.

Lamya'al-Faruqi, Lois. *Islam and Art.* Islamabad, Pakistan: National Hijra Council, 1985.

Lancaster, Chet S. *The Goba of the Zambezi: Sex Roles, Economics, and Change.* Norman, OK: University of Oklahoma Press, 1981.

Laqueur, Thomas. *Making Sex: Body and Gender from the Greeks to Freud.* Cambridge, MA: Harvard University Press, 1990.

Leach, Edmund. "Aryan Invasions over Four Millennia." In *Culture Through Time: Anthropological Approaches*, ed. Emiko Ohnuki-Tierney, 227–45. Stanford: Stanford University Press, 1990.

Leach, Edmund. "Virgin Birth." In *Genesis as Myth and Other Essays.* London: Jonathan Cape, 1969.

Leacock, Eleanor Burke. "Interpreting the Origins of Gender Inequality: Conceptual and Historical Problems." *Dialectical Anthropology* 7 (1983): 263–83.

———. *Myths of Male Dominance.* New York: Monthly Review Press, 1981.

———. "Women in Egalitarian Societies." In *Becoming Visible: Women in European History*, ed. Renate Bridenthal, Claudia Koonz, and Susan Stuard. 2d ed. Boston: Houghton Mifflin, 1987.

———. "Women's Status in Egalitarian Society: Implications for Social Evolution." *Current Anthropology* 19/2 (1978): 247–75.

Lee, Susan/Susanah Libana. *You Said, What Is This For, This Interest in Goddess, Prehistoric Religions?* Austin, TX: Plain View Press, 1985.

Lefkowitz, Mary. "The New Cults of the Mother Goddess." *The American Scholar* 62 (1993): 261–68.

———. "The Twilight of the Goddess." *The New Republic*, 3 August 1992, 29–33.

———. *Women in Greek Myth.* Baltimore: Johns Hopkins University Press, 1986.

Lehmann, W. P. "Frozen Residues and Relative Dating." In *Varia on the Indo-European Past: Papers in Memory of Marija Gimbutas*, ed. Miriam Robbins Dexter and Edgar C. Polomé. Washington DC: Journal of Indo-European Studies Monograph No. 19, 1997.

Leibowitz, Lila. "Origins of the Sexual Division of Labor." In *Woman's Nature: Rationalization of Inequality*, ed. Marian Lowe and Ruth Hubbard, 123–47. New York: Pergamon, 1983.

Lerner, Gerda. *The Creation of Patriarchy*. New York: Oxford University Press, 1986.

——. "Writing Women into History." *Woman of Power* 16 (Spring 1990): 6–9.

Leroi-Gourhan, André. "The Evolution of Paleolithic Art." *Scientific American* 218 (February 1968): 59–70.

Leslie, Jacques. "The Goddess Theory." *Los Angeles Times Magazine*, 11 June 1989, 22–24, 26.

Levin, Harry. *The Myth of the Golden Age in the Renaissance*. Bloomington, IN: Indiana University Press, 1969.

Levy, Gertrude Rachel. *The Gate of Horn: A Study of the Religious Conceptions of the Stone Age, and their Influence upon European Thought*. London: Faber and Faber, 1948.

Lincoln, Bruce. *Discourse and the Construction of Society: Comparative Studies of Myth, Ritual, and Classification*. New York: Oxford University Press, 1989.

Lo Russo, Guiditta. "Origine e Diffusione dell'Idea d'una Societa Matriarcale." *Revue Internationale de Sociologie* 8/203 (Aug.-Dec. 1972): 34–56.

Loraux, Nicole. *The Children of Athena: Athenian Ideas about Citizenship and the Division Between the Sexes* [1984]. Translated by Caroline Levine. Princeton: Princeton University Press, 1993.

Lorde, Audre. *Sister Outsider*. Trumansburg, NY: Crossing, 1984.

Mack, Rainer. "Reading the Archaeology of the Female Body." *Qui Parle* 4/1 (1990): 79–97.

Mackey, Mary. *The Fires of Spring*. San Francisco: HarperSanFrancisco, 1998.

——. *The Horses at the Gate*. San Francisco: HarperSanFrancisco, 1995.

——. *The Year the Horses Came*. San Francisco: HarperSanFrancisco, 1993.

Magli, Ida, ed. *Matriarcato e Potere delle Donne*. Milano: Feltrinelli, 1978.

Makkay, János. "The Linear Pottery and the Early Indo-Europeans." In *Proto-Indo-European: The Archaeology of a Linguistic Problem*, ed. Susan Nacev Skomal and Edgar C. Polomé. Washington DC: Institute for the Study of Man, 1987.

Malinowski, Bronislaw. *The Father in Primitive Psychology*. New York: W. W. Norton, 1927.

——. *Myth in Primitive Psychology* [1926]. Westport, CT: Negro Universities Press, 1971.

——. *Sex, Culture, and Myth*. New York: Harcourt, Brace, and World, 1962.

Mallory, J. P. *In Search of the Indo-Europeans*. London: Thames & Hudson, 1989.

Mann, Judy. *The Difference: Growing up Female in America*. New York: Warner Books, 1994.

Marcus, Joyce. "The Importance of Context in Interpreting Figurines." In "Can We Interpret Figurines?" *Cambridge Archaeological Journal* 6/2 (1996): 285–91.

Marinatos, Nanno. *Minoan Religion: Ritual, Image, and Symbol*. Columbia: University of South Carolina Press, 1993.

Marler, Joan, ed. *From the Realm of the Ancestors: An Anthology in Honor of Marija Gimbutas*. Manchester, CT: Knowledge, Ideas & Trends, Inc., 1997.

Marshack, Alexander. *The Roots of Civilization: The Cognitive Underpinnings of Man's First Art, Symbol and Notation*. Rev. ed. Mount Kisco, NY: Moyer Bell Ltd., 1991.

Mason, Jim. *An Unnatural Order: Uncovering the Roots of Our Domination of Nature and Each Other*. New York: Simon and Schuster, 1993.

Mathews, Zena Pearlstone. "Seneca Figurines: A Case of Misplaced Modesty." In *Studies on Iroquoian Culture*, ed. Nancy Bonvillain. Occasional Publications in Northeastern Anthropology, 6. Ridge, NH: Franklin Pierce College, 1980.

Matriarchy Study Group, ed. *Politics of Matriarchy*. London: Matriarchy Study Group, 1979.

McCall, Henrietta. *Mesopotamian Myths*. London: British Museum Publications, 1990.

McCoid, Catherine Hodge, and LeRoy D. McDermott. "Toward Decolonizing Gender: Female Vision in the Upper Paleolithic." *American Anthropologist* 98/2 (June 1996): 319–26.

McLennan, John Ferguson. "The Early History of Man." *North British Review* 50 (1869): 516–49.

Meigs, Anna S. *Food, Sex, and Pollution: A New Guinea Religion*. New Brunswick, NJ: Rutgers University Press, 1984.

Mellaart, James. *Çatal Hüyük: A Neolithic Town In Anatolia*. New York: McGraw-Hill, 1967.

———. *The Neolithic of the Near East*. London: Thames and Hudson, 1975.

Merlan, Francesca. "Gender in Aboriginal Social Life: A Review." In *Social Anthropology and Australian Aboriginal Studies*, ed. Ronald M. Berndt and Robert Tonkinson, 17–76. Canberra: Aboriginal Studies Press, 1988.

Meskell, Lynn. "Goddesses, Gimbutas, and 'New Age' Archaeology." *Antiquity* 69 (1995): 74–86.

Miles, Rosalind. *The Women's History of the World*. New York: Harper and Row, 1990.

Milisauskas, Sarunas. *European Prehistory*. Orlando, FL: Academic Press, 1978.

Miller, Barbara Diane, ed. *Sex and Gender Hierarchies*. Cambridge: Cambridge University Press, 1993.

Millett, Kate. *Sexual Politics*. Garden City, NY: Doubleday, 1970.

Min Jiayin, ed. *The Chalice and the Blade in Chinese Culture: Gender Relations and Social Models*. Beijing: China Social Sciences Publishing House, 1995.

Moltmann-Wendel, Elisabeth. *A Land Flowing with Milk and Honey: Perspectives on Feminist Theology*. Translated by John Bowden. London: SCM, 1986.

Montagu, Ashley. *Coming into Being among the Australian Aborigines* [1937]. 2d rev. ed. London: Routledge, 1974.

———. *The Natural Superiority of Women*. Rev. ed. New York: Macmillan, 1974.

Moore, Albert C. *Iconography of Religions: An Introduction*. Philadelphia: Fortress Press, 1977.

Moore, Henrietta L. *Feminism and Anthropology*. Minneapolis: University of Minnesota Press, 1988.

Moore, Jenny, and Eleanor Scott, eds. *Invisible People and Processes: Writing Gender and Childhood into European Archaeology*. London: Leicester University Press, 1997.

Mor, Barbara, and Monica Sjöö. "Respell the World." *Woman of Power*, no. 12 (Winter 1989).

Morelli, Gilda A. "Growing up Female in a Farmer Community and a Forager Community." In *The Evolving Female: A Life-History Perspective*, ed. Mary Ellen Morbeck, Alison Galloway, and Adrienne L. Zihlman. Princeton: Princeton University Press, 1997.

Morgan, Lewis H. *Ancient Society or Researches in the Lines of Human Progress from Savagery through Barbarism to Civilization*. New York: Henry Holt and Company, 1878.

Morris, Rosalind C. "All Made Up: Performance Theory and the New Anthropology of Sex and Gender." *Annual Review of Anthropology* 24 (1995): 567–92.

Motz, Lotte. *The Faces of the Goddess*. New York: Oxford University Press, 1997.

Murdock, Maureen. *The Heroine's Journey: Woman's Quest for Wholeness*. Boston: Shambhala, 1990.

Murphy, Robert F. "Social Structure and Sex Antagonism." *Southwestern Journal of Anthropology* 15/1 (1959): 89–98.

Murphy, Yolanda, and Robert F. Murphy. *Women of the Forest*. New York: Columbia University Press, 1974.

Murray, Margaret A. "Female Fertility Figurines." *Journal of the Royal Anthropological Institute* 64 (1934): 93–100.

Múten, Burleigh, ed. *Return of the Great Goddess*. Boston: Shambhala, 1994.

Nelson, Sarah M. "Diversity of Upper Palaeolithic 'Venus' Figurines and Archaeological Mythology." In *Powers of Observation: Alternative Views in Archaeology*, ed. Sarah M. Nelson and Alice B. Kehoe, 11–22. Washington DC: American Anthropological Association, 1990.

———. *Gender in Archaeology: Analyzing Power and Prestige*. Walnut Creek, CA: Sage Publications, 1997.

Neslen, Kristie. *The Origin: An Investigation into Ancient Matriarchal Societies, the Patriarchal Takeover and its Effect on Society Today, and the Building of a Just and Egalitarian Post-Patriarchal Society*. San Francisco: Venusian Propaganda, 1979.

Neumann, Erich. *The Great Mother*. Translated by Ralph Manheim. 2d ed. Princeton: Princeton University Press, 1963.

Neusner, Jacob. "Studying Ancient Judaism through the Art of the Synagogue." In *Art as Religious Studies*, ed. Douglas Adams and Diane Apostolos-Cappadona. New York: Crossroad, 1987.

Noble, Vicki. "Authorizing Our Teachers: Teaching in a Feminist Spiritual Context." *Woman of Power* 24 (Summer 1995): 71–75, 84.

———. "Marija Gimbutas: Reclaiming the Great Goddess." *Snake Power* 1/1 (1989): 5–7.

———. *Motherpeace: A Way to the Goddess through Myth, Art, and Tarot*. San Francisco: Harper and Row, 1985.

———. "The Shakti Woman." *Snake Power* 1/1 (1989): 12–13, 26–28.

———. *Shakti Woman: Feeling our Fire, Healing our World. The New Female Shamanism*. San Francisco: HarperSanFrancisco, 1991.

————, ed. *Uncoiling the Snake: Ancient Patterns in Contemporary Women's Lives*. San Francisco: HarperSanFrancisco, 1991.

Olsen, Kirstin. *Chronology of Women's History*. Westport, CT: Greenwood, 1994.

Orenstein, Gloria Feman. *The Reflowering of the Goddess: Contemporary Journeys and Cycles of Empowerment*. New York: Pergamon Press, 1990.

Orphanides, Andreas G. "A Critique of Suggested Interpretations of Prehistoric Anthropomorphic Figurines." *Journal of Business and Society* 1 (1988): 164–71.

Ortner, Sherry. "Is Female to Male as Nature Is to Culture?" *Feminist Studies* 1/2 (Fall 1972): 5–32.

————. *Making Gender: The Politics and Erotics of Culture*. Boston: Beacon Press, 1996.

Ortner, Sherry, and Harriet Whitehead, eds. *Sexual Meanings: The Cultural Construction of Gender and Sexuality*. Cambridge: Cambridge University Press, 1981.

Osborne, Lawrence. "The Women Warriors." *Lingua Franca* 7/10 (Dec./Jan. 1998): 50–57.

Owen-Smith, Patti, Shirley A. Stave, and Ina Jane Wundram. "Feminist Teaching Across the Curriculum: Reclaiming the Goddess." Paper presented at the National Women's Studies Association Annual Meeting, Washington DC, June 1993.

Panoff, Michel. "Patrifiliation as Ideology and Practice in a Matrilineal Society." *Ethnology* 15 (1976): 175–88.

Pantel, Pauline Schmitt, ed. *A History of Women in the West*. Vol. 1, *From Ancient Goddesses to Christian Saints*. Translated by Arthur Goldhammer. Cambridge, MA: Belknap Press of Harvard University Press, 1992.

Paper, Jordan. *Through the Earth Darkly: Female Spirituality in Comparative Perspective*. New York: Continuum, 1997.

Parker, Seymour, and Hilda Parker. "The Myth of Male Superiority: Rise and Demise." *American Anthropology* 81 (1979): 289–309.

Pateman, Carole. *The Sexual Contract*. Stanford: Stanford University Press, 1988.

Pembroke, Simon. "Women in Charge: The Function of Alternatives in Early Greek Tradition and the Ancient Idea of Matriarchy." *Journal of the Warburg and Courtald Institutes* 30 (1967): 1–35.

Penniman, T. K. *A Hundred Years of Anthropology*. 2d ed. London: Duckworth, 1952.

Perera, Sylvia Brinton. *Descent to the Goddess: A Way of Initiation for Women*. Toronto: Inner City Books, 1981.

Perkins, Sally J. "The Myth of the Matriarchy: Annuling Patriarchy through the Regeneration of Time." *Communication Studies* 42/4 (Winter 1991): 371–82.

Pesando, F. J. *Sisters of the Black Moon*. New York: Penguin, 1994.

Pestalozza, Uberto. "The Mediterranean Matriarchate: Its Primordial Character in the Religious Atmosphere of the Paleolithic Era." *Diogenes* 12 (1955): 50–61.

Pipher, Mary Bray. *Reviving Ophelia: Saving the Selves of Adolescent Girls*. New York: Putnam, 1994.

Plaskow, Judith, and Carol Christ, eds. *Weaving the Visions: New Patterns in Feminist Spirituality*. San Francisco: Harper and Row, 1989.

Poewe, Karla O. "Universal Male Dominance: An Ethnological Illusion." *Dialectical Anthropology* 5/2 (1980): 111–25.

Pollack, Rachel. *The Body of the Goddess: Sacred Wisdom in Myth, Landscape, and Culture.* Rockport, MA: Element Books, 1997.

Pomeroy, Sarah B. *Goddesses, Whores, Wives, and Slaves: Women in Classical Antiquity.* New York: Schocken, 1975.

———. *Goddesses, Whores, Wives, and Slaves: Women in Classical Antiquity.* 2d ed. New York: Schocken, 1994.

Poth, Dee. *The Goddess Speaks: Myths and Meditations.* Portland, OR: Sibyl Publications, 1994.

Powell, H. A. *An Analysis of Present Day Social Structure in the Trobriands.* London: Thesis, 1956.

Prentiss, Charlotte. *Children of the Ice.* New York: Penguin, 1993.

Preston, James J., ed. *Mother Worship: Themes and Variations.* Chapel Hill, NC: University of North Carolina Press, 1982.

Purkiss, Diane. *The Witch in History: Early Modern and Twentieth-Century Representations.* New York: Routledge, 1996.

Rabinowitz, Nancy Sorkin, and Amy Richlin, eds. *Feminist Theory and the Classics.* New York: Routledge, 1994.

Ranck, Shirley. *Cakes for the Queen of Heaven.* Boston: Unitarian Universalist Association, 1986.

———. *Cakes for the Queen of Heaven: An Exploration of Women's Power Past, Present, and Future.* Chicago: Delphi Press, 1995.

Raymond, Janice. Review of *The Subordinate Sex*, by Vern L. Bullough and Bonnie Bullough. *Christian Century* 91 (1974): 457–59.

Read, Donna. *Goddess Remembered.* Videocassette. 55 minutes. National Film Board of Canada. Distributed by Direct Cinema, Santa Monica, California, 1989.

Redmond, Layne. "Rhythm and the Frame Drum." *Woman of Power* 15 (Winter 1989).

———. *When the Drummers Were Women: A Spiritual History of Rhythm.* New York: Crown Publishing, 1997.

Reed, Evelyn. *Problems of Women's Liberation: A Marxist Approach.* Enl. ed. New York: Pathfinder Press, 1970.

———. *Woman's Evolution: From Matriarchal Clan to Patriarchal Family.* New York: Pathfinder Press, 1975.

Reich, Wilhelm. *The Invasion of Compulsory Sex-Morality* [1931]. New York: Farrar Straus Giroux, 1971.

Reichel-Dolmatoff, Gerardo. "Anthropomorphic Figurines from Columbia: Their Magic and Art." In *Essays in Pre-Columbian Art and Archaeology*, ed. S. K. Lothrop et al., 229–41. Cambridge, MA: Harvard University Press, 1961.

———. *Amazonian Cosmos: The Sexual and Religious Symbolism of the Tukano Indians.* Chicago: University of Chicago Press, 1971.

Reis, Patricia. *Through the Goddess: A Woman's Way of Healing.* New York: Continuum, 1991.

Renfrew, Colin. *Archaeology and Language: The Puzzle of Indo-European Origins.* New York: Cambridge University Press, 1987.

————. Review of *Archaeology and Language* (with reviews by David Anthony, Bernard Wailes, P. Baldi, Graeme Barker, Robert Coleman, Marija Gimbutas, Evžen Neustupný, and Andrew Sherratt). *Current Anthropology* 29/3 (June 1988): 437–68.

Rice, Patricia C. "Prehistoric Venuses: Symbols of Motherhood or Womanhood?" *Journal of Anthropological Research* 37/4 (1981): 402–14.

Rice, Patricia C., and Ann L. Paterson. "Anthropomorphs in Cave Art: An Empirical Assessment." *American Anthropologist* 90 (1988): 664–74.

Rich, Adrienne. *Of Woman Born: Motherhood as Experience and Institution* [1977]. Tenth anniversary ed. New York: Norton, 1986.

Rigoglioso, Marguerite. "Awakening to the Goddess." *New Age Journal* 14/3 (June 1997): 60–69, 144–48.

————. "Interview with Luisah Teish." *Goddessing Regenerated* 7 (Summer/Fall 1997): 11–14, 16.

Riley, E. M. Denise. *"Am I That Name?" Feminism and the Category of "Women" in History.* Minneapolis: University of Minnesota Press, 1988.

Robb, Christina. "In Goddess They Trust: Feminists Eschew Tradition in Pursuit of 'Deeper' Worship." *Boston Globe*, 9 July 1990, Living/Arts Section, 32, 36.

Robbins, Tom. *Skinny Legs and All.* New York: Bantam, 1990.

Rodriguez, Jeanette. *Our Lady of Guadalupe: Faith and Empowerment among Mexican-American Women.* Austin: University of Texas Press, 1994.

Rohrlich, Ruby. "State Formation in Sumer and the Subjugation of Women." *Feminist Studies* 6/1 (1980): 76–102.

Rohrlich-Leavitt, Ruby. "Women in Transition: Crete and Sumer." In *Becoming Visible: Women in European History*, ed. Renate Bridenthal and Claudia Koonz, 36–59. Boston: Houghton Mifflin, 1977.

Roosevelt, Anna C. "Interpreting Certain Female Images in Prehistoric Art." In *The Role of Gender in Precolumbian Art and Architecture*, ed. Virginia E. Miller, 1–34. Lanham, MD: University Press of America, 1988.

Rosaldo, Michelle Zimbalist. "The Use and Abuse of Anthropology: Reflections on Feminism and Cross-Cultural Understanding." *Signs* 5/3 (1980): 389–417.

Rosaldo, Michelle Zimbalist, and Louise Lamphere, eds. *Woman, Culture, and Society.* Stanford: Stanford University Press, 1974.

Rose, Deborah. "Black Madonnas: From Ancient Dark Ancestress to Blessed Virgin Mary." *Goddessing Regenerated* 5 (Summer/Fall 1996): 17.

Rose, H. J. "On the Alleged Evidence for Mother-Right in Early Greece." *Folk-Lore* 22 (1911): 277–91.

————. "Prehistoric Greece and Mother-Right." *Folk-Lore* 37 (1926): 213–44.

Rowbotham, Sheila. "When Adam Delved, and Eve Span." *New Society*, 4 January 1979, 10–12.

Ruether, Rosemary Radford. *Gaia and God: An Ecofeminist Theology of Earth Healing.* San Francisco: HarperSanFrancisco, 1992.

————. *Sexism and God-Talk: Toward a Feminist Theology.* Boston: Beacon Press, 1983.

Rufus, Anneli S., and Kristan Lawson. *Goddess Sites: Europe*. San Francisco: HarperSanFrancisco, 1991.

Ruth, Sheila. *Take Back the Light: A Feminist Reclamation of Spirituality and Religion*. Lanham, MD: Rowman and Littlefield, 1993.

Rybakov, B. A. "Cosmology and Mythology of the Agriculturalists of the Eneolithic." *Soviet Anthropology and Archeology* 4 (1965–66): 2/16–36; 3/33–52.

Sacks, Karen. *Sisters and Wives: The Past and Future of Sexual Equality*. Westport, CT: Greenwood, 1979.

Samson, Ross. "Superwomen, Wonderwomen, Great Women, and Real Women." *Archaeological Review from Cambridge* 7/1 (1988): 60–66.

Sanday, Peggy Reeves. *Female Power and Male Dominance: On the Origins of Sexual Inequality*. Cambridge: Cambridge University Press, 1981.

Schlegel, Alice, ed. *Sexual Stratification: A Cross-Cultural View*. New York: Columbia University Press, 1977.

Schmerl, Christiane, and Cordula Ritter. "Stand und Bedeutung der Matriarchatsdebatte." In *Philosophische Beiträge zur Frauenforschung*, ed. Ruth Grossmass and Christiane Schmerl, 83–98. Bochum: Germinal-Verlag, 1981.

Schor, Naomi A. "Feminist and Gender Studies." In *Introduction to Scholarship in Modern Languages and Literature*, ed. Joseph Gibaldi, 262–87. 2d ed. New York: Modern Language Association, 1992.

Schuler, Alfred. "Mutterdunkel." In *Johann Jakob Bachofen (1815–1887): Eine Begleitpublikation zur Ausstellung im Historischen Museum Basel*. Basel: Historical Museum of Basel, 1987.

Sempowski, Martha L. "Differential Mortuary Treatment of Seneca Women: Some Social Inferences." *Archaeology of Eastern North America* 14 (1986): 35–44.

Sered, Susan Starr. "Ideology, Autonomy, and Sisterhood: An Analysis of the Secular Consequences of Women's Religions." *Gender and Society* 8/4 (December 1994): 486–506.

Shannon, Jacqueline. *Why It's Great to Be a Girl: Fifty Eye-Opening Things You Can Tell Your Daughter to Increase Her Pride in Being Female*. New York: Warner Books, 1994.

Sherfey, Mary Jane. *The Nature and Evolution of Female Sexuality*. New York: Vintage, 1973.

Sherratt, Andrew. "Mobile Resources: Settlement and Exchange in Early Agricultural Europe." In *Ranking, Resource, and Exchange*, ed. Colin Renfrew and Stephen Shennan. Cambridge: Cambridge University Press, 1982.

———. Review of *The Language of the Goddess*, by Marija Gimbutas. *Antiquaries Journal* 69/2 (1989): 345–46.

Shlain, Leonard. *The Alphabet Versus the Goddess: The Conflict Between Word and Image*. NY: Viking, 1998.

Shreeve, James. *The Neandertal Enigma: Solving the Mystery of Modern Human Origins*. New York: Morrow, 1995.

Silverblatt, Irene. "Women in States." *Annual Review of Anthropology* 17 (1988): 427–60.

Singer, Philip, and Daniel E. Desole. "The Australian Subincision Ceremony Reconsidered: Vaginal Envy or Kangaroo Biped Penis Envy." *American Anthropologist* 69 (1967): 355–58.

Sjöö, Monica. *New Age and Armageddon: The Goddess or the Gurus? Towards a Feminist Vision of the Future.* London: The Women's Press, 1992.

———. "A Poem in Memory of and in Tribute to Marija Gimbutas." *Goddessing Regenerated* 5 (Summer/Fall 1996): 30.

Sjöö, Monica, and Barbara Mor. *The Great Cosmic Mother: Rediscovering the Religion of the Earth.* San Francisco: Harper and Row, 1987.

Skinner, Marilyn. "Greek Women and the Metronymic." *The Ancient History Bulletin* 1 (1987): 39–42.

Snell, Daniel C. *Life in the Ancient Near East, 3100–322 BCE.* New Haven, CT: Yale University Press, 1997.

Spaeth, Barbette Stanley. *The Roman Goddess Ceres.* Austin: University of Texas Press, 1995.

Spector, Janet D. "Male/Female Task Differentiation among the Hidatsa: Toward the Development of an Archaeological Approach to the Study of Gender." In *The Hidden Half: Studies of Plains Indian Women*, ed. Patricia Albers and Beatrice Medicine. Washington DC: University Press of America, 1983.

Spencer, Anna Garlin. *Woman's Share in Social Culture* [1917]. New York: Arno Press, 1972.

Spiro, Melford E. "Virgin Birth, Parthenogenesis, and Physiological Paternity: An Essay in Cultural Interpretation." *Man (n.s.)* 3 (1968): 242–61.

Spretnak, Charlene. *Lost Goddesses of Early Greece: A Collection of Pre-Hellenic Myths.* Boston: Beacon Press, 1981.

———, ed. *The Politics of Women's Spirituality: Essays on the Rise of Spiritual Power Within the Feminist Movement.* Garden City, NY: Anchor Books, 1982.

———, ed. *The Politics of Women's Spirituality: Essays by Founding Mothers of the Movement.* Rev. ed. Garden City, NY: Anchor Books, 1994.

———. "The Spiritual Experience of the Female Psyche/Soma." Lecture in Los Angeles, 24 April 1982. Audiotape.

Sreenivasan, Jyotsna. *The Moon Over Crete.* Duluth, MN: Holy Cow! Press, 1994.

Stanton, Elizabeth Cady. "The Matriarchate or Mother-Age: Address of Mrs. Stanton before the National Council of Women." *The National Bulletin* 1/5 (February 1891) 1–12.

Starhawk. *Dreaming the Dark: Magic, Sex, and Politics.* Boston: Beacon Press, 1982.

———. *Truth or Dare: Power, Authority, and Magic.* San Francisco: Harper and Row, 1987.

———. "Witchcraft and Women's Culture." In *Womanspirit Rising*, ed. Carol P. Christ and Judith Plaskow. San Francisco: Harper and Row, 1979.

Stein, Diane. *Dreaming the Past, Dreaming the Future: A Herstory of the Earth.* Freedom, CA: Crossing Press, 1991.

———. *The Women's Spirituality Book.* St. Paul, MN: Llewellyn Publications, 1987.

Steinem, Gloria. *Wonder Woman.* New York: Holt, Rinehart, and Winston, and Warner Books, 1972.

Steinfels, Peter. "Idyllic Theory of Goddesses Creates Storm." *New York Times*, 13 February 1990.

Stephenson, June. *Women's Roots.* 4th ed. Napa, CA: Deimer, Smith, 1993.

Stern, Philip Van Doren. *Prehistoric Europe: From Stone Age Man to the Early Greeks.* New York: Norton, 1969.

Stoliar, A. D. "On the Sociohistorical Decoding of Upper Paleolithic Female Signs." *Soviet Anthropology and Archaeology* 16 (1977/78): 36–77.

Stone, Merlin. *The Return of the Goddess.* Four audiocassettes. Montreal: Canadian Broadcasting Corporation, 1985.

———. *When God Was a Woman.* New York: Harcourt, Brace, Jovanovich, 1976.

Streep, Peg. *Sanctuaries of the Goddess: The Sacred Landscapes and Objects.* Boston: Little, Brown and Co., 1994.

Sturgeon, Noël. *Ecofeminist Natures: Race, Gender, Feminist Theory, and Political Action.* New York: Routledge, 1997.

Swain, Tony. "The Mother Earth Conspiracy." *Numen* 38 (June 1991): 3–26.

Szemerényi, Oswald. "Studies in the Kinship Terminology of the Indo-European Languages with Special References to Indian, Iranian, Greek, and Latin." *Acta Iranica* 16 (1977): 1–240. Leiden: E. J. Brill, 1977.

Talalay, Lauren E. "A Feminist Boomerang: The Great Goddess of Greek Prehistory." *Gender and History* 6 (1994): 165–83.

Tambiah, Stanley Jeyaraja. *Magic, Science, Religion, and the Scope of Rationality.* Cambridge: Cambridge University Press, 1990.

Tavris, Carol. *The Mismeasure of Women: Why Women Are Not the Better Sex, the Inferior Sex, or the Opposite Sex.* New York: Simon and Schuster, 1992.

Taylor, Sarah. "'Brothers' in Arms? Feminism, Poststructuralism and the 'Rise of Civilisation.'" In *Writing the Past in the Present,* ed. Frederick Baker and Julian Thomas, 32–41. Lampeter, England: St. David's University, 1990.

Taylor, Timothy. *The Prehistory of Sex: Four Million Years of Human Sexual Culture.* New York: Bantam, 1996.

Teish, Luisah. *Jambalaya: The Natural Woman's Book of Personal Charms and Practical Rituals.* San Francisco: Harper and Row, 1985.

Thomas, C. G. "Matriarchy in Early Greece: The Bronze and Dark Ages." *Arethusa* 6 (1973): 173–95.

Thomas, Elizabeth Marshall. *Reindeer Moon.* New York: Simon and Schuster, 1987.

Thomson, George. *Studies in Ancient Greek Society.* London: Lawrence and Wishart, 1949.

Thurer, Shari L. *The Myths of Motherhood: How Culture Reinvents the Good Mother.* New York: Penguin Books, 1995.

Tiffany, Sharon W. "The Power of Matriarchal Ideas." *International Journal of Women's Studies* 5/2 (1982): 138–47.

Tolstoy, P. "Morgan and Soviet Anthropological Thought." *American Anthropologist* 54 (1952): 8–17.

Tooker, Elisabeth. "Women in Iroquois Society." In *Extending the Rafters: Interdisciplinary Approaches to Iroquoian Studies,* ed. Michael K. Foster, Jack Campisi, and Marianne Mithun, 109–23. Albany: State University of New York Press, 1984.

Townsend, Joan B. "The Goddess: Fact, Fallacy, and Revitalization Movement." In *Goddesses in Religions and Modern Debate*, ed. Larry W. Hurtado, 179–203. University of Manitoba Studies in Religion. Atlanta: Scholars Press, 1990.

Trump, David. *The Prehistory of the Mediterranean*. New Haven, CT: Yale University Press, 1980.

Trump, David, Anthony Bonanno, Tancred Gouder, Caroline Malone, and Simon Stoddart. "New Light on Death in Prehistoric Malta: The Brochtorff Circle." In *Illustrated History of Mankind*, vol. 2, ed. Göran Burenhult. San Francisco: HarperSanFrancisco, 1993.

Tuzin, Donald F. *The Voice of the Tambaran: Truth and Illusion in Ilahita Arapesh Religion*. Berkeley: University of California Press, 1980.

Tylor, Edward Burnett. *Primitive Culture: Researches into the Development of Mythology, Philosophy, Religion, Language, Art, and Custom* [1871]. New York: Holt, 1889.

Tyrrell, William Blake. *Amazons, a Study in Athenian Mythmaking*. Baltimore: Johns Hopkins University Press, 1989.

Ucko, Peter J. *Anthropomorphic Figurines in Predynastic Egypt and Neolithic Crete with Comparative Material from the Prehistoric Near East and Mainland Greece*. London: A. Szmidla, 1968.

———. "Mother, Are You There?" In "Can We Interpret Figurines?" *Cambridge Archaeological Journal* 6/2 (1996): 300–304.

Unterman, Alan. "Judaism." In *A New Handbook of Living Religions*, ed. John R. Hinnells. Oxford: Blackwell, 1997.

Ventris, Michael, and John Chadwick. *Documents in Mycenaean Greek: Three Hundred Selected Tablets from Knossos, Pylos and Mycenae with Commentary and Vocabulary*. Cambridge: Cambridge University Press, 1956.

Vermeule, Emily. *Greece in the Bronze Age*. Chicago: University of Chicago Press, 1964.

Veyne, Paul. *Did the Greeks Believe in Their Myths?* Chicago: University of Chicago Press, 1988.

Vidal-Nacquet, Pierre. "Slavery and the Role of Women in Tradition, Myth, and Utopia." In *Myth, Religion, and Society*, ed. R. L. Gordon. Cambridge: Cambridge University Press, 1981.

von Cles-Reden, Sibylle. *The Realm of the Great Goddess*. Englewood, NJ: Prentice-Hall, 1962.

von Kellenbach, Katharina. *Anti-Judaism in Feminist Religious Writings*. Atlanta: Scholars Press, 1994.

Wakeman, Mary K. "Ancient Sumer and the Women's Movement: The Process of Reaching Behind, Encompassing, and Going Beyond." *Journal of Feminist Studies in Religion* 1/2 (Fall 1985): 7–27.

Walker, Barbara G. *The Skeptical Feminist: Discovering the Virgin, Mother, and Crone*. San Francisco: Harper and Row, 1987.

Walters, Suzanne Danuta. "Caught in the Web: A Critique of Spiritual Feminism." *Berkeley Journal of Sociology* 30 (1985): 15–40.

Ward, Martha C. *A World Full of Women.* Needham Heights, MA: Allyn and Bacon, 1996.

Washburn, Sherwood L., and C. S. Lancaster. "The Evolution of Hunting." In *Man the Hunter,* ed. Richard B. Lee and Irven DeVore, 293–303. Chicago: Aldine, 1968.

Webster, Paula. "Matriarchy: A Vision of Power." In *Toward an Anthropology of Women,* ed. Rayna R. Reiter, 141–56. New York: Monthly Review Press, 1975.

Weiner, Annette B. *Women of Value, Men of Renown: New Perspectives on Trobriand Exchange.* Austin, TX: University of Texas Press, 1976.

Wendt, Herbert. *In Search of Adam: The Story of Man's Quest for the Truth about his Earliest Ancestors.* Translated by James Cleugh. Boston: Houghton Mifflin, 1956.

Weston, Kath. "Lesbian/Gay Studies in the House of Anthropology." *Annual Review of Anthropology* 22 (1993): 339–67.

Whyte, Martin King. *The Status of Women in Preindustrial Societies.* Princeton: Princeton University Press, 1978.

Wilber, Ken. *Up From Eden: A Transpersonal View of Human Evolution.* Boulder: Shambhala, 1983.

Wilford, John Noble. "What Doomed the Maya? Maybe Warfare Run Amok." *New York Times,* 19 November 1991, section C, 1, 10–11.

Willetts, R. F. *Cretan Cults and Festivals.* London: Routledge and Kegan Paul, 1962.

Wilshire, Donna. *Virgin Mother Crone: Myths and Mysteries of the Triple Goddess.* Rochester, VT: Inner Traditions, 1994.

Wolf, Joan. *The Horsemasters.* New York: Penguin, 1993.

Woolger, Jennifer Barker, and Roger J. Woolger. *The Goddess Within: A Guide to the Eternal Myths that Shape Women's Lives.* New York: Fawcett Columbine, 1987.

Worthman, Carol M. "Hormones, Sex, and Gender." *Annual Review of Anthropology* 24 (1995): 593–616.

Wynne, Patrice. *The Womanspirit Sourcebook.* San Francisco: Harper and Row, 1988.

Yanagisako, Sylvia Junko, and Jane Fishburne Collier. "Toward a Unified Analysis of Gender and Kinship." In *Gender and Kinship: Essays Toward a Unified Analysis,* ed. Jane Fishburne Collier and Sylvia Junko Yanagisako, 14–50. Stanford: Stanford University Press, 1987.

Young, Katherine K. "Goddesses, Feminists, and Scholars." *Annual Review of Women in World Religions.* Vol. 1, 105–79. Albany, NY: SUNY Press, 1991.

Younger, J. S. *The Iconography of Late Minoan and Mycenaean Sealstones and Finger Rings.* Bristol, England: Bristol Classical Press, 1988.

Zeitlin, Froma I. "Signifying Difference: The Case of Hesiod's Pandora." In *Playing the Other: Gender and Society in Classical Greek Literature,* 53–86. Chicago: University of Chicago Press, 1996.

Zhang Zhong-Pei. "The Social Structure Reflected in the Yuanjunmiao Cemetery." *Journal of Anthropological Archaeology* 4 (1985): 19–33.

The following illustrations have been reprinted with permission: **1.1.** Courtesy of Andrea Evans, Declarations of Emancipation. **2.1.** Courtesy of Hélène de Beauvoir. **2.2.** Courtesy of Adrienne Momi, AnaTours. **7.1.** From Marija Gimbutas, *Goddesses and Gods of Old Europe*, new and updated ed. (London: Thames and Hudson, 1981, and Berkeley: University of California Press, 1982), 90, fig. 46. By permission of Thames and Hudson and University of California Press. **7.2.** From André Leroi-Gourhan, "Evolution of Paleolithic Art," *Scientific American* 218 (February 1968): 67. Courtesy of Nelson H. Prentiss and Mme. Leroi-Gourhan. **7.3.** From Layne Redmond, *When the Drummers Were Women* (New York: Crown, 1997), 29. Courtesy of Tommy Brunjes. **7.4.** From Marija Gimbutas, *The Language of the Goddess* (San Francisco: HarperSanFrancisco, 1989), 68, fig. 107. By permission of Harper-Collins Publishers, Inc. **7.5** and **7.6.** From Alexander Marshack, *The Roots of Civilization* (New York: McGraw Hill, 1972), 284, fig. 156, and 309, fig. 179. Courtesy of Alexander Marshack. **7.7.** From Marija Gimbutas, *Goddesses and Gods of Old Europe*, new and updated ed. (London: Thames and Hudson, 1981, and Berkeley: University of California Press, 1982), 139, figs. 120 and 121. By permission of Thames and Hudson and University of California Press. **7.8** and **7.9.** From Alexander Marshack, *The Roots of Civilization* (New York: McGraw Hill, 1972), 289, fig. 161a, and 330, fig. 198. Courtesy of Alexander Marshack. **7.10.** From Alice B. Kehoe, "No Possible, Probable Shadow of Doubt," *Antiquity* 65 (1991): 129, fig. 2. By permission of Alice B. Kehoe and Antiquity Publications Ltd. **7.11.** From Helena Wylde Swiny and Stuart Swiny, "An Anthropomorphic Figurine from the Sotira Area," *Report of the Department of Antiquities* (Nicosia, Cyprus, 1983), 57, fig. 1. Courtesy of Stuart Swiny. **7.12.** "Venus of Willendorf," © Naturhistorisches Museum Wien. **7.13.** "Venus of Lespugue," © Musée de l'Homme, Paris. **7.14.** From Björn Kurtén, *How to Deep-Freeze a Mammoth* (New York: Columbia University Press, 1986), 114–15. Courtesy of Dr. Gregory S. Pepper. **7.15.** From Max Geisberg, *The German Single-Leaf Woodcut: 1500–1550*, vol. 1 (New York: Hacker Art Books, 1974), 376, fig. G410. By permission of Hacker Art Books. **7.16.** Courtesy of Museum of Anatolian Civilizations, Ankara, Turkey. **7.17** and **7.18.** From James Mellaart, *Çatal Hüyük* (London: Thames and Hudson, 1967), 116, fig. 28, and 128, fig. 41. Courtesy of James Mellaart. **7.19.** From Dorothy Cameron, *Symbols of Birth and Death in the Neolithic Era* (London: Kenyon-Deane, 1981). By permission of

ACKNOWLEDGMENTS

My first debt of gratitude goes to the Center for the Study of American Religion (now the Center for the Study of Religion) at Princeton University. The CSAR has been unfailingly supportive and unstintingly generous over the past four years, giving me access to a wonderful community of scholars and an unparalleled research library. I want to thank Robert Wuthnow and Anita Kline in particular, who have done a great deal to smooth my path at Princeton. The members of the CSAR workshop, especially Ann Braude and Marie Griffith, have provided much encouragement and helpful criticism. Ann Taves and Grey Gundaker deserve a special thank you for continuing to insist over my protests that I was really writing two books rather than one, until I finally came to believe them.

Many librarians have shared their passion for information by tracking down obscure sources for me. Lois Nase, Robert G. Margolis, and Patti Ponzoli of the Firestone Library Interlibrary Services have enriched this project enormously, as have Nancy Janow, Joyce McKee, Lindita Cani, and Catherine Sullivan of the South Orange Public Library. Jo Ann Troncone of Summit Bank walked me through the labyrinthine process of sending international money orders, and I thank her for her expertise. For translations, I am indebted to Rosa Zagari-Molinari, Tamara Schoenbaum, Teresa Shaw, Pamela Klassen, and Vondah Sheldon.

Readers of this manuscript have provided an invaluable service to me (and to all future readers). Lauren Bryant, Faulkner Fox, Elizabeth Reis, Teresa Shaw, and Sylvia Wolfe took on the thankless task of wading through a sprawling first draft. With patience and tact, they helped me to see how it could be reworked and cut down to size, and I am extremely appreciative of their efforts. Alice Kehoe and Wayne Eastman read a considerably trimmer manuscript and zeroed in on remaining peculiarities at a time when I had become blind to them.

Susan Worst nurtured this project in its early stages, as did Doug Abrams. Amy Caldwell of Beacon Press later took on this project with much grace and offered many valuable suggestions. I would also like to thank Lynn Meskell, Grey Gundaker, Lauren Talalay, Donna Maeda, Marie Griffith, and Robert Wolfe for providing helpful readings of individual chapters; Susan Meigs, who copyedited the manuscript; and Lori Krafte, who proofread it.

I owe long overdue debts to two mentors: Robert Ellwood, who has had a deep and lasting influence on how I think about religion, myth, society, and the funny business of writing about people's deepest spiritual commitments; and John Collins, who at a crucial point in my life insisted that it was worth every penny it took to have my own space in which to work.

Truly wonderful combinations of support, distraction, and much-needed perspective were offered by family and friends as I worked on this project. I owe my mental health, such as it is, first and foremost to Teresa Shaw, who tolerates endless whiny phone calls with remarkable patience, and never fails to send me back out into the world feeling better able to take it on. Other friends who have lent encouragement and a listening ear to the development of this project include Elizabeth Reis, Sylvia Wolfe, Lori Krafte, Jody Shapiro Davie, Janna Southworth, Carol Hansen, Kathy and Jesse Carliner, Carolyn and Tom McGee, Deborah Campbell, Michael Brzozowski, Lynn and Paul Woodruff, Holly and Tomm Scalera, Jane Hurwitz, Stephen Moore, Magda and Bernard Greene, and of course my darling Sophia.

All the staff at the Blue Moon Diner kept me fed, watered, and in touch with the twentieth century when I threatened to permanently drift off to 6000 BCE. And the teachers and administrators of the South Mountain YMCA—particularly Marguerite McDougal, Elaine Lyons, Rachel Mondalto, April Pray, Kirbee Stern, Tameka Pullen, Judith Hannah, Julia Dixon, Estelle Fields, Marie Papageorgis, Diane DiGiovanni, Christine La Rosa, Ellie Maziekien, Keyana Rogers, Kathleen Jones, Kathleen Shaw, and Elissa Lombardo—left my mind free to wander by taking my daughter into their loving and very professional arms.

The Marlin Eller Foundation for the Support of Siblings made the illustrations in this volume possible, and I am most grateful for the Foundation's continued financial underwriting of my work.

This book, and most of my life, would not be possible without the love, laughter, and periodic infusions of cash I have received from Jonathan Greene, the best patron a writer could wish for and a terrific husband besides. It is to him and our daughter Sophia that this book is dedicated.

INDEX

abortion, 99

Acheulean hand axes, 39

Aeschylus, 170–71, 173

Africa, 29, 41, 109, 159, 192n. 29, 197n. 28

Afrocentrism, 29, 197n. 29

Agamemnon, 170–71

agriculture: associated with goddess worship, 138, 223n. 42; in matriarchal societies, 48; women's invention of, 33, 42, 93, 107, 111–12, 217–18n. 49. *See also* horticulture, plow agriculture.

Albania, 96

Alpert, Jane, 42, 57

Alphabet Versus the Goddess, The, 29, 206–207n. 1

Amazons, 172, 178, 200n. 57, 230–31n. 34, 231–32n. 53

Americas, the, 159, 163; as site of prehistoric matriarchy, 40, 197n. 28, 214n. 29

Anat, 104

Anatolia, 40, 146, 161, 165, 227n. 10

Ancient Society, 32

Anima Mundi Dance Company, 191n. 25

animal husbandry, 46, 47–48, 157, 160

animals, as represented in prehistoric art, 119, 121, 123, 124, 128, 138, 143, 144. *See also* bucrania.

Ann, Martha, 15

Anthony, David, 113, 114

anthropology: and study of gender, 85–87; as champion of matriarchal myth, 31; cultural, 82–87; evolutionary, 31–32, 82–83; feminist, 34–35, 86–87, 216–17n. 44; socialist feminist, 198n. 37, 199–200n. 54, 204n. 25

anthropomorphic figurines, 126–42, 143–44, 148, 219n. 4, 223n. 39; ascertaining sex, 126–28, 138–39, 147, 148, 221nn. 15, 25, 225n. 57; as dolls, 139; as fertility symbols, 134, 138; as goddess icons, 124–26, 129, 133, 134, 139, 143, 147–48, 153–55, 181; fatness of, 134–36, 138; find spots of, 139, 143, 153; interpretation of prehistoric, 124–33, 139–40, 156; magical or ritual uses of, 136, 139; male, 143, 153–54; question of pregnancy, 134, 138, 143, 222n. 34, 223n. 38; variety among, 134, 136–38, 143. *See also* art; "bird goddess"; "goddess with leopards"; Paleolithic "Venus" figurines; "phallic goddesses"; "pillar deities"; "sleeping goddess" of Malta; "snake goddess."

anti-Semitism, 50, 201n. 64

Aphrodite, 106

apocalypticism, 27, 33, 54, 202n. 73

Apollo, 171, 173

Appiah, Kwame Anthony, vii, 64, 75, 205n. 34, 206n. 47

archaeology: as champion of matriarchal myth, 32, 36, 90, 142, 151, 195n. 6, 220n. 7; as resource for uncovering the past, 87–89; feminist, 89, 134; methodology, 90–91; study of gender in, 88–89

architecture. *See* palaces, of Minoan Crete; temples, Maltese.

Ariadne, 22, 43, 47, 192n. 27

Aristotle, 95, 168, 211n. 5

arrowheads, 113, 114